THE
RETURN
FROM AVALON

THE RETURN FROM AVALON

A Study of the Arthurian Legend in Modern Fiction

RAYMOND H. THOMPSON

CONTRIBUTIONS TO THE STUDY OF
SCIENCE FICTION AND FANTASY, NUMBER 14

Greenwood Press
WESTPORT, CONNECTICUT • LONDON, ENGLAND

Copyright Acknowledgment

Grateful acknowledgment is hereby given for permission to quote excerpts from *Arthur Rex: A Legendary Novel* by Thomas Berger. Copyright © 1978 by Thomas Berger. Reprinted by permission of Delacorte Press/Seymour Lawrence and Don Congdon Associates, Inc.

Library of Congress Cataloging in Publication Data

Thompson, Raymond H. (Raymond Henry), 1941-
  The return from Avalon.

  (Contributions to the study of science fiction and fantasy, ISSN 0193-6875 ; no. 14)
  Bibliography: p.
  1. English fiction—20th century—History and criticism. 2. Arthurian romances—History and criticism. 3. American fiction—20th century—History and criticism. 4. Middle Ages in literature. 5. Fantastic fiction—History and criticism. I. Title. II. Series.
PR888.A76T45 1985   823'.91'09351   84-10853
ISBN 0-313-23291-1 (lib. bdg.)

Library of Congress Catalog Card Number: 84-10853
ISBN: 0-313-23291-1
ISSN: 0193-6875

First published in 1985

Greenwood Press
A division of Congressional Information Service, Inc.
88 Post Road West
Westport, Connecticut 06881

Printed in the United States of America

10 9 8 7 6 5 4 3 2 1

To

Hilary, Gareth, Katie, and Gawen,

companions on the quest

CONTENTS

ACKNOWLEDGMENTS

Working on the Arthurian legend is, for me, a labor of love, but the task has been made considerably easier by the courtesy and assistance of the following: Jean Beveridge of the Acadia University Library; Joyce Day of the Science Fiction Foundation Library; Glyn Davies and David Hughes of the Clwyd County Library; Mary Flagg of the University of New Brunswick Library; and Cynthia Peters of the Newberry Library.

I should also like to express my thanks to Joy Cavazzi for typing the manuscript with her usual skill and good humor, and to my family for their encouragement and understanding.

Research for and preparation of this study have been assisted by a Research Grant from the Social Sciences and Humanities Research Council of Canada.

THE
RETURN
FROM AVALON

1

INTRODUCTION

Since Nathan Comfort Starr wrote his pioneering study, *King Arthur Today: The Arthurian Legend in English and American Literature, 1901–1953*,[1] the quantity of Arthurian literature has grown substantially. This growth, however, has taken place primarily in the field of prose fiction, particularly the novel, for although short poems have remained popular, long poetry and drama have declined sharply from their earlier rate of appearance.[2] Whereas the first half of this century produced less than fifty novels of Arthurian provenance, the last thirty years have yielded more than twice that number. Moreover this period has seen the rapid growth in popularity of fictional forms such as science fiction and fantasy, the latter of which has been particularly attractive to authors dealing with Arthurian legend. These developments reflect a change in literary taste, and they indicate that it is high time to update and augment Starr's work with a study of Arthurian prose fiction published from 1882 to 1983.[3]

What strikes readers of modern Arthurian fiction most forcefully is the sheer variety of the treatment. In the close to two hundred novels and short stories that have appeared in the past one hundred years, the variations seem endless.[4] The vision may be heroic, as we admire the triumphs of Arthur and his warriors in their struggle against heavy odds; it may be tragic, as we witness their final failure and defeat; or it may be ironic, as we discover the humorous gap between their aspirations and their actual achievements. Arthur and his followers may be the central subject of the story, or they may play but a minor role in events.

These events may take place in post-Roman Britain during the Saxon invasions;[5] or in the timeless world of medieval romance; or even in modern times. The grim brutality of Arthur's world may appall us, or its glittering splendor dazzle. Arthur himself may be an idealistic hero, an opportunistic tyrant, or a simple-minded buffoon; Guenevere may be proud and self-indulgent, or merely the lovely victim of circumstances; Merlin may be a cynic or a sage.

Yet amidst the seemingly endless contradictions, groupings do emerge. The fiction can be divided into five recognizable categories: retellings, realistic fiction, historical fiction, science fiction, and fantasy. What distinguishes them is their attitude towards setting.

First there are retellings, either translations or modernizations of the Arthurian story for an audience unskilled in the language of the medieval versions. Since most of these are aimed at younger readers, they tend to simplify their material to varying degrees. The setting of the sources is reproduced unchanged except by this process of simplification.

The second category places events in a contemporary setting. These are either thrillers that make use of an Arthurian site or artifact in the plot, or else they are consciously modeled upon key elements of the Arthurian legend, such as the Grail, or the love affairs of Lancelot and Guenevere, of Tristan and Iseult.[6] The original Arthurian figures are not involved in the latter group, though their stories may be explicitly recalled. Instead a new cast of characters acts out the ancient pattern in a modern world, thereby demonstrating its archetypal power. Although often mystical and romantic in the treatment of their subject matter, these novels differ from fantasy in that they offer what are intended to be rational explanations for the Arthurian element that is borrowed.

Historical novels endeavor to recreate the spirit of the age of Arthur through attention to authentic detail. Setting is carefully constructed, based upon the latest knowledge of the period, and this setting—physical, political, and social—largely determines the conduct of the characters. Events may be set in the Dark Ages of the fifth and sixth centuries, after the withdrawal of Roman protection from Britain; or during the High Middle Ages pictured in the romances that were the literary sources for these works. Regardless of period, however, two poles exist. One is ruthlessly realistic, presenting a bleak picture of life in a harsh age. Since it exposes the coarse reality behind the glorious legend, it is usually pessimistic in mood. The other is romantic, and it stresses the noble aspirations and achievements of Arthur's rule. Characters seem larger than life, and since they have more success in triumphing over adversity, they create an optimistic mood. Because it recedes in importance, setting is often less clearly depicted. The difference is between the novel and the romance, between Northrop Frye's low mimetic, or even ironic, mode and his romance mode.[7] Few historical novels are pure examples of any one mode, however. Most are located at points between the two poles, blending elements typical of both.

Science fiction offers a picture of how life might be, provided that certain scientific or societal developments could have taken place. Once these developments are accepted, the logic of events should follow naturally, indeed inevitably. Science fiction provides a rational explanation for the apparently supernatural powers of figures like Merlin and Nimue, the Lady of the Lake, or for the Arthurian roles that characters find themselves acting out in some distant future. When the focus falls upon the apparently magical causality, rather than the scientific, however, then the work may become science fantasy, a form located somewhere between science fiction and fantasy proper.[8]

Fantasy constitutes the fifth and final category of modern Arthurian fiction. Here supernatural events play a significant role, and no effort is made to explain them in rational terms. Numinous powers intervene directly in the affairs of men, for purposes that are not always immediately clear. Numerous types or strains of fantasy have been identified, although critics still argue about which labels to use. Arthurian fantasy, however, falls readily into four groups, which I have chosen to call low, heroic, ironic, and mythopoeic.[9] In low fantasy inexplicable supernatural occurrences intrude upon our ordinary rational world, where they do not fit. They remain mysteries. By contrast high fantasy, of which the latter three groups are subcategories, offers us a secondary world in which magical or supernatural powers do operate by their own rules, however alien they may be to our world. Heroic fantasy measures the achievements of Arthur and his knights to discover the heroic heights which the resolute human spirit can scale despite apparently insurmountable odds. Ironic fantasy measures these same achievements against their high-minded aspirations to expose a comical gap. Mythopoeic fantasies find that both the triumphs and failures are rooted in the contradictory nature of humanity itself, and they express this dichotomy in terms of an eternal conflict between good and evil, waged at a supernatural level.

These groupings suggest a means of approaching modern Arthurian fiction in order to discover the directions in which it has been evolving over the past one hundred years. Moreover, this approach should help us to understand the relationship between form and Arthurian tradition, a relationship that has always been important. In the Middle Ages it is readily apparent that the chronicles preserve a more warlike image of Arthur than do the romances. Thus when a work draws upon this tradition, as does the fourteenth-century English alliterative poem, *Morte Arthure*, then it presents him as an aggressive emperor, conquering his enemies with ruthless vigor. In the romances, by contrast, focus upon the deeds of his knights pushes the king into the background. Here he dwindles to little more than a figurehead, helpless without the support of his greatest champions, like Gawain, Lancelot, and Perceval. However, in the verse romances this gradual evolution follows an ironic direction that invites us to share in often covert humor at Arthur's foibles. Thus in Raoul de Houdenc's *La Vengeance Raguidel*, a French poem of the early thirteenth century, the disgruntled monarch wanders off to bed supperless because the marvel that convention dictates must precede a high feast fails to materialize; and in the fourteenth-century English alliterative poem, *Sir Gawain and the Green Knight*, his immature impetuousness betrays him into discourtesy to the Green Knight. In prose romances, on the other hand, Arthur's decline is judged more severely, and it often alienates his noblest followers. Thus in the *Perlesvaus*, a French Grail romance from the early thirteenth century, Arthur's best knights avoid the court, disgusted at his slothful inactivity, while in the Vulgate *Lancelot*, another French romance from the same period, they dispute his misjudgment in the episode of the false Guenevere.

Even more significantly, the concluding section of this latter romance, *La Mort Artu*, introduces into tradition Arthur's great sin, the incest with his half-sister Morgause that produces Mordred. Prior to this Mordred had been no more than Arthur's nephew.[10]

Obviously, attitudes vary from work to work, as each author adopts his or her own unique approach to the traditional material, and this necessitates a broad survey of the fiction in order to appreciate the full scope and variety of Arthurian legend today.[11] Yet broad trends remain, and they suggest that the relationship between form and tradition should yield valuable insights into that most joyous mystery, the return of Arthur from Avalon. For he has indeed come again, with all his noble knights of the Round Table and their magnificent ladies, to inspire his latter-day followers by their glorious example. And nowhere is the evidence of their return so dynamic as in the pages of modern Arthurian fiction.

NOTES

1. Nathan Comfort Starr, *The Arthurian Legend in English and American Literature, 1901–1953* (Gainesville: University of Florida Press, 1954).

2. Since 1954 about forty short poems have been published, eleven long poems, ten plays, five short stories, and over one hundred novels.

3. I have chosen this period since it encompasses all the major fiction since Tennyson restored the popularity of Arthurian legend. Earlier works, such as Thomas Love Peacock's *The Misfortunes of Elphin* (1829), are dealt with by James Douglas Merriman in *The Flower of Kings: A Study of the Arthurian Legend in England between 1485 and 1835* (Lawrence: University Press of Kansas, 1973), and in "The Other Arthurians in Victorian England," *Philological Quarterly*, 56 (1977), 249–53; and by David Staines, "King Arthur in Victorian Fiction," in *The Worlds of Victorian Fiction*, ed. Jerome H. Buckley (Cambridge, Mass., and London: Harvard University Press, 1975), pp. 267–93. See also Beverly Taylor and Elisabeth Brewer, *The Return of King Arthur: British and American Literature Since 1900* (Woodbridge, Suffolk: Boydell and Brewer; Totowa, N.J.: Barnes and Noble, 1983).

4. For a bibliographical listing of modern Arthurian literature, see Clark S. Northup and John J. Parry, "The Arthurian Legends: Modern Retellings of the Old Stories," *Journal of English and Germanic Philology*, 43 (1944), 173–221; Paul A. Brown and John J. Parry, "The Arthurian

Legends: Supplement to Northup and Parry's Annotated Bibliography," *Journal of English and Germanic Philology*, 49 (1950), 208–16; Stephen R. Reimer, "The Arthurian Legends in Contemporary English Literature, 1945–1981," *Bulletin of Bibliography*, 38 (1981), 128–38, 149; Mary Wildman, "Twentieth-Century Arthurian Literature—an annotated bibliography," in *Arthurian Literature I*, ed. Richard Barber (Woodbridge, Suffolk: Boydell and Brewer, 1982).

5. The Germanic invaders actually consisted of three major groups: the Jutes who first settled in Kent and the Isle of Wight; the Saxons who settled in the southern areas, founding the kingdoms of Essex, Sussex and Wessex; and the Angles who settled in East Anglia, the midlands (Mercia), and north (Northumbria). See John Morris, *The Age of Arthur: A History of the British Isles from 350 to 650* (London: Weidenfeld and Nicolson, 1973), especially pp. 317–32. Since the British referred to all these enemies as Saxons, and since most modern authors allow their characters to follow this practice, I have decided to retain it for the sake of convenience.

6. Modern authors use as many variants to spell their characters' names as do their medieval predecessors. When discussing a particular work, I have chosen to follow the author's spelling. Elsewhere I have used a common standardized form, such as Arthur, Gawain, Bedivere, etc. Where a variant spelling seems particularly obscure, I have identified the character in brackets. All the variants used in this study are listed in the appendix.

7. See *Anatomy of Criticism: Four Essays* (Princeton, N.J.: Princeton University Press, 1957), pp. 33–34.

8. Fuller discussion of this and other categories takes place in the relevant chapters below.

9. I have used these terms elsewhere: see "Arthurian Legend and Modern Fantasy," in *Survey of Modern Fantasy Literature*, ed. Frank N. Magill (Englewood Cliffs, N.J.: Salem Press, 1983), 5, 2299–2315. The first is borrowed from Kenneth J. Zahorski and Robert H. Boyer as used in their introduction to *Fantasy Literature, A Core Collection and Reference Guide* (New York and London: R. R. Bowker, 1979), which they compiled together with Marshall Tymn: see pp. 5–7. The remainder are taken from Diana Waggoner, *The Hills of Faraway: A Guide to Fantasy* (New York: Atheneum, 1978), but are more broadly encompassing. Mythopoeic is roughly equivalent to the type called myth fantasy by Zahorski and Boyer, and to what J.R.R. Tolkien calls high myth in "On Fairy-Stories" (first published in *Essays Presented to Charles Williams*, Oxford: Oxford University Press, 1947, reprinted in *Tree and Leaf*, London: George Allen and Unwin, 1964, and in *The Tolkien Reader*, New

York: Ballantine Books, 1966); heroic fantasy equates with faery-tale fantasy in the former, low myth in the latter. It is the grouping that is important rather than the label, which is a critical convenience. However, the terms low, mythopoeic, heroic, and ironic are useful for this study in that they indicate the distinctive thrust of each group.

10. Rosemary Morris has recently completed a study entitled *The Character of King Arthur in Medieval Literature* (Woodbridge, Suffolk: Boydell and Brewer, 1982).

11. By choosing to focus upon the Arthurian element and how it is used, and upon its links with earlier tradition, I have, of necessity, been generally forced to ignore how these works fit into the authors' canons. However, studies of the works of important individual authors, like John Cowper Powys and Mark Twain, have been done, and should be consulted by those interested in this dimension of Arthurian tradition.

Some works are unavoidably omitted, either because they have eluded the search of bibliographers, or because I have been unable to find a copy to examine. Because many Arthurian novels fall into the category of popular literature they are less likely to have been collected in libraries than more serious writings. I have included these missing items in the bibliography of Arthurian fiction, indicating their status accordingly. They are mainly sentimental historical romances. They are few in number. Rarity has also compelled the use of editions other than the first at times. This is indicated in footnotes whenever it occurs.

2

RETELLINGS

On the face of it, retellings of earlier versions contribute little to the growth of Arthurian legend. They are, after all, strictly limited by what is included in their sources. Whenever they go beyond them they become more than a retelling. This latter process can be observed in John Steinbeck's *The Acts of King Arthur* (1976).[1] In his Introduction Steinbeck proposes "to set the stories down in meaning as they were written, leaving out nothing and adding nothing....In no sense do I wish to rewrite Malory, or reduce him, or change him, or soften or sentimentalize him" (p. xiii). The author does indeed start out by adding very little; but in the second half of his book he departs increasingly from Malory, "opening it out" (p. 350), as he admits in a letter to his literary agent. What begins as a modernization thus concludes as a new literary creation, and will be dealt with as such later.

It is fascinating to observe this imaginative development in an author, and to conjecture upon the extent to which it may have taken place in many of the medieval versions of the legend, including that of Malory himself. However our concern in this chapter is with close retellings of earlier versions, and although they are not, strictly speaking, "modern," they do merit brief attention in this study for two reasons. In the first place they contribute indirectly but significantly to developments within the body of the legend; and in the second the same process of selection of material that recurs in more independent creations takes place in many retellings, particularly those that are aimed at younger readers.

Retellings acquaint the reading public with stories that might otherwise remain inaccessible, either from scarcity or for linguistic reasons. Many medieval romances survive in rare or even unique manuscripts, now carefully guarded to ensure their preservation. It has been the task of generations of scholars to prepare definitive editions of these works. These, however, are of help only to other specialists, trained to read languages and dialects that may be very different from those of today. The gap between specialists and more general readers is bridged, therefore, by modern retellings, whether they be translations from foreign languages, or modernizations of archaic forms of their own language.

Their value to Arthurian tradition is two-fold. On the one hand, they encourage an interest in the legend that can lead readers back to study original texts or to read other versions, modern as well as ancient. They help create the audience without which a legend fades from sight. On the other, they serve as valuable sources for creative writers who wish to treat Arthurian subjects. For several centuries almost the only Arthurian work familiar to the educated elite was Sir Thomas Malory's *Le Morte Darthur* (1470), and those authors who chose to deal with King Arthur used it as their point of departure.[2] Malory continues to exercise by far the greatest influence upon modern authors, as is apparent not only from a scrutiny of their works, but also by their own admission. To cite but two examples, Steinbeck speaks of his childhood fascination with Malory in the introduction to his *Acts of King Arthur* (pp. xi-xii), and Clemence Housman constantly refers to him as "my most dear Master" in *Sir Aglovale de Galis* (1905).

However, other accounts of the Arthurian legend have become increasingly available. One of the earliest, and still deeply influential, is the collection of medieval Welsh tales found in *The Mabinogion*, first translated into English by Lady Charlotte Guest (1838–49). Readers now may compare the chronicles of Geoffrey of Monmouth, composed originally in Latin, of Wace, composed in Old French, and of Layamon, composed in early Middle English; although much remains untranslated, the greatest achievements of Old French romance are available in the poetry of Marie de France and Chrétien de Troyes, and in the prose of the Vulgate *Mort Artu*; the fatal love of Tristan and Iseult is told by Béroul and Thomas in Old French, by Gottfried von Strassburg in Middle High German; and the varying accounts of the Grail quest have been translated from the French verse of Chrétien de Troyes' *Le Conte du Graal*, from the French prose of the Vulgate *Queste del Saint Graal*, from the German verse of Wolfram von Eschenbach's *Parzival*, and from the Welsh prose of *Peredur Son of Efrawg*.

The task of selection from among the often contradictory stories found in these close translations, as well as in modernized versions of Middle English romances, is one that confronts not only the authors of fiction, but also those who adapt their material in the process of retelling. Since most are aimed at younger readers, adaptation most commonly involves simplifying the often confusing body of tradition. This is usually achieved by focusing upon a few important and largely self-contained episodes, such as Arthur drawing the sword from the stone, or Gareth's quest to rescue a besieged lady.

Another noticeable trend is the removal of all traces of sexual immorality, a practice Steinbeck berates in the Introduction to *The Acts of King Arthur*. Considering the amount of illicit sexuality in Arthurian tradition and how crucial it is to the meaning of certain key events, this effort to protect the innocence of young people cannot but rob the legend of much of its power.

An example of this kind of writing can be found in *King Arthur and his Knights*, a version published in 1964 by Parents' Magazine Press, New York. This uses the adaptation of Mary MacLeod which was first published in 1900. The Preface announces that "Arthur was a king above reproach, and the gentlest, most honorable knight who ever lived," and this assessment is borne out by omitting embarrassing details of his career. We are not told that Arthur was conceived out of wedlock. Rather, we are informed only that Uther entrusts the infant to Merlin in return for an unspecified "great service" (p. 1). We later learn that Igraine had been married to the Duke of Cornwall prior to her marriage to Uther, but we are told nothing more. Having cleaned up her hero's past, MacLeod then tackles his youthful incest with his half-sister Morgause. She acknowledges no more than that King Lot's wife "quite won the heart of King Arthur" (p. 15). The suspicious may wonder why Mordred is only a half-brother of Gawaine and his brothers, but although she is silent about his paternity, MacLeod insists stoutly that he is no more than Arthur's nephew. She veils in similar silence the adultery of Lancelot and Queen Guinevere, and of Tristram and Iseult. That they do love each other is acknowledged, but for all that MacLeod allows to happen between them, their passion might have been pure of all blame. The lovers are trapped by treacherous enemies—but no details are supplied that even hint at any misdoing on their part. That Lancelot is the father of Galahad is also admitted, but how this was achieved is ignored.

The effect of this tampering with tradition is to weaken the tragic power of the original stories, and at times to leave the reader confused as to what all the fuss is about. The vengefulness of characters like King Mark, Mordred, and Morgan le Fay is much harder to account for in the absence of the adultery of Tristram, Arthur, and Uther. Yet even where the process of selection is less damaging, it may still give a shape to a story that differs quite markedly from that of the source. By including or omitting certain details, characterization may be subtly altered, and even the very spirit of the original transformed. The process is explained by Rosemary Sutcliff, the finest practitioner of the art of retelling.

In the Author's Note to *The Sword and the Circle* (1981), Sutcliff informs her reader that, although she follows Malory "in the main" she has not done so "slavishly." Every minstrel "adds and leaves out and embroiders and puts something of himself into each retelling" (p. 8). She goes on to list other sources that she uses for various stories, including two English poems from the fourteenth and fifteenth centuries respectively, *Sir Gawain and the Green Knight* and *The Wedding of Sir Gawain and Dame Ragnell*.

Blending material from disparate sources, however, does create problems. For example the concept of Sir Gawain in the English poems is much more favorable than that found in Malory, and Sutcliff is forced to resolve this inconsistency in characterization by making some adjustments to her materials.[3] Since

Gawain is the finest champion at Arthur's court in *Sir Gawain and the Green Knight*, it is only appropriate that he be subjected to the complex test of loyalty, courage, and courtesy represented by the combination of the beheading game and chastity test. His remarkable achievement and the final failure caused by his human love of life thus serve as a comment upon mankind's potential for perfectibility. Much may be achieved if we try hard enough, yet the limitations of our imperfect human nature ultimately doom us to failure. The best in mankind—Gawain—has been tried and found wanting. However, in *Le Morte Darthur* Gawain is by no means the finest knight at Arthur's court, and Sutcliff follows Malory in this, though she is somewhat more generous in her portrayal of Arthur's nephew. Gawain is chosen to respond to the Green Knight's challenge, not because he is most fitted by his eminence among the knights of Arthur's court, but because he is newly knighted and still needs to prove that he is worthy to sit at the Round Table. Lancelot is clearly his superior, but he is absent from the court on a quest when the challenge is issued. Since King Arthur behaves with greater dignity than he does in the poem, he is protected from stigma of failure. By diminishing Gawain's stature Sutcliff changes the significance of his experience. Since the hero is no longer the best that mankind has to offer, his encounter with the reality of human limitations loses much of its force and universality. It becomes just one more adventure among the many that occur in Arthur's kingdom, albeit stranger and more thoughtful than most.

Gawain's achievement is also reduced in the story of his marriage to Dame Ragnell, the Loathely Lady. The medieval version is a test of loyalty and courtesy, requiring not only that Gawain save Arthur's life by marrying the hideous creature, but also that he treat her with kindness and respect if the spell that holds her in this guise is to be broken. His success on both counts is made all the more impressive by the selfishness of everyone else, including Arthur himself in one account. However, in Sutcliff's adaptation Gawain seems to be prompted as much by pride as by courtesy and loyalty. His initial promise to wed the lady seems partly a response to his brother's taunt about his many protestations of loyalty to the king. This impression of bravado is reinforced by his conduct during the wedding celebrations. His assurance to Ragnell that he can guard both her and himself against insult is a gesture of warlike defiance, emphasized when he "glared round him at the others with his fighting face upon him" (p. 237). Even his response to the choice the lady offers him, to be fair by night or by day, is less impressive than in the source. Gawain has to be reminded of the consequences of both decisions before he offers to leave the choice to her, and thereby breaks the spell.

This is not a failure on the part of Sutcliff to appreciate her sources. Rather she is adapting the material to fit her own artistic purposes. First of all, she is concerned to create a reasonably consistent character for Gawain out of the conflicting traditions which she has utilized. Her Gawain is close to Malory's: well-intentioned, but flawed by pride and quick temper. Consequently his famed courtesy is diminished in order to bring out these qualities. Even in Sutcliff's account of the coming of Percival to Arthur's court, Gawain's courtesy to the young hero is marred by his jealous protest against so untried a warrior being made knight.

Second, the author is concerned to explain the implications of certain events to the young audience at which the book is aimed. This is why she chooses to spell out the implications of the choice offered Gawain by the Loathely Lady, and she repeats the technique when Percival abandons the feud between his family and that of Gawain. As a result of this process of clarification, Gawain's role becomes less noble than in the English poems that are the sources of these two episodes. That this clarification serves the purpose of characterization is a tribute to Sutcliff's control over her complex material. Nevertheless it also demonstrates how so apparently straightforward a process as retelling a story can produce important changes in the material.

A comprehensive list of retellings would be tedious to rehearse, but it is interesting to note some of the better-known authors who have written adaptations for children. They include Enid Blyton, Brian Kennedy Cooke, Antonia Fraser, Andrew Lang, Sidney Lanier, Barbara Leonie Picard, Eleanor Price, and Dorothy Senior. The best-known versions are probably Roger Lancelyn Green's adaptation for Puffin Books in 1953, and of course Howard Pyle's superbly illustrated series for Scribner, 1903–10. However, the finest are Rosemary Sutcliff's series for The Bodley Head, which combine a keen sensitivity to the spirit of the legend with a simple yet elegant prose style. Apart from *The Sword and the Circle*, already cited, which deals with the early days of Arthur's kingdom, she has written *Tristan and Iseult* (1971), where "she tried to get back to the Celtic original as much as possible" (p. 7); *The Light Beyond the Forest: The Quest for the Holy Grail* (1979), a medieval Christian story "shot through with shadows and half-light and haunting echoes of much older things" (p. 10); and *The Road to Camlann* (1981) where she concludes the tragic story.

Authors like Sutcliff research their material with great care, examining various original texts and works of scholarship. Indeed some, like Gillian Bradshaw, Douglas Carmichael, Sanders Anne Laubenthal, Francis Owen, and Mary Stewart have themselves been trained as scholars. However, the large number of retellings now available can be of great value to writers. They broaden and diversify modern Arthurian tradition, allowing greater freedom of choice in approaching the legend. They contribute valuably to the flexibility that has been one of the legend's greatest strengths.

The effect can be appreciated by looking again at the figure of Gawain. His reputation varied greatly in medieval literature, as we saw in Sutcliff's *The Sword and the Circle*. While most novels follow Malory and Tennyson in their blame of Arthur's nephew, some of the more recent fantasies are clearly influenced by the more favorable treatment that he receives in the verse romances, both English and French. In *The Green Knight* (1975), a modern fantasy based upon *Sir Gawain and the Green Knight*, Vera Chapman resolves the problem of conflicting views on Gawain by making her hero another knight with the same name. He is the son of Gareth, hence nephew to the original figure. However, both Thomas Berger in *Arthur Rex* (1978) and Gillian Bradshaw in her Arthurian trilogy, *Hawk of May* (1980), *Kingdom of Summer* (1981), and *In Winter's Shadow* (1982), rehabilitate Gawain, or Gwalchmai as Bradshaw calls him. Though not without faults, he is a hero truly worthy of the respect and love with which he was regarded in the verse romances.

Other characters are similarly affected by the rich diversity of Arthurian tradition made accessible in retellings. Early Welsh tradition in *The Mabinogion* presents Kay as the most feared warrior of Arthur's following, whereas in the romances he becomes the ill-tempered seneschal whose rudeness is so regularly rebuked. The chronicles condemn Guenevere for adultery with Mordred, even though the prose romances generally defend her affair with Lancelot. And the impact of different traditions upon the reputation of King Arthur himself was pointed out in the last chapter. Retellings are invaluable as sources to authors of modern Arthurian fiction. It is to these that we now must turn to consider the fruits of their labor.

NOTES

1. Bibliographical data are cited in the footnotes only where editions other than the first are used. In all other cases the full information will be found in the bibliography of primary material. Where both British and American editions are included in the bibliography, quotations are from the first one listed. This practice has been dictated by the availability of texts. As noted in note 11 to Chapter 1, many modern Arthurian novels are considered popular fiction and do not find their way into academic libraries.

2. These works are examined by Merriman, *The Flower of Kings*, and by Taylor and Brewer, *The Return of King Arthur*.

3. The fluctuations in Gawain's reputation are examined by B. J. Whiting, "Gawain, His Reputation, His Courtesy and His Appearance in Chaucer's *Squire's Tale*," *Medieval Studies*, 9 (1947), 189–237. For more detailed studies see Keith Busby, *Gauvain in Old French Literature* (Amsterdam: Editions Rodopi, 1980), and my Ph.D. thesis for the University of Alberta, "Sir Gawain and Heroic Tradition" (1969).

3

REALISTIC FICTION

In recent years most novels that introduce elements of the Arthurian legend into a contemporary setting have been fantasies, reflecting the growth in popularity of that form. However, there have always been a few authors who continue to borrow from the legend in the course of writing realistic fiction. Realistic is a term few scholars like to use, and it can be particularly misleading when applied to this category of Arthurian literature, since so many of the novels adopt a romantic approach to their material. Nevertheless it does describe the treatment of the Arthurian element in the novel, as opposed to such elements as character and plot. Rather than introduce magic to account for the intrusion of the Arthurian world upon ours, or to enable people from our world to visit that of Arthur, these novels offer rational explanations for the Arthurian element. The explanation may not be convincing, but it is generally intended to be.

These novels can be divided into two general groups: mystery thrillers, and modern transpositions. The first, mystery thrillers, are few in number and they merely make use of items with Arthurian associations in the course of constructing their plots.[1] Alice Campbell's *The Murder of Caroline Bundy* (1932) is a poorly written murder mystery in which the villain tries to swindle his victim into leaving him her money so that he can search for the Holy Grail on her estate near Glastonbury. Gerard Francis' *The Secret Sceptre* (1937) is another undistinguished detective story involving the Holy Grail. Elizabeth Peters includes a treasure trove reputed to be Arthurian in her playful suspense mystery,

The Camelot Caper (1969). Anthony Price uncovers an ingenious Russian plot to blame both the American and British intelligence services for desecrating the site of the battle of Badon in *Our Man in Camelot* (1975).

The best-written of this group is the most recent, a mystery by Jonathan Gash called *The Grail Tree* (1979). Murder is committed to gain possession not of the battered pewter cup said by legend to be the Grail, but of the tree-shaped silver casket in which it is placed. The value lies in the decorations to this casket by great silversmiths of the past. The Grail possesses no mystical qualities, and its Arthurian associations are barely mentioned. Lovejoy, the Norfolk antique dealer and amateur sleuth, is an unlikely Grail quester, though he does remind us of Perceval in earlier verse tradition, with his essential innocence, his repeated involvement with women, and his surprising fighting skill. However, the book is memorable rather for the lively interaction of a humorous cast of characters which bears little resemblance to Arthur's court. None of the novels in this group contributes to Arthurian tradition as such, though they do give indirect evidence of its popularity.

Other authors transpose the legend to a modern setting, re-creating such popular features as the Grail quest and the love triangles formed by Lancelot-Guenevere-Arthur and Tristan-Iseult-Mark. The main difficulty here is to determine whether the adherence to the Arthurian model is close enough to warrant a book being considered Arthurian, and scholars have differed in their opinions. Clark S. Northup and John J. Parry list J. H. Shorthouse's nineteenth-century version of the Grail quest, *Sir Percival: A Story of the Past and of the Present* (1886), among the rejected items in their modern Arthurian bibliography.[2] However, both David Staines and James Merriman include it in their respective articles on the Arthurian legend in Victorian fiction,[3] although the former admits that it does little other than use Tennyson's Arthurian world as "a suggestive frame of reference" (p. 292). Parry also rejects John Steinbeck's *Tortilla Flat* (1935) with the observation, "According to the author it is based on an Arthurian theme, including the Grail quest, but this is not obvious."[4] By contrast, Arthur F. Kinney concludes that it is "a successful transposition of the legend" that avoids "the dangers of too close a parallel. . . . *Tortilla Flat* is quite possibly the best Arthurian story for which a modern society can serve as basis."[5] More recently Arthurian parallels have been discerned in Franz Kafka's *The Castle* (1926) and John Le Carré's Smiley trilogy.[6] Novels in this group thus range from close transpositions to borrowing of so general a nature that the Arthurian element remains no more than a tantalizing analogy. An example of this last is Charles Mason's *Merlin: A Piratical Love Story* (1896). This describes the hopeless passion of an artist named Mr. Merlin for an aristocratic young woman. He boldly rescues her from pirates, but since he is already unhappily married, he cannot claim her. Merlin's futile pursuit of Nimue/Vivien is explicitly recalled when he paints a picture called "Merlin and his Vivien," using the heroine as his model for the latter. However, although some details fit, notably Merlin's misfortune with women, and his preoccupation with his "art," the story as a whole has more differences than similarities. Merlin is ennobled, not degraded, by his love in Mason's sentimental story which, as Staines remarks, owes more to Victorian stage melodrama than to Arthurian legend.

Far more popular as a model is the love story of Tristan and Iseult. It serves as a frame of reference for both Mary Elizabeth Braddon's *Mount Royal* (1882) and Charles Morgan's *Sparkenbroke* (1936), but in neither case are the parallels close. Mary Ellen Chase makes the links explicit in *Dawn in Lyonesse* (1938) by having the narrator read the story of Tristan and Iseult. Her understanding of, and sympathy for, the lovers' plight gives her insight into the comparable attachment of her husband and friend, an awakening of the sympathetic imagination through literature that parallels the awakening of the lovers' emotions. Here, too, however, the similarities are only those of general situation.

The two most recent novels based on this romance have gone much further in attempting to provide details that match those found in the legend. Originally published in Polish in 1967, Maria Kuncewicz's *Tristan: A Novel* (1974) tells the story of Michael Gaszynski (Tristan), a Polish partisan who escapes to London. There he is nursed back to health by Kathleen McDougal (Iseult). Despite their attraction to each other, he allows her to marry the eminent Professor Bradley (Mark). They meet later in

Cornwall, where Michael's mother owns a cottage, fall uncontrollably in love while drinking wine (love potion), and run away to London together (abduction). Poverty eventually forces them to part, despite their recognition that they belong to each other (return). They meet a final time in the United States (Brittany) where Michael has married another Kate (Iseult of the White Hands). The story becomes quite involving, capturing something of the power of its original. Moreover, it is intriguing to observe how traditional details of the legend are provided with modern equivalents. As Michael lies wounded, he sends a messenger from America to Cornwall with an earring for identification. If Kathleen will agree to come, the messenger is to cable white, if not, black. This recalls the story of the white and black sails, and the link is reinforced when Michael's wife misreports the message, although the consequences are not so tragic.

The finest modern transposition of the Tristan and Iseult story, however, is *Castle Dor* (1961). Begun by Sir Arthur Quiller-Couch, this novel was completed from his notes by Daphne du Maurier. The story is set in the nineteenth century in the vicinity of Castle Dor, which has been identified as the historical site of Mark's fortress.[7] As he reflects upon the legend, Dr. Carfax is moved to ponder that "the pattern of events, curiously intermingled as they were, followed a course uncannily similar to that which was happening on the same terrain today. Thought transference seemed the only possible explanation" (p. 224).

He cannot but wonder whether he had been "so imbued with the spirit of a place that. . .he breathed into her his own sense of haunting tragedy, dooming her to unwilling repetition of a story that was not hers" (p. 224). As a man of science the doctor is unwilling to venture further into the realms of the nonrational, and the reason for the repetition of events remains an enigma. Yet some kind of explanation for what is happening is certainly needed, for the parallels between past and present are striking.

The characters are all present. Amyot Trestane, a Breton fisherman, plays the role of Tristan. Linnet Lewarne, who is descended from royalty and is crowned Harvest Queen, acts out Iseult's part. The betrayed husband is the innkeeper Mark Lewarne, old, suspicious, rich. Deborah Brangwyn is the faithful maid who eventually betrays her mistress in an attempt to help her. Farmer Bosanko, who discovers that he is descended from Hoel of Little Britain, plays the part of that king, harboring Amyot during his "banishment"; his children, Mary and Johnny, are Iseult of the White Hands and Kaedin. Even Dr. Carfax finds himself cast in the character of Dinas, Tristan's good friend. The spying dwarf is there too in the shape of Ned Varcoe, the hunchbacked bartender.

Not only are the characters closely linked with the past by these various devices, but so also is the plot, including an astonishing number of specific motifs. Amyot's mother, like Tristan's, "had borne him in sorrow" (p. 113). He is nursed back to health following an injury by Linnet, just as Iseult healed Tristan. He drinks Linnet's special potion, a secret recipe handed down to her by her mother, just as Tristan drank the love potion, and declares, "it's as though when we drank, something magic had entered into me" (p. 148). He kills the massive Captain Fouguereau, as Tristan slew the giant Urgan, and like his predecessor he gives his lady the gift of a dog. Here too is Iseult's misleading oath (p. 143) and Tristan's leap (p. 256); Tristan's banishment (pp. 190, 198, 225), madness (pp. 246–49), and death from a poisoned spear (pp. 253, 266). Even the motif of the black and white sails (p. 269) is included, along with many others from the legend.

The connection between past and present is made explicit through Carfax's researches and, as he observes, the details fit together like "puzzle pieces" (p. 256). Much of the book's fascination comes from identifying these puzzle pieces. However, they also contribute to the sense of fate that gives the novel its power. Even as he perceives the direction in which events are turning, the doctor is unable "to stay a senseless repetition of one of the saddest love stories in the world" (p. 273). He is as helpless to keep the lovers apart as he is to remain aloof from the tragedy. The triumph of fate over human will is epitomized at the end when it is from his own well-meaning hand that Amyot receives his unintentional death wound. The legend not only forces unsuspecting characters into their prepared roles, but at times even takes possession of them, dragging their minds into the past until they become like Amyot, "a wanderer in time, caught up in a past that was not of his own seeking" (p. 268).

Novels that transpose the love triangle formed by Lancelot-Guenevere-Arthur have been less numerous, and they usually incorporate the Grail quest in some form or other. The earliest, *Arthur: or a Knight of Our Own Day* (1876) is a sentimental romance by Mary Neville that predates the period of this study. There follows a long gap before the next, Babs H. Deal's *The Grail: A Novel* (1963). This ingeniously transposes the Arthurian legend to the setting of U.S. college football, where the Grail is a perfect season without loss. Coach Arthur Hill of Castle University, hailed as "a king" (p. 161) because of his successful career, puts together a winning team, led by Lance Hebert, his brilliant quarterback. Unfortunately Lance falls in love with the coach's wife, Jennie, and their affair disrupts the team's unity. They lose their final game.

It is fascinating to identify traditional characters in their new roles. Buck Timberlake, the handsome, guitar-playing fullback, is Tristan the harpist. Wayne and Dwayne O'Hara, twins playing as linebackers, represent Gawain and Gareth. Like their predecessors they come from the north, recruited from Pennsylvania. With two other friends from the same state they form a distinct group within the team, the equivalent of the Orkney faction in the Round Table. They also identify Arthur Hill with their uncle. Even the feud with Lancelot is recalled: Wayne abandons his earlier support of Lance after the quarterback strikes Dwayne for challenging him about his affair with Jennie.

Despite the ingenuity with which traditional characters are transposed, and they include Mordred, Agravain, Iseult, Elaine of Corbenic, and Morgan le Fay, the cumulative effect is to reduce the significance of events. Most of the players and their sorority girl friends simply lack the necessary depth and stature. Moreover, the loss of one football game, no matter how crucial, just does not seem all that important to most people, and the action is not so involving that we lose sight of this. Nevertheless the similarities between modern team sports and medieval warfare as portrayed in romance, especially where attitudes to codes of behavior and to heroes and leaders are concerned, are intriguingly close, and fans and participants alike can take competition very seriously indeed.

Nicole St. John has treated the story most recently in *Guinever's Gift* (1977). This is a gothic romance with most of the familiar trappings: a dark, gloomy house with locked rooms and mysterious secrets, a crippled aristocratic owner brooding about the past, hostile servants and suspicious relatives, and an innocent young heroine whose life is in danger. The supernatural overtones are eventually rationalized, e.g., visions are explained as "scrying," a form of self-hypnosis. However, they do contribute to the atmosphere of brooding mystery.

The Grail sought here is archeological proof of Arthur's existence. More important, however, is the fatal triangle that occurs not once but twice. On the first occasion the heroine's mother and father represent Guinever and Arthur, while the young Lord Charles Ransome plays Lancelot. Later, Charles finds himself in the role of Arthur, while the heroine and his archeological assistant are cast in the role of the lovers. His cousin serves as a fusion of Elaine of Corbenic and Morgause, and she bears him an illegitimate child who functions as Mordred. The crippled Charles also evokes elements of the Fisher King legend.

The parallels are perceived by the characters themselves, since they are engaged in Arthurian research, and their struggle to resist the preordained pattern, to assert their individuality and independence by living their own lives, gives this novel a thoughtful potential. Unfortunately, it is squandered by the failure to develop character more fully and to raise plot above the level of melodrama. This latter weakness is epitomized in the final bizarre struggle on the cliffs opposite Tintagel, where the invalid Charles charges to the rescue by pushing his heavy wheelchair up a rough and grassy slope.

This group of novels, based upon the loves of Tristan and Iseult, Lancelot and Guenevere, contributes to the legend by enlarging our appreciation of the traditional characters and situations. In the first place they challenge us to identify the traditional characters in their new guise, teaching us more about them in the process. Beyond that, however, by transposing characters and situations into a modern context, they breathe fresh life into both, arousing our sympathy and understanding. They invest these characters and events with an immediacy and relevance that serve as proof positive of their universality. Love can still drive people to irrational acts, can still transport them with ecstasy, or crush them with despair. There is something of Tristan and Iseult, of Mark and Mordred, in all of us should events move in a particular direction. Our sympathy is gained, however, not only because the characters are recreated in a contemporary setting, but also because they are seen as prisoners of a preordained destiny. Their attempts to avoid fate thus arouse our pity and admiration, whereas their offenses are more readily excused. This sympathy may even extend to characters who play a traditionally destructive role, as is demonstrated by the treatment of the modern counterparts of Mordred and Morgause in *Guinever's Gift*, and of Morgan le Fay in *The Grail: A Novel*. *Castle Dor* preserves a more dispassionate perspective: Mark and his dwarf spy are unpleasant creatures, and even the lovers can be ruthless in order to be together, especially Linnet/Iseult. Yet the overpowering sense of possession by a power beyond their control continues to mitigate their actions.

The third group of novels deals with the Grail quest, and they often contain mystical elements that relate them to fantasy. The earliest is J. H. Shorthouse's sanctimonious Victorian novel, *Sir Percival: A Story of the Past and of the Present* (1886). Here good triumphs over evil in the feminine guise so traditional in later medieval versions of Percival's quest. Not only does she tempt the hero from his holy destiny, but she is guilty of being a socialist and an atheist. For these dire sins she is carried off by a fever. Which is no more than she deserves for visiting sick people, it would appear. Percival eventually wins salvation through martyrdom in West Africa, recalling his predecessor's death fighting in the Holy Land in the English verse *Sir Perceval of Gales*.

Arthur Machen includes the Grail in two works. *The Great Return* (1915) describes the confusion and excitement caused by a visitation of the Holy Grail to modern Wales. The critical objectivity of the reporter, from whose point of view the story is told, contrasts starkly with the supernatural phenomenon whose impact he is struggling to report. This contrast between the material and spiritual worlds is developed more fully in *The Secret Glory* (1922). The young hero is modeled upon Perceval, and he too is martyred by infidels, this time in the East. As a child he is taken to see the Grail, which is in the possession of a descendant of its traditional keepers. Thereafter his youth is filled with ecstatic visions that contrast sharply with his surroundings: the ugliness of the factory town and the arrogant insensitivity of the public school. Machen is particularly scathing about the latter and its inability to appreciate the rapture that transforms the hero. "It is very probable that if, in the nature of things, it had been possible for an English schoolboy to meet St. Francis of Assisi, the boy would have concluded that the saint had just made 200 not out in first-class cricket" (p. 109). The Grail serves to reveal the limitations of modern society, its cruelty, stupidity, and hypocrisy in the guise of morality.

In his preface to the 1955 edition, John Cowper Powys describes the Grail as the "heroine" (p. xiii) of his mystical work, *A Glastonbury Romance* (1933). This is a complex book and it uses Arthurian symbols complexly. Some idea of this can be seen in the character of "Holy Sam" Dekker. His affair with Nell Zoyland initially recalls the Lancelot-Guenevere-Arthur triangle. Like Arthur the husband is the illegitimate son of an aristocratic father. Crummie Geard, who plays Elaine of Astolat in the great pageant staged in Glastonbury, ironically plays a comparable role in life, for she is in love with Sam, yet sacrifices her own interests to the welfare of Sam and Nell, albeit in her case willingly. However, when Sam leaves Nell for his Grail quest, he is closer to Perceval abandoning Blancheflor. Moreover his vision of the Grail occurs on a barge that reminds one of the barges that bear the successful Grail knights in the Vulgate *Queste del Saint Graal* and in Malory. As one critic has pointed out, the novel uses "Arthurian myth to point, though not to control, the development of the themes.... At certain moments and occasions the myth is re-enacted."[8]

Other characters also evoke Arthurian prototypes. John Geard, after seeing the ghost of Merlin in a house called Mark's Court for its associations with that monarch, takes upon himself aspects of the old enchanter. A child called Morgan Nelly is related to the enchantress by her fierce courage and power over her friends as well as by her name. Geard's two daughters and Mad Bet seem to function as Grail-bearers. Other analogies exist too, for the author compares Philip Crow's speech to the Dolorous Blow in Chapter XII. Nor is the Grail the only Arthurian vision, for John Crow sees Arthur's sword cast into the river.

Powys' approach to the Arthurian material certainly invests his book with mystical power, and the reaction of the different characters to the mystical experience symbolized by the Grail provides valuable insight into their personalities. However the complexity of this approach also reflects a structural weakness that has been strongly criticized in Powys' work. The Arthurian elements fit into a rich tapestry to which they add both color and strength, but the patterns formed are not always easy to discern. They demand a sympathetic eye.

The only juvenile novel in this category is *The Flowering Thorn* (1961) by Elizabeth Yunge-Bateman. Inspired by a quiet faith, five young people set out to track down the Grail, a wooden cup at Nanteos reputed to have been brought to Britain by Joseph of Arimathea.[9] They do not find it, but one at least experiences a Grail vision and all achieve spiritual contentment from their charitable deeds along the way. This is a sentimental tale, but it avoids offensive piety enough for the children to remain attractive characters.

The most recent Grail novel is in many respects also the most impressive. Lancelot Lamar, the narrator-hero of Walker Percy's *Lancelot* (1978),[10] had been a college football hero, then a liberal lawyer who supported racial equality in the U.S. South. However his early promise and idealism fade after an unhappy marriage. Like the Lancelot of tradition, after whom he was named by his father, he is distracted from the Holy Grail of a noble cause by a woman. She too is one he should avoid. Impressed by his status and his family mansion, she seduces him with her sexuality and they marry. Yet though he genuinely loves her, she soon tires of him, aspiring to a career as a film actress. To compensate for her meagre talents, she sleeps with the director. Meanwhile the betrayed husband sinks into alcohol and impotence, no longer the noble champion who wins the queen's heart, but rather the maimed Fisher King. He tries to blunt his anguish with drink, yet as he sits in the midst of the Waste Land that is modern America he cannot but recognize the desolation that surrounds him. Society, however, ignores the evil and ugliness, blinding itself with the dazzling illusion provided by and symbolized by Hollywood. Thus Lancelot renews his quest, though this time he plans to punish society for its betrayal of the ideals that he cherished as young man.

Viewing himself as the "Knight of the Unholy Grail" (p. 144), he comments, "So Sir Lancelot set out, looking for something rarer than the Grail. A sin" (p. 147). Rarer, that is, in the eyes of a society blinded by illusion, as is witnessed by the town's fascination with the film company. Lancelot achieves his vision, recording on video tape the sexual promiscuity of both his wife and his daughter. Moreover, just as his predecessor's vision of the Grail was partially veiled, so is his hindered by the poor quality of the recording, with its images reversed as is only appropriate for an unholy quest. Both questers are barred by their own sin.

Herein lies the irony. Lancelot's quest inevitably involves his own destruction, because he too has been corrupted, more deeply than he realizes. It is not enough that he is an injured party, nor that he temporarily lays off alcoholic drink. He did, after all, succumb to the seductive advances originally, and his moral failure is seen in both the neglect of his law practice and the paternalistic attitude which he adopts toward "his" blacks. He too manipulates people for his own ends, and that he chooses to find proof of sin on video tape, using the very techniques of the film world which he so despises, is a potent symbol of his corruption. He shares in the moral blindness of society. He must therefore be destroyed in the final cataclysm, though typically he is incapable of confronting the full truth. He must escape into madness.

There are other Arthurian echoes also: Merlin, the producer-director, is the creator of stars, bringing new heroes from obscurity to fame on the wide screen, just as the Merlin of tradition served as Arthur's mentor; and Lancelot narrates his story to an old college friend called Percival, now a psychiatrist and priest. This is a symbolic novel, and the Arthurian borrowings serve to deepen the significance of the symbols. Elements from tradition are transformed to fit the vision of the author. And a powerful vision it is, despite its flaws. It presents us with a world of spiritual desolation, a modern Waste Land that gives fresh meaning to the myth of the Grail quest. This is not the only novel in which Percy reveals a preoccupation with the world of film and film making, but here he succeeds impressively in integrating it into the Grail legend. Moreover, as a setting it is ideally suited to explore the theme of illusion and reality that is as central to Arthurian legend as it is to this particular novel. Like many of the greatest works of Arthurian literature, Percy's *Lancelot* explores the gap between illusion and reality to reveal that failure and sin exist not only in the outside world, but also within those who seek to improve it. It is a mortifying and ever-timely lesson.

These novels as a group develop the symbolic significance of the Grail, using it to measure the human condition. Both Powys and Yunge-Bateman stress the positive spiritual achievements that are rewarded by the Grail vision. Shorthouse, Machen and Percy write largely cautionary tales that focus upon the spiritual shortcomings of the world. Perceval is the most popular model among the Grail knights, since his youthful innocence forms a striking contrast with a materialistic world. The message that the world corrupts is confirmed by Percy's novel, where the middle-aged hero is so deeply infected by the very sins he despises that he is destroyed.

These novels strengthen the universality of the Grail legend, revealing its continuing relevance. It is not just a curious medieval tale, but an expression of that basic spiritual yearning that is so important to mankind. It is precisely because these novels view this spiritual dimension as vital to man that they are considered among the "realistic" treatments of the Arthurian legend. The Grail visions experienced in the books by Shorthouse, Machen, Powys and Yunge-Bateman are all genuine. The authors' view of life in these works may be more mystical than that held by many people, but for them it is not fantasy.[11]

Where Arthurian characters are transposed in these Grail novels they gain an immediacy from their modern context. Identity with traditional models is less close than in the Guenevere-Iseult love stories, since the roles are less clearly defined. Indeed medieval concepts of the Grail were quite vague and contradictory.

This permits greater flexibility in transposing the legend and the characters involved. In place of the inexorable fate that controls the lovers, we find freedom of choice. The Grail quester must choose whether or not he wishes to pursue the spiritual values that are folly in the eyes of the world. Moreover, the conflict between innocence and corruption that is at the heart of the Grail legend may be confronted in many different ways. It is significant that those authors who transpose the Grail material most freely, namely Powys and Percy, have also been most successful in their handling of it. Conversely Quiller-Couch and du Maurier, who adhere most closely to the details of the original love story, have been most effective in retelling it. The reason for this difference is inherent in the material they have chosen to work with: the Grail legend reveals basic human failings that manifest themselves in different ways as society changes, whereas the love story gains its power from its sense of inevitability, of characters swept forward by emotions they cannot control.

NOTES

1. For mysteries in a traditional Arthurian setting, see Maxey Brooke's "Morte D'Alain: An Unrecorded Idyll of the King," which is discussed in Chapter 4, and Phyllis Ann Karr's *Idylls of the Queen*, which is discussed in Chapter 6.

2. Northup and Parry, "The Arthurian Legends: Modern Retellings of the Old Stories," p. 220.

3. Staines, "King Arthur in Victorian Fiction," and Merriman, "The Other Arthurians in Victorian England."

4. Brown and Parry, "The Arthurian Legends: Supplement to Northup and Parry's Annotated Bibliography," p. 216.

5. Arthur F. Kinney, "The Arthurian Cycle in *Tortilla Flat*," in *Steinbeck: A Collection of Critical Essays*, ed. Robert Murray Davis (Englewood Cliffs, N.J.: Prentice-Hall, 1972), pp. 36–46; see p. 46. See also *Steinbeck and the Arthurian Theme*, ed. Tetsumaro Hayashi (Muncie, Ind.: Ball State University Press, 1975).

6. The former was the subject of a paper delivered by Eugene Green, entitled "The Pursuit of the Grail as Burlesque in Kafka's *The Castle*," on 7 May 1983 to the Eighteenth International Congress on Medieval Studies at Kalamazoo, Michigan. The latter was argued in a paper by Veatrice C. Nelson, entitled "Between Two Merlins: The Quest of a Modern Arthur in John Le Carré's Smiley Trilogy," delivered on 13

March 1982 to the Third International Conference on the Fantastic in the Arts at Boca Raton, Florida.

7. See C. A. Ralegh Radford, "Romance and Reality in Cornwall," in *The Quest for Arthur's Britain*, ed. Geoffrey Ashe (London: Pall Mall Press, 1968), pp. 75–100; Geoffrey Ashe, *A Guidebook to Arthurian Britain* (Wellingborough, Northamptonshire: Aquarian Press, 1983), pp. 76–78. Quotations are from the American edition of *Castle Dor* (Garden City, N.Y.: Doubleday, 1962).

8. Glen Cavaliero, *John Cowper Powys: Novelist* (Oxford: Clarendon Press, 1973), p. 65. Cf. Taylor and Brewer, *The Return of King Arthur*, p. 285.

9. See Ashe, *A Guidebook to Arthurian Britain*, pp. 163–64.

10. Quotations are from the paperback edition of Walker Percy's *Lancelot* (New York: Avon, 1978).

11. One might draw an analogy with legend and mythology which similarly assume at least a measure of belief. However, the distinction is a fine one, and these novels might just as easily have been grouped with low fantasy.

4

HISTORICAL FICTION

Whereas the realistic novels are set in the modern period, historical novels are set in the past, in King Arthur's day. They recreate the spirit of that earlier time so that it comes alive once again for the readers. They can thus re-experience that world as it might have existed, with all the social, political, and human forces that created and finally destroyed it.

However, Arthur is not just a figure from history. Indeed some scholars deny that Arthur ever existed. They argue that his story was borrowed from the Romanized Britons of an earlier era, or from the Dalriada Scots, or even from Sarmatian mercenaries serving under a Roman officer named Lucius Artorius Castus on Hadrian's Wall. Many of the adventures attached to Arthur are drawn from myth and legend, and from the deeds of other historical personages.[1] Among his followers can be discerned Celtic deities who are only partly euhemerized, and heroes from other eras and other lands.[2] Certainly hard historical data are very scarce, and much of what has been gleaned is either suspect or circumstantial. Nevertheless, most scholars continue to believe in a post-Roman war leader who led the British to a temporary victory over the Germanic invaders during the late fifth and early sixth centuries, and they offer various theories to account for his successes and ultimate failure.

The very uncertainty about what really happened has, in fact, proved a considerable asset to the authors of historical fiction, since it allows them greater freedom in shaping the various details to fit their own literary purposes. Historical novelists usually place a figure of minor importance at the center of the action, since the deeds of major figures are often well documented. To tamper with historical data to suit thematic development might weaken the credibility of the novel. Since Arthur and the other important figures of his day are so shadowy, historical novels about them are not so restricted in their dealings. While minor characters remain popular as narrators, and as vital actors in the events described, often these functions are performed by an important follower, such as Bedivere, Lancelot, Guenevere, Merlin, or even by Arthur himself.

However, this freedom has given rise to other problems for the historical novelist. Earlier writers and storytellers have seized the golden opportunity to offer their own interpretations and inventions. And many of these features have become integral parts of the story that cannot be easily ignored without losing some of the power it possesses. The tyranny of literary tradition has replaced that of history.

This is most apparent when we look at two motifs that are later accretions to the legend: the love between Lancelot and Guenevere, and the incestuous birth of Mordred. Initially Mordred was no more than Arthur's nephew, the son of his sister Anna. Appointed regent during his uncle's expedition against Rome, he rebelled, married Guenevere, and died fighting Arthur at Camlann. Lancelot was one of Arthur's less important captains, with no links whatsoever to the Queen. However, changes were introduced by medieval romance in the twelfth and thirteenth centuries, and because they proved popular they became firmly attached to Arthurian tradition. When modern novelists retell the story of Arthur, they often retain both motifs even though they strive for historical authenticity. However, this is not only because their audience expects these motifs. The love affair and the incest have been preserved precisely because they add a tragic dimension to the story of Arthur's rise and fall. The hero and his followers scale great heights against insurmountable odds, only to be destroyed by their own innate failure. To discard these motifs is to rob the story of some of the very elements that attracted the authors in the first place.

Precisely because the traditional shape of the story exercises such powerful fascination, many historical novelists choose to preserve the setting of the High Middle Ages found in Malory and his predecessors. Unlike those who strive to recreate an authentic post-Roman Britain as the setting for events, they retain the trappings of a later era made familiar in the retellings described in Chapter 2. In their novels we find feudalism, courtly love, monasticism, chivalry, castles, and tournaments. Moreover, these features are treated as they are in medieval romance rather than reality: real castles were much more cramped and crowded than those in romance; and real knights were much less faithful in keeping their word.[3]

Although such a setting is clearly unhistorical, nevertheless its familiarity to readers serves as some compensation, especially to those whose knowledge of early periods of history is imprecise. More important, the suspension of disbelief can be achieved by developing characters whose actions are psychologically plausible. However, many of the writings set in the High Middle Ages make relatively few attempts to establish either historical or psychological authenticity. They are historical *romances*, not historical *novels*.

In the romance mode of writing the focus falls upon the activities of characters who are larger than life. Northrop Frye describes "the typical hero of romance" as "superior in *degree* to other men and to his environment, . . . whose actions are marvellous but who is himself identified as a human being."[4] Such heroes are not intended to be credible as ordinary people. Rather they represent certain standards of behavior, and it is as representatives that their actions should be judged. We are invited to observe their conduct, and to learn from the trials and tribulations through which they must pass before they achieve success. Like all literature, romance must still say something relevant about the human condition, but it does so primarily through the thematic pattern thus evolved, rather than by creating the illusion of reality through convincing characterization and authentic setting.

I have thus divided the historical novels into two groups: those set in the Dark Ages, and those set in the High Middle Ages.

THE DARK AGES

To date well over thirty historical novels and short stories have set Arthur in post-Roman Britain. From a mere trickle of less than one novel a decade, the numbers have grown steadily: two each in the 1930s and 1940s; from 1950 to 1964, they appeared at the average rate of a novel every second year; since 1965 the rate has doubled to one every year. It is tempting to attribute some of this attention in the historical Arthur to interest aroused by the archeological excavations at South Cadbury Castle in the late 1960s. Certainly they have encouraged speculation among scholars upon the historicity of Arthur.[5]

Among the novels and stories, several give Arthur and his warriors a very minor role, usually because their focus is upon either earlier or later events. Warwick Deeping's sentimental romance, *The Man on the White Horse* (1934), has the earliest setting, Britain during the disastrous collapse of order under combined barbarian invasions in A.D. 367. Against this background unfolds the love story of Guinevra and Geraint, a stalwart Roman landowner. Like Gawaine and Caradoc, two of Geraint's lieutenants, they bear Arthurian names, and the story of the rise of a champion against external invasion and internal disorder anticipates Arthur's career. However the Arthurian influence seems only of a very general kind.

The Count of the Saxon Shore (1887) by the Reverend Alfred J. Church is a highly idealized and melodramatic romance about Britain immediately after the departure of the legions early in the fifth century. The last chapter, however, jumps ahead to the Battle of Mount Badon, here given the early date of A.D. 451. In his ironic short story, "The Last of the Legions" (1911), Sir Arthur Conan Doyle describes the scene as the Romans receive the order to withdraw the remaining legions from Britain at the beginning of the fifth century. The British leaders, who arrive to ask for greater independence, are given more than they bargained for, and they soon fall prey to invaders. The wife of one ends up as mistress to one "Mordred, the wild chief of the western Cymri" (p. 100). This idea is carried a step further by Adam Fergusson in *Roman Go Home* (1969). This political satire upon the post-colonial experience is modeled upon contemporary African rather than historical experience, though the suggested parallels are fascinating. Thus the Roman Empress, very much the representative of the royal family at independence celebrations, observes, "Ingratitude and incompetence were the first and invariable manifestations of liberty from colonial rule; and it was never long before corruption, poverty and repressive legislation set in, followed by popular rising, *coups d'état* and the disintegration of the body politic" (p. 203). This proves a depressingly accurate prediction, as the unscrupulous Vortigern seizes power by murdering his brother Constans, only to become a puppet of the Marxist Saxon mercenaries whom he hires to prop up his corrupt regime.

Two works published in 1926 are set in the years shortly after Arthur's death, when the Saxon invaders resumed their conquest of what was to become England. Both "The Last Legion and Gray Maiden, the Sword" by Arthur D. Howden Smith and *The Altar of the Legion* by Farnham Bishop and Arthur Gilchrist Brodeur recall the valor of Arthur with nostalgia in a highly idealized and sentimental picture of heroic resistance against overwhelming odds. The latter story includes King Owain ap Urien and his ravens—here black-cloaked Irish cavalry—figures developed from *The Dream of Rhonabwy* in the Welsh *Mabinogion*.

Anya Seton's *Avalon* (1965) is set still later, in the tenth century. The hero comes to England in search of the Holy Grail and the peace of Avalon, and there he meets a Cornish girl who claims to be the last living descendant of Arthur. The story succeeds in capturing some of the yearning expressed in the myth.

Although it describes events contemporary with Arthur's career, Alfred Duggan's *Conscience of the King* (1951) allows Arthur and his followers no more than a brief appearance. The protagonist is Cerdic, who survives defeat at Mount Badon to establish the kingdom of Wessex. The strength of the novel is the vivid picture it paints of the political disintegration of Britain. Cerdic, a British renegade, is the embodiment of those qualities which Gildas castigates in his compatriots.[6] Although not unmoved by nobler sentiments, his actions are governed by expediency and unscrupulous self-interest. To further his ambition, he kills his brother, his wife, and (indirectly) his father. Cerdic powerfully demonstrates the political problems that doomed Arthur's attempt to preserve Britain.

Among those historical novels that give Arthur a major role in events, four make use of the device of an objective written report. In John Masefield's *Badon Parchments* (1947), an officer loaned by Justinian, the Emperor of Byzantium, to help the British organize against the invaders presents a rather self-conscious report on the military and political developments leading up to the battle on Mount Badon. Perhaps the most interesting aspects of the novel are its parallels with World War II. The barbarians recall the Nazis in their political tactics and rhetoric, claiming provocation for their attacks which, they insist, are purely defensive. Like their descendants, the members of the Council of Britons waste valuable time in futile debate, listening to arguments for appeasement even as they delude themselves about the extent of the danger, for they underrate the external threat even as they overrate their own preparedness. The progress of the war also suggests parallels with the campaigns of World War II. No attempt is made to develop character. Instead the novel focuses upon its political message: that a valiant and alert defense is the only way to deal with an unscrupulous enemy.

In Walter O'Meara's *The Duke of War* (1966) events are chronicled by a young Romano-British girl at the request of her grandfather. Since their villa serves as Arthur's headquarters for the few weeks of the campaign that culminates in the victory at Mount Badon, she is well placed to observe his domestic, as well as his political and military, problems. Moreover, she reports tales told about his followers, such as Geraint's neglect of valor and suspicions of his wife. This provides a fuller picture of the difficulties confronting Arthur as he tries to keep his forces united against the enemy, despite the quarrelsome pride, impatience, selfishness, and even treachery that threaten to divide them.

However, the narrative distancing deprives the story of the intensity that comes from personal involvement. This is most noticeable when the narrator falls in love with a young warrior who is slain in the battle. Her initial excitement and subsequent sense of loss contrast with the detachment of her views of Arthur's household.

In George Finkel's *Twilight Province* (1967), published as *Watch Fires to the North* (1968) in the United States, Bedwyr sets out to provide an accurate version of what happened during a period of rapid change. Events are set in the North of Britain during the first part of the sixth century, a date that is later than that usually assigned to Arthur. This allows a British mission led by Bedwyr to learn heavy cavalry tactics from Belitzar (Belisarius), the brilliant general of Justinian, Emperor of Byzantium. He returns to apply them with devastating effect against the Saxons.

As son of the Romano-British ruler of what eventually becomes a kingdom along the River Tees, Bedwyr is in many ways more powerful than Artyr (Arthur), a Dumnonian refugee of royal birth. He is appointed war leader of the North British confederation because he has no local interests, but since he has no warband of his own he is totally dependent upon their support. The heavy cavalry, many of whom are mercenaries, are raised by the Teesiders and led in battle by Bedwyr. In keeping with his position, Artyr remains a remote figure. Bedwyr admits that he was "not an easy man to know. He was an indifferent warrior but a great general...most wise in council" (p. 311). Bedwyr also comments upon the various stories about Artyr, rejecting them as exaggeration. Thus he insists that the relationship between his cousin Gwenyfer (Guenevere) and the Gothic mercenary Olans (Lancelot) was no more than friendship. The novel is interesting for the ingenuity with which it adapts traditional features to fit its historical framework, for its picture of ordinary people fighting to preserve a way of life that is threatened with violent destruction, and for the sense of rapid change taking place as Britain is transformed from a Roman to an English land.

John Gloag's *Artorius Rex* (1977) is cast in the form of a report by Caius Geladius (Kay) to Justinian, the Emperor of Byzantium, who is contemplating reconquering the former province of Britain. The focus is upon political events, the internal conflicts that ultimately prove Artorius' downfall. Here, however, Arthur just fades out of the picture. The independent kings grow in strength, while he loses most of his warband following the banishment of Gwinfreda (Guenevere) and Wlenca (Lancelot).

Since all four novels focus upon the political divisions that ultimately defeated the British, they present a generally foreboding picture. This is strengthened by the detachment of the narrators from the events they relate. Both the Byzantine officers and the young woman are outsiders, the former because they are foreigners, the latter because she encounters Arthur and his household but briefly; all three regard the internal dissensions and ruinous self-interest with grave misgivings. Since they view the characters from the outside, measuring the consequences of their actions rather than their noble aspirations, they do not balance the negative vision with more positive achievements. The consequence of this particular perspective is most noticeable in O'Meara's novel, where the narrator's romantic involvement engages our sympathy for the lovers in a way that contrasts with our response to the other characters.

The negative vision is less pronounced in Finkel's novel where the narrator, Bedwyr, is more closely involved in developments. Yet here too the author tries to create a sense of historical authenticity by preserving narrative detachment. Bedwyr is always concerned with "setting the record straight," and he refutes many of the romantic tales that circulate about Artyr. Unfortunately, the account he offers is not entirely convincing, and so the price of his demythologizing objectivity is a reduction in reader involvement.

The wide focus upon broad political developments in all four novels also leads to a reduction in attention to character. There is simply less room to develop individual figures, and so we do not see much of them. Even in battle the warriors tend to get lost in the crowd, partly because acts of heroism are so common that very few stand out. This shift of emphasis from character reflects a philosophical stance. The individual matters less in these novels because he or she is subject to forces beyond his or her control. A hero may struggle for a while and win both our admiration and a temporary respite: Cador in *Badon Parchments* resists doggedly until Arthur arrives to save the day at Mount Badon; and Arthur in *The Duke of War* asserts, "I hold it a man's part to stand up to his fate" (p. 51). Yet the tides of history inevitably sweep away both them and their achievements, and it is these tides of history that are the subject of the narratives. They are, in many respects, latter-day pseudo-chronicles, heirs to the tradition of Geoffrey of Monmouth.

The next group preserves the dark anti-romantic perception of these chronicles, but they describe events with an intensity that is very different. The earliest are two works by Edward

Frankland. "Medraut and Gwenhwyvar" (1944) is one of a series of stories set in a particular place at different times in history. This tale provides a glimpse of Arthur and his army marching south to fight the Saxons. They are fiercely determined, but they carry with them the seeds of their own destruction as Medraut and Gwenhwyvar plot betrayal. In *The Bear of Britain* (1944) this glimpse is expanded into a full-blown vision of corruption, selfishness, treachery, folly, and greed, inspired by Gildas' diatribe against the rulers of Britain. Indeed he is frequently the source of the quotations at the beginning of each chapter. Arthur is too honorable to seize absolute power after his victory at Mount Badon. He refuses to use "lies and treachery" (p. 177) as a means to an end, however important. His heroism is proclaimed: "Of all the heroes that have come up out of the race of Britons, this man sought least for himself and was most basely betrayed" (p. 262). However, his achievements are overshadowed by the ominous warnings voiced by Medraut, and by the treachery that abounds everywhere: in his brother Modron, his nephew Medraut, his wife Gwenhwyvar, the tyrant kings whom he too generously spares, and the renegade Cerdic.

Henry Treece continued this anti-romantic tradition in *The Eagles Have Flown* (1954), *The Great Captains* (1956), and *The Green Man* (1966). The first, which is written for juveniles, tells the story of two idealistic youths, a Romanized Briton and a Jute, who encounter Arthur. The former saves Arthur's life and serves him in the battles of Glein and Dubglas, engagements listed by Nennius. However, the brutal reality of warfare and betrayal leads to disillusionment. Recognizing that a true friend is more important than political and military expediency, no matter how worthy its purpose, the British lad saves the Jute and they flee together to Brittany.

Treece changed many of the details of this novel when he wrote *The Great Captains* (1956), but he retained the same vision of a violent and cruel age. We are shown strong men, who love and hate fiercely, whose pride prompts them to take heedless risks. They chew their knuckles or pound the table in their fury, and they die brutal and often senseless deaths. The novel covers the entire career of Artos, but he shares the stage with Medrawt (Mordred).

Arthur also figures in *The Green Man* (1966), which retells the story of Hamlet with typically brutal realism. Arthur is an aging leader here, and the crumbling power of the British is matched by his own physical decay: "He was fifty-four now. The teeth on the right side of his mouth had gone in a sudden sword sweep outside Caerwent. He could hardly see from his left eye by reason of a blow from a lance butt. . . . Arthur mourned far less the loss of hair, the rheumatism in his left hand which made shield-holding intolerable, his jumped-up right hip from a horse-fall" (p. 113). He is a pragmatist in his efforts to muster support against the invaders, tolerating conduct that he deplores. Yet the self-honesty and dignity with which he responds to the condemnation of the hero wins our admiration. The energy of the younger hero and the Germanic peoples that he represents may contrast with the weary decadence of Arthur and the British, but their arrogance blinds them to the fact that their morality is no better.

The most recent of these anti-romantic novels is Peter Vansittart's *Lancelot: A Novel* (1978). The story is narrated in an impressionistic style by Ker Maxim (Lancelot), a Briton of Roman family, and the dominant perception is of people's folly and pettiness: "history is a compendium of rumour, misunderstanding, inaccurate translation, error and fraud" (p. 165). Arthur displays talent as a commander of cavalry, but none as a strategist or administrator. Not only does he lack vision, but he compounds this limitation by refusing to trust others and delegate authority. Surly, unprincipled, murderous, suspicious of the ability of others, he maintains his power through the Owls, a network of secret police led by Kei: "The doomed merely vanished" (p. 111). Yet if Arthur emerges as a petty tyrant, the narrator fails to inspire much enthusiasm either. That he is resented as a representative of the Romans and for his administrative skills implies an attitude of superiority on his part that probably sharpens many of his criticisms. Typically, he dismisses as exaggeration many of the stories that were to build the noble legend of Arthur: Merlin is considered a charlatan who "exploited the general ignorance" (p. 120). Unlike Treece's novels where the figures loom larger than life despite their faults, this book's bitterly ironical perspective leaves no room for heroics.

In these dark visions of Arthur's world, the characters are predictably unattractive, and it is no accident that the most prominent are Mordred, Guenevere and Kay, three of the least admirable figures in Arthurian legend. Kay is the quick-tempered warrior of early Welsh tradition, and though his courage is impressive, it is his violence that one most remembers from these accounts. The negative view of Guenevere found in some medieval versions is found here also.[7] Frankland makes her proud and selfish; Treece develops the Welsh tradition of the three Gueneveres and makes at least one of them a prostitute; Vansittart makes her a high-priced whore before her marriage to Arthur. She is almost invariably deceitful and lustful.[8] Mordred is bloodthirsty, unscrupulous, and unreliable, but only in *The Green Man* does he lack some appeal. Vansittart even has him die fighting on Arthur's behalf. Where there is so little to admire, his cynicism and brilliance show to some advantage. Gawain and, more especially, Bedivere possess more amiable qualities, but they are kept in the background where they do not disturb the patterns of pride and anger, of selfishness and betrayal, of cruelty and lust.

Nevertheless, most of the novels set in the Dark Ages preserve a more traditional and benevolent view of Arthur, his followers, and the world that they inhabit. As the vision grows more romantic, so mystical elements start to intrude. The earliest are two rambling sentimental romances, *Cian of the Chariots* (1898) by William H. Babcock, and *Pendragon* (1930) by W. Barnard Faraday. The former offers a tediously self-righteous warning against religious intolerance, but the latter is redeemed by some entertaining passages of humor. These are generated by the verbal irony of characters such as Gwendaello (Guenevere) and the two bards Aneurin and Merddin (Merlin). But the finest sallies come from the sarcasm of Gildas. As he sets out for a battle between the Britons and Irish, he announces, "the souls of the Irish are best saved when at the point of death. I hope to save many" (p. 239). The effect is heightened by the frequent failure of the valiant, but not too quick-witted, Artorius to perceive the irony. The book also presents an attractive picture of Gwendaello, whose quick wit and sharp tongue match her personal courage and astuteness as a ruler.

Very different is John Cowper Powys' *Porius: A Romance of the Dark Ages* (1951). Its structure is badly flawed, especially toward the end when it becomes almost incoherent, but like *A Glastonbury Romance* it offers a wealth of riches. Perhaps the most interesting features from the point of view of Arthurian tradition are the anti-romantic view of Arthur and his followers, the mysticism of Myrddin Wyllt (Merlin), and the political conflict that influences the action. Of Arthur we learn, "That fabulous hero with that historic sword was gone. The courtly emperor bestowing names upon brave steeds, and learning the names of beautiful ladies was gone too. The man who dominated them now was a man of pure undiluted generalship, realistic, practical, and competent" (p. 351). By contrast Myrddin is perceived as an incarnation of Cronos, God of the Golden Age. "What the world wants," he declares, "is more common-sense, more kindness, more indulgence, more leaving people alone. . . . I never took arms against anything but the tyranny of heaven" (pp. 276–77). The political struggle pits the matriarchal leaders of the pre-Celtic forest people, who form an alliance with the marauding Saxons, against the Celtic tribes ruled by the House of Cunedda who support the inheritors of Roman tradition, led by Arthur. This reflects the internal divisions which eventually lost the British most of their land, and it explores some intriguing philosophical differences that may well have been as important in Arthur's time as they have been since.

Five of the remaining novels are written in the third person, and virtually all place Arthur firmly at the center of the story. The exception is Victor Canning's *The Crimson Chalice* (1976) which tells instead the story of his parents. However Canning went on to write about the youth and early triumphs of Arturo (Arthur) in *The Circle of the Gods* (1977), and of his later achievements, culminating at Mount Badon, before leaping ahead to conclude briefly with his death in *The Immortal Wound* (1978). All three were published in 1978 as *The Crimson Chalice*. Douglas Carmichael traces events from the conception of Artorius to his triumph at Mount Badon in *Pendragon: An Historical Novel* (1977). Gil Kane and John Jakes combine to carry the tale to his departure for Avalon in *Excalibur!* (1980).

The characters in *Excalibur!* are the high-minded idealists of romance: Arthur, recognizing too late before their marriage that Guinevere loves Lancelot, promises never to touch her; for their part, the lovers never betray him. The king consciously embraces the cause of good, recognizing that "the enemy was the darkness in them all" (p. 143). Unfortunately, like many a medieval romance the novel remains preoccupied with adventure for its own sake. Consequently the plot is not only loosely episodic, but also does too little to explore the conflict between good and evil, except in a general and simplistic way. Carmichael's plot structure is tighter, but much of his attention is occupied with the task of rendering traditional features plausible. This is fascinating for those familiar enough with the legend to recognize these features and the occasional wry touches of humor enliven an intelligent and involving story. Unfortunately, it leaves too little opportunity to explore character and theme, e.g., the reasons for, and implications of, the rebelliousness of the British kings.

This challenge is met more successfully by Canning's trilogy. This takes greater liberties with tradition, especially in the first book where the hero is given totally new parents, Baradoc and Gratia.[9] Like his father Arturo is moved by a strong sense of destiny, as one of his companions soon realizes: "in all things Arturo saw the hands and the will of the gods and believed without any shadow of doubt that he had been chosen to foster their work and their dreams for this country" (p. 381). This, however, comes into conflict with the ties of love—for wife, for comrade, for servant. Action generally mirrors this theme: the attempt upon Arturo's life by his father's cousin is a symptom of the internal rivalry of the British whom he is pledged to unite against the Saxon invader.

These conflicts generate tensions and crises, yet the general mood remains optimistic. This effect is achieved by having serious reversals reported briefly, whereas long struggles that are ultimately crowned by success are witnessed dramatically. Thus the disasters that throw Arturo's parents together happen before the story begins, whereas their long and painful struggle to safety is followed step by step; the slow death of Arturo's first wife takes but two sentences to describe, whereas the gradual stages by which he builds his warband at the villa are recounted in detail. The victory at Mount Badon forms the climax of Canning's story, the reward of years of patient dedication and self-sacrifice. By contrast Arturo's death, here reduced to a skirmish involving but eighteen men, seems a fulfilment and brief epilogue: "The gods had worked... this day of golden fruitfulness which was to die into the long darkness of the rest they decreed for him" (p. 642). The emphasis upon achievements gained through adherence to duty despite the cost and suffering creates a spirit of true heroism that is still further elevated by the essential humanity and nobility of Arturo: "to keep that peace he had had to shape himself anew and found many times when the iron of his pitilessness seared him more sharply than his victims" (p. 643). His belief in destiny may be an illusion, but his faith transforms it into reality.

Like Faraday's *Pendragon*, Edison Marshall's *The Pagan King* (1959) and Rosemary Sutcliff's *Sword at Sunset* (1963) are narrated by Arthur himself. The former is a lively, if at times rambling and contrived, novel that is distinguished by its development of the theme of illusion and reality. Arthur's career is a process of education. He sheds the illusion that he is a predestined leader when he discovers the reality that the ancient auguries were manipulated by Merdin (Merlin), here his great-uncle as well as mentor. And he finally discovers how much his early credulity has allowed him to be deceived by the fair Vivain, his dire foe at almost every turn. Magic exists only in the human imagination. Yet, paradoxically, as he grows more realistic he also learns to appreciate what illusion can achieve, and at the end he resigns his kingship, makes a personally stage-managed exit on a barge with three queens, and sets off with Elaine, his true love, to wander as an anonymous bard, transforming historical fact into glorious legend: "What is any king without an excellent bard to lie about him?... do not let the singer tell the truth about you... And let him not tell the dread violence of our dark age... for century beyond century our earth will remain uninhabitable, and life intolerable without kind lies" (p. 373). True to his own dictum, the author relates a stirring tale that takes many liberties with tradition, e.g., Vortigern is made Arthur's father, and Modred, his half-brother, a noble and valiant foe. Indeed the half-brothers are such kindred spirits that they are forever sparing each other's lives!

Sword at Sunset has been one of the most admired historical novels about Arthur, and deservedly so for it is a fine work. Some traditional features are retained, but Sutcliff strips away many. This is partly an attempt to get at the historical truth behind romance and legend, but also to focus upon the most important patterns of the story. In the Author's Note she describes these as "The Sin which carries with it its own retribution; the Brotherhood broken by the love between the leader's woman and his closest friend.... [and] the Sacred King, the Leader whose divine right, ultimately, is to die for the life of the people" (p. vii).[10] Of the traditional warriors only Cei, Gwalchmai (Gawain), and Bedwyr remain, and the last is given Lancelot's role of close friend to Artos and lover of Guenhumara (Guenevere).[11] The missing characters are replaced by new creations of Sutcliff's invention. This allows her to achieve a greater sense of historical authenticity, and at the same time to focus more clearly upon the major patterns that she perceives.

Sutcliff's novel has many virtues, including the clear prose that makes all her books a joy to read and the plausibility of the Dark Age world that she creates, both in setting and characterization. However, what really distinguishes the novel is the powerful sense of caring. Artos genuinely cares for others, and it shows most poignantly in his response to death: of his successive hounds, each named Cabal, one whose "valiant heart wore out" (p. 82), and another who lies wounded to the death for Artos' sake, yet who begins "a whisper of the old deep throat-song that had always been his way of showing his contentment in my company" (p. 395); of his warriors, "the young men who will never grow old" since the "flame is too bright" (p. 84); of his oldest and dearest friends, like Aquila, Gwalchmai, and Ambrosius. Yet even amidst his grief he can still feel for others. Over the horribly torn corpse of the beloved Ambrosius he looks at "the ashen face and quivering mouth of Ambrosius's young armor-bearer, and knew that the boy must instantly be got away and given something to do" (p. 356). When he learns of Medraut's rebellion, he sends off his own armor-bearer with a message that will keep him from the last fatal battle. The young man's grandfather, Aquila, had died fighting at Badon; his father was to accompany Artos. "Three were too many to take in direct succession from one man's line" (p. 453). Artos even feels distress at the suffering of his enemies, unwisely sparing Cerdic on two occasions, and avoiding torture, not out of pity but because he himself feels "too sharply" (p. 99) the pain of others.

This may seem a strange quality in a war leader until we recall that Artos' struggle is to protect his people. His role as the Sacred King, who must sacrifice his own life for his people, is recalled throughout the story, and before the last battle he reflects, "I could only hope that my death might serve also as a ransom for the people" (p. 464). Artos, like so many he has mourned, goes to meet his death with a quiet courage and resolve that bring tears to the eyes. At the last charge he tells his remaining loyal few, "If it is given to men to remember in the life we go to, remember that I loved you, and do not forget that you loved me" (p. 473).

Yet Artos is not a guiltless sacrifice. Not only does he relax his vigilance when he is seduced by his half-sister, Ygerna, but he neglects his wife. He marries her with frank reluctance, and he pays too little attention to her emotional needs—and her pride. Typically, he is absent when their daughter dies. Artos has good reasons for his conduct, however. As he makes clear to Guenhumara, he wishes to avoid marriage because he anticipates that his other responsibilities will leave too little time for his personal life. And he arrives after their daughter's death because he was busy fighting the enemy. Artos, thus, may have his faults, but they are faults that humanize him as he struggles with an impossible task. As a result of this humanity we can admire and appreciate his self-sacrifice all the more deeply. Arthur is almost always portrayed as a hero in modern fiction, but never is he more compassionate.

The remaining novels set in the Dark Ages are all told from the point of view of various narrators. The only invented character is Aquila in another Sutcliff novel, *The Lantern Bearers* (1959). This novel is also the best. It is a book for younger readers and a Carnegie Medal winner. Aquila, who appears later in *Sword at Sunset*, is a young officer with the last body of Roman legionaries when they are withdrawn from Britain. He chooses to remain, but is captured soon after by Jutish raiders. After several years as a thrall, he escapes and joins Ambrosius in the war against the invaders. This is a story of the days before Artos' rise to power, and so it is dominated by figures like Hengest and Rowena, Vortigern and Vortimer, but the young Artos plays a significant role in the later part of the book. Although narrated in the third person, the point of view never shifts from Aquila.

What makes this another fine performance by the author is the care with which the theme of forgiveness is worked out. Aquila suffers grievous wrong at the invader's hand: his father and their faithful servants are slain, his sister abducted, and he himself left for the wolves to devour until rescued by a different band of raiders and carried off as a slave or thrall. To make matters worse, when he eventually finds his sister he discovers not only that she has married the son of their father's slayer and borne him a son, but that she is unwilling to leave them and join him in escape. To him, this is betrayal. His soul is warped by the bitterness of his hatred and it nearly costs him the love of his own family. Fortunately, he gradually learns that love is more important than hate, and he is able eventually to grant full forgiveness to his sister and his Jutish enemies, forgiveness symbolized by his saving the life of his Jutish nephew. It is a final redemption that anticipates the compassion of *Sword at Sunset.* Both books share the image of keeping the light of civilization shining in the darkness of cruel barbarity, but for Sutcliff civilization means love.[12] Aquila's father deserves our respect, not for his aristocratic Roman descent but because he freed his slaves and treated his servants kindly. Both Artos and Ambrosius win our admiration for the concern they show for others. This heightens the paradox of their situation, forced to fight to preserve peace and love.

The narrator of Godfrey Turton's *The Emperor Arthur* (1967) is Pelleas, the warrior who eventually marries Vivian. Merlin, by contrast, is an evil priest who plots with the Saxon invaders. The political conflict is between the noble Arthur and rivals ambitious for power, notably the Church. At a thematic level this is reflected by the conflict between consideration and loyalty on the one hand, and selfish ambition on the other, but it is not seriously explored. The refusal of the good-natured characters like Gareth and Lancelot to suspect plotting endangers Britain's security, but this paradox is ignored. The lack of care is mirrored by the weak plot structure.

The narrator in Mary Stewart's Merlin trilogy is, of course, Merlin. *The Crystal Cave* (1970) starts with his own conception, seen in a vision, and concludes with the begetting of Arthur; *The Hollow Hills* (1973) continues the story up to Arthur's crowning; *The Last Enchantment* (1979) concludes with the final withdrawal of Merlin from the world. The author integrates and reinterprets many traditional features into an absorbing and plausible story, no mean task given the amount of magic associated with Merlin. The supernatural does enter into these novels: Merlin is a vehicle through which his god accomplishes his purpose; and he, like Nimue, has the sight, which makes him a seer and a prophet. Yet though rare, such abilities are not incredible. Most of the remaining magic is explained away as the superstitious response of other people to things they do not understand, e.g., Merlin's skill as a physician and as an engineer.

The main theme in the trilogy is the importance of accepting fate, or, as Merlin calls it, the will of the god. Over this Merlin has no control, and much of the action throughout the trilogy stems from his attempts to handle situations where it is assumed he has more power than he really has. This pattern culminates in the third book where Merlin faces his final loss of power and the fading of his visions. It is time for a new generation, which he himself has carefully and lovingly taught, to come to the fore: Nimue assumes the power of vision, Arthur the responsibility of rulership. Partly because Merlin has had to come to terms with the reality of his gift throughout his life, he has the wisdom to accept without struggle this ultimate fate: in effect, death. Indeed the distress and anguish are felt more keenly by those who love him, Arthur and Nimue, and he worries more about consoling them than he does about his own loss. Their struggle to accept is muted for the reader because it is witnessed through Merlin's eyes. It is a wise lesson on how to face the passing of power and death, but the tranquility of Merlin's acceptance robs the process of drama. Moreover, this mood of golden fulfilment and calm acceptance, though profoundly suggestive, is not fully reconciled with the pattern of political conflict that continues to disturb Arthur's kingdom and is destined finally to destroy it. This destruction is accomplished in *The Wicked Day* (1983), which tells the story of Mordred in the third person. Since Mordred is intelligent, he is quick to appreciate both the dangers and advantages of his situation as the son of Arthur, the High King. Yet as Nimue recognizes, "there is no treachery here, only ambition and desire" (p. 328). In fact, Mordred is perceptive and cautious enough to recognize that his best hope lies in winning the trust of the king. At Arthur's request, he keeps close watch upon Agravain and Gaheris, and he spies upon the disaffected younger element at court, posing as a sympathizer. Yet despite his ambition he possesses a genuine affection for his father, and the two develop a bond of mutual trust.

What destroys his bright hopes of succession is the inexorable working of fate, which first raises Mordred to prominence, then brings about his downfall, not through any fault of his own, but through an unfortunate sequence of circumstances. All his life Mordred has struggled to control his own destiny, first against the manipulation of his mother, Morgause, then against the mistrust of others: "he was Mordred, and Mordred depended on Mordred, and on no man else" (p. 109). Thus he recognizes a kindred spirit in the young wildcat which Morgause carries south as a gift, and he releases it from its cage. Yet he himself cannot escape so easily from the prophesy that he will cause his father's death, abhorrent though the idea is. Eventually, however, he learns to accept what must be: "It would come, yes, but only as, soon or late, all deaths came. He, Mordred, was not the instrument of a blind and brutal fate, but of whatever, whoever, made the pattern to which the world moved. *Live what life brings; die what death comes*" (p. 224; cf. pp. 193, 196).

The sense of golden fulfilment that this acceptance brings to the close of the Merlin trilogy is missing here, because the final disaster seems so wasteful. The new order that Mordred starts to create as Arthur's successor offers a reasonable hope for the future peace and prosperity of all the inhabitants of Britain, Celtic and Saxon alike, and Arthur is wise enough to recognize this. Yet this prospect is shattered by mischance, and by the selfish behavior of those, like Constantine, Morgause, and her sons, who are moved to rash deeds by pride and ambition. This frustration is captured by the image of Mordred lying injured and helpless while events unfold that he sought to prevent: after he is wounded by Bedwyr while trying to prevent conflict;[13] when he is left at the monastery by Gaheris while the latter makes good his escape; and when he lies dying at the end while Arthur is borne off in the barge by weeping women.

Mordred may not win our affection, but certainly he deserves our sympathy and understanding. Stewart explains in the Author's Note, "I have not made a 'hero' out of Mordred, but in my tale he is at least a man who is consistent in his faults and virtues, and has some kind of reason for the actions with which the legend has credited him" (p. 348). Stewart certainly achieves this aim, and she manages to generate some suspense from Mordred's struggle against his fate. However, like the Merlin trilogy, the novel lacks drama and intensity. Mordred is so guarded and self-preoccupied that it is not easy to get involved with him. Rather than identify with his actions, we judge them with the same detachment that he himself displays. Moreover Stewart focuses most sharply upon episodes like the attack upon Bedwyr and the deaths of Mordred's foster-parents, of Morgause, and of Lamorak, all of which show the failure of his attempts to achieve positive goals. The final effect is a sombre and cautionary tale of mankind's futility in the face of an implacable fate.

Anna Taylor's *Drustan the Wanderer* (1971), based upon the legend of Tristan and Iseult, is narrated by Drustan (Tristan). Precisely because he is a wanderer, the plot seems disjointed; and because of his inability to live fully without Essylt (Iseult) he experiences little character development. Drustan is very self-preoccupied, moving at times almost in a dream detached from the world about him. This captures that sense of the lovers' helplessness to resist a fate beyond human control—and it is significant that the love potion is one of the few mystical elements retained. However, it also reduces the hero to a more passive role in events, reflected by his directionless wanderings.

Although it shifts into third-person narrative in parts two and three, Jayne Viney's *The Bright-Helmed One* (1975) opens with a first-person account of Arthur's rise to power by Anwas, one of Arthur's followers in Welsh tradition. The second part follows the fortunes of his half-Jutish wife Winifrith (Guenevere) during the subsequent campaigns that culminate in the victory at Badon. The third part focuses upon the role of Cai in the events leading to the last battle against Medraut. The author uses these shifting points of view to explore different aspects of Arthur's life, but she is not in control of the technique. The personal preoccupations of the central characters intrude too much, and the limited point of view prevents the reader from establishing a bond of sympathy with Arthur. The result is a disjointed narrative structure that obscures rather than illuminates the theme of loyalty and betrayal, especially between father and son. This is particularly unfortunate in that the novel makes an interesting attempt to reconcile the conflicting traditions concerning Cai: his fierce and loyal service, as opposed to his treacherous murder of Arthur's son.

The remaining two novels set in the Dark Ages are both narrated by Bedivere. Roy Turner's *King of the Lordless Country* (1971) is an involving, if improbable, version of Arthur's rise to power, culminating in the victory at Mount Badon. Gwenhwyfer (Guenevere) is chief of the Circle, a band of warriors dedicated to noble ideals. Bedwyr and Arthur are recruited into it by a convoluted process that recalls the initiation rites of some secret society, and the latter marries Gwenhwyfar. This is a story of love and war, with the focus upon the narrator rather than Arthur. Bedivere loves three women, each in a different way: one platonic, one as wife and mother of his family, the third as a fellow warrior and lover. Whatever potential lessons exist in his experience seem to be lost on the narrator, however.

Catherine Christian's *The Sword and the Flame* (1978), published in the United States as *The Pendragon*, follows the traditional story more closely. One result of this is that the novel sprawls at such length that the pace suffers and the broader patterns blur. As its subtitle proclaims, it consists of "Variations on a theme of Sir Thomas Malory," and the situations and characters are often more romantic than realistic. Since it also tries to provide some historical authenticity, however, the effect can be confusing. The author falls between two stools, demythologizing too rigorously for romance, yet creating characters and situations that strike one as rather farfetched and contrived. Nevertheless, there is much to enjoy in this reconstruction, and the leisurely pace allows time to relish the way in which tradition has been modified and integrated, e.g., the fusion of Perceval and Galahad into the naive and mystical Peredur, the son of Lancelot and Elaine (another fusion, in this case of the two Elaines); Arthur's love for his half-sister, Ygern, which accounts for his inability to find happiness with Guinevere, is suggested by his traditional love-hate relationship with Morgause and Morgan le Fay.

Although not a novel, Joy Chant's *The High Kings* (1983) focuses briefly upon certain significant episodes in Arthur's career to create a narrative frame for a beautifully illustrated book. Within this frame bards recite traditional stories of past rulers, drawn from Geoffrey of Monmouth's twelfth-century Latin chronicle, *The History of the Kings of Britain,* and from early Welsh tradition recorded in the Triads and *The Mabinogion,* but told stylistically "in the way in which they might have been told in the last days of Britain" (p. 9). It concludes with a series of tales about Arthur himself, reconstructed from hints in these same sources. Each episode and its accompanying story is preceded by a short explanation of some aspect of Celtic life that sheds light upon the fictional material that follows.

The Arthurian frame is highly dramatic, sketching a sharp picture of a great and beloved leader struggling to unite Britain against the invaders. However, the power of the book comes from the interaction of its three elements. Thus the discussion of marriage customs and the status of women is followed by a scene from the celebration for both Arthur's victory over the Saxons at Lindum and his forthcoming marriage to Gueneva, then by the story of "The Two Queens of Locrin." As Merdyn points out, this tale warns "that jealous queens harm their rivals. You pledged your faith twelve years ago, Arthur, when you took your weapons. Britain is your bride" (p. 55).

Blending historical fact with historical fiction and legend is an imaginative concept that illuminates all three with often exciting results. It helps us to enter more fully into the world of Celtic Britain, and to understand the process by which the Arthurian legend grew: "As the years darkened, his glory shone even brighter, and the sorrow of his passing was felt more bitterly" (p. 207).

Almost all the historical novels thus preserve a sympathetic view of Arthur as a heroic leader struggling to unite his feuding people in the face of the grave danger posed by Saxon invasion. Only Vansittart makes him a cruel tyrant with no redeeming features, a portrait which recalls that found in the saints' legends.[14] Others criticize his failings, however: Treece depicts an arrogant leader, capable of unnecessary savagery and acts of expediency in his earlier novels, though he is a nobler figure in *The Green Man*; conversely, Frankland blames him for being too high-minded to do what is necessary to unite his country, while Babcock suggests that he is too credulous and easily fooled. Most, however, make Arthur a well-intentioned and honorable man, flawed like all humans, yet willing to learn from his mistakes.

Where he wins most sympathy and admiration is in those novels that develop his compassion for others. This places him in an impossible dilemma, for in order to protect his people from attack he must call upon many of them to give their lives. The deep suffering that this causes him culminates when he finally lays down his own life for his people. We catch glimpses of Arthur's self-sacrifice in the novels of Canning, Marshall, Stewart, and even Treece's *The Green Man*, but only in Sutcliff is it developed fully.

Since the other characters in the historical novels are defined by their relationship to Arthur, their portrayal depends upon the author's approach to the king. This is most noticeable in Treece's novels. Mordred's betrayal is much more acceptable in *The Great Captains* where Arthur's faults are striking, than it is in *The Green Man* where his virtues are emphasized. Arthur is usually viewed sympathetically, however, and so we tend to approve of those characters who support his goals, and disapprove of those who oppose them, sometimes with confusing results where tradition is concerned. Thus Mordred in Marshall's *The Pagan King* is a noble antagonist who saves Arthur's life, whereas Vivian opposes him with ill-justified malice; yet in Turton's *The Emperor Arthur* the former is selfishly ambitious, whereas the latter works untiringly to help Arthur in her role as Lady of the Lake. Turton's Merlin is a traitor, whereas in Stewart's trilogy he strives to bring Arthur to the throne. Stewart's Morgause plots constantly against Arthur and her legitimate sons wreak havoc with their rash pride; whereas in *Excalibur!* by Kane and Jakes she commits incest under the influence of drugs and dies in childbirth sickened by guilt, while her legitimate sons are Arthur's loyal captains. Their Morgan hates Arthur because his father killed hers, but in Christian's *The Sword and the Flame* she is a loyal agent of Arthur and the Merlin, here a bardic office.[15] The variations seem endless, but always their attitude towards Arthur colors our view of them.

The better works go beyond merely approving or disapproving of characters on this simple basis, however. The human reasons behind their failing are explored to deepen our understanding of human nature and the meaning of the legend. Thus Guenevere in Canning's trilogy sleeps with other men because she is desperate to beget an heir; in Sutcliff's *Sword at Sunset* she seeks consolation in Bedwyr's arms because of her husband's neglect. In *Porius* Powys reveals the political pressures that drive the pre-Celtic people to join with the Saxon invaders against Arthur; in her Merlin trilogy Stewart explains why Merlin must leave Arthur to rule alone. Characters may win redemption, through forgiving others, as do Aquila in Sutcliff's *The Lantern Bearers*, Modred and Arthur in Marshall's *The Pagan King*. More often, however, they must walk paths that are predestined, as do Arthur in Sutcliff's *Sword at Sunset* and Canning's Crimson Chalice Trilogy, and both Merlin and Mordred in Stewart's four novels.

The novelists make ample use of the freedom to choose between variants in Arthurian legend. Yet they also feel free to reject legendary material in the interests of historicity. Those who have been boldest in stripping away traditional material in order to focus upon a few essential elements have also been the most successful. Sutcliff, Powys, and Canning are sparing in their choice of threads when they weave the fabric anew and the results are striking. By contrast Carmichael, Christian, and even Stewart allow attention to an excessive number of traditional details to blur the outlines of their stories. The problems of structure, however, are endemic in the material because of its complexity. Seduced by their fascination with the legend, too many novels ramble from one adventure to another as they try to explain too many disparate details. Since the range of Arthur's experience over a long career is so varied, it is difficult to reduce it to tidiness. It is, perhaps, no accident that the tightest structure has been achieved by Sutcliff in *The Lantern Bearers*, a novel that focuses upon a newly created character set in the Arthurian world. Because he is unhampered by a traditional role, Aquila can more comfortably reflect the important dilemmas and conflicts of the age. However, Sutcliff's success in recounting Arthur's career in *Sword at Sunset* makes it clear that a coherent plot structure can be drawn from the legend by those who exercise tight discipline in selecting material.

Most of the historical novels have difficulty in successfully integrating characterization, plotting, and theme. Marshall's development of the theme of illusion and reality is exciting, but both characterization and plotting are weak. Stewart's characterization is convincing, the theme of inexorable fate powerful, but plotting is diffuse by contrast. Powys and Treece have the same problem. Sutcliff alone manages to integrate all three into a profound and moving vision of a hero who chooses to sacrifice himself for his people.

HIGH MIDDLE AGES

Most historical novelists have, in recent years, chosen to set their stories of Arthur in the Dark Ages, but this has not always been the case. Over two dozen novels and almost as many short stories follow the tradition established by medieval romance and adopt the High Middle Ages as their setting. Interestingly, about half were published during the decade immediately following World War II. They can be broadly divided into four groups: psychological novels, which focus primarily upon the motivation and interaction of convincing characters; sentimental romances that share many of the techniques of medieval prose romance; juvenile adventure stories, intended to amuse and instruct younger readers; and finally sentimental comedies that bring out the humor inherent in the exaggerations of romance.

Earliest of the group of psychological novels are by John Er-skine, who wrote *Galahad* (1926) and *Tristan and Isolde: Restoring Palamede* (1932), as well as a series of seven tales which were published in *American Weekly* during February and March, 1940. *Galahad* shows how Guinevere may have trapped herself into the role of inspiring great deeds: first by Arthur, then Lancelot, and finally Galahad, whom she encourages to undertake the Grail quest. Unfortunately, she never really recognizes her self-deception, and although this failure lends itself to some enter-taining irony, it also hinders the development of a sense of direction. Thus despite some interesting insights into idealism and the predicament of women in an insensitive male-oriented society, the novel remains too slow moving.

Erskine was more successful with his second Arthurian novel. This is the story of Palamede, a romantic young Saracen whose imagination has been captivated by stories of idealized love. His gradual realization that his view is a romantic illusion marks his growth into maturity: "youth will attach its dream to anything that is at hand. If love is hardy enough to survive extreme youth its eyes will gradually open, until it can recognize merit in one particular woman. Love will then be grown-up.... At that mo-ment, riding through the darkening forest, rudely awakened for the first time to his own inadequacy, he became, had he but known it, mature" (pp. 295–96). This clear development pro-vides not only a structure for the novel, but also opportunity for gentle irony at the hero's expense. Moreover this irony serves as both a comment upon Palamede's folly and a means to heighten his own awareness of it.

Erskine's favorite instrument for this dual purpose is Bran-gain, Isolde's beautiful cousin. She delights in teasing Palamede about his unrealistic view of love, and she encourages him to be more honest and direct about his feelings. The object of *her* devotion, she confides, would "never escape my admira-tion....Even if he did not want me, there I'd be, to the ends of the earth!" (p. 210). This is sage advice to the overly tentative lover, but he responds with typical naivete by asking if she means that he should pursue Isolde despite her love for Mark. This is a double misunderstanding, for not only does Isolde love Tristan rather than Mark, but also Brangain is herself in love with Palamede and offering gentle encouragement: "That was not my meaning!" (p. 210) she replies with a laugh. The verbal irony provokes the deeper reflection necessary for the hero's development. However, there is also irony of situation that comments upon the impracticality of his sentiments. While he adopts the romantic dreams common to women trapped in a man's world, she takes on the active male role, advising vigorous pursuit of the object of affection. Her actions suit her words. When she learns, at the conclusion of the novel, that the young Saracen has left for home, she cries, "where is the Holy Land? Get me a horse!" (p. 347). This role reversal thus provokes not only humor, but also insight into the nature of love.

Brangain's good-humored wisdom and generous devotion also make her such an attractive character that one measure of Palamede's growth is his appreciation of her. As he rides home, his thoughts reveal how his judgment has improved: "he knew how steady her kindness had been, he remembered her warm cheerfulness. It would be hard never to see her. He had loved Isolde, he still did love her of course, but it was Brangain he missed" (p. 298).

The tragic love of Tristan and Isolde suffers from this shift in focus. Not only does their lack of scruple make them less attractive as characters than Palamede and Brangain, but their love serves as an object lesson to the young hero, demonstrating the dangers of heedless passion. What seems glorious in story is revealed to be selfish in reality. Since the hero ultimately learns to appreciate more enduring qualities, the love of Tristan and Isolde is reduced by its association with the delusions of his youth.

Like *Galahad* this novel moves at too leisurely a pace, but it has a much stronger structure and sense of direction. Moreover, it effectively uses Arthurian legend to explore the ironic interplay between illusion and reality. It is this exploration that distinguishes the better novels in this group.

Unfortunately there is too little of it in the first two Arthurian novels by Dorothy James Roberts, *The Enchanted Cup* (1953) and *Launcelot, My Brother* (1954). The former tells the story of Tristram and Isoud, focusing upon the conflict between love and duty, but it fails to probe the issues in depth. The latter deals with

the love of Launcelot and Guenivere, as told by Bors, here Launcelot's brother. The mood is sombre as the characters struggle
unavailingly against the fate imposed by their own personalities.
Her third novel, *Kinsmen of the Grail* (1963), is more successful,
largely because the subject matter is more suitable to her talents
for developing alienated characters.

Events are based largely upon the twelfth-century French romance of *Perlesvaus*, and Roberts uses Gawin (Gawain) as her
narrator and principal actor. He has lost some of his enthusiasm
for knight-errantry, since the problems always seem to recur
despite all that Arthur has been struggling to build. Yet though
drawn to the Grail, he finds himself confused by its significance
and frustrated in his attempts to achieve positive goals during
his quest. Depression, confusion, and frustration are traditional
barriers in the search for the Grail, and they certainly dominate
Gawin's state of mind. The problems of illusion and reality are
inherent in Gawin's experience, but they are never clearly confronted. The final effect, therefore, as in the earlier novels, is of
a character defeated by forces that he never fully understands.
These novels approach the existential, but lack the philosophical
depth. One experiences the depression of alienation without any
of the illumination.

The Queen's Knight (1956) by Marvin Borowsky also presents
us with characters defeated by the forces against which they
struggle. Like Treece and Frankland the author creates a darkly
anti-romantic world, dominated by pride and ambition, jealousy
and treachery, anger and passion. Even Arthur is presented as
a country oaf, set up by the powerful Lords of the Council as a
puppet king. Yet though clumsy and slow-witted he has a vision
of peace and justice that gains often reluctant support and respect. Thus despite his scorn for Arthur as a person, Launcelot
is won by his dream, and he is the great leader and warrior who
wins Arthur's battles for him. The main focus of the novel,
however, falls upon negative aspects: the awkwardness of Arthur, the pride of the nobility, the suffering of the ordinary
people. The final effect, thus, is that man's dream of a better
world is inevitably doomed by a brutal reality—in itself a reflection of his flawed nature. Yet the dream still beckons, however flawed the dreamers, and the cruel reality serves as a foil

to their transitory achievements. Their hope may be an illusion, but it is also a tribute to the human spirit that endures despite disappointment and suffering.

The last two psychological novels in this group both make powerful use of impressionistic and streams of consciousness techniques to achieve a heightened sense of reality. In her *Tristan* (1940) Hannah Closs often filters events through the mind of her hero. Thus the fight with Morholt is recalled by Tristan in a series of striking images as he rows back to land, wounded and dazed (pp. 116–20). Such series of images are, in their turn, woven into a brilliant tapestry that creates once again the lovers' timeless tale.

For Closs, Tristan is more than just a fine warrior. In him, "imaginative passion and active deed vied ceaselessly with one another as the eternal conflict between two selves—a battle vain and hopeless as the struggle of the rocks with the sea" (p. 263). The former seeks outlet in harping and singing, which sway the hearts and souls of his listeners. Yet as he himself recognizes, "Fighting and song... spring from the same impulse—the power to spend oneself utterly—the power to die" (p. 292). As the author herself declares, Tristan is a dreamer and a poet. Thus the images that pass through his mind gain an imaginative intensity that vividly evokes the lovers' passions. Since these passions must be concealed, they burn with dizzying heat. Consequently, the lovers move in a dreamworld that captures the mythic quality of their story. Their experience transcends the bounds of mere material reality, entering into an eternal realm beyond. Here passion burns more ardently, isolation pains more acutely, yearning aches more keenly, anguish bites more sharply. It is the Platonic reality of which our world is but the shadow.

In Jim Hunter's *Percival and the Presence of God* (1978) Percival narrates the account of his quest for the Holy Grail through the device of allowing his thoughts to travel back in time as present events evoke memories of past experiences. Episode by episode there unfolds the story of a man impelled on his search by spiritual yearnings, despite temptations to desist. He rescues Whiteflower and learns to love her, finding in her "God's kindness" (p. 70); yet he leaves her and all the love and security that she offers to pursue his quest. Other obstacles are less seductive. In a ruined chapel, the Chapel Perilous of tradition, he is trapped by falling timber and comes close to death before he is finally rescued.

Such experiences teach him valuable lessons. Of his relationship with Whiteflower, he realizes, "She might have said: God could not rebuke you, for remaining to cherish this. I believed that too. But only, perhaps, since he is a forgiving God" (p. 71). After he has been rescued from the ruined chapel and nursed back to health by peasants, Percival discovers "that the heroic quester, whatever self-sacrifice he shows, must depend for his career on the unobtrusive sacrifices and support of many unheroic labouring people. I had spent nearly two years being fed by others" (p. 136).

Yet while these experiences bring Percival closer to God, it is not an easy journey, and he remains deeply puzzled by many things. He wonders at the wastefulness and arbitrariness of death, which claims his mentor Mansell, a generous-hearted and valuable member of society, yet spares him when he seemed doomed in the ruined chapel. Confronted by "death and absurdity" (p. 131), Percival struggles to understand. "I think I do now accept that either things are truly arbitrary, an utter haphazardness of God, or their direction is likely to be too difficult for us to understand, so that they appear arbitrary though they are not so. . . . To some this is cynicism, and to others it is faith" (p. 138).

What Hunter has succeeded in doing is transforming Percival's experience on the Grail quest into a Christian existential novel. Faced by the absurdity of life, he pursues his search for spiritual meaning—for the Holy Grail. The novel closes, however, with the quest incomplete. Percival finds no clearcut answer that will satisfy him, as perhaps must inevitably prove the case in this life. How can the limited understanding of human beings comprehend God's pattern? By persisting in his quest despite its apparent hopelessness and the suffering that it causes, Percival proves that he is truly God's fool. Yet it is a folly that raises profound and disturbing questions about life.

These two novels pierce the fabric of reality, taking us into a dreamworld that is in many ways more real than the one that surrounds us. In so doing they capture the essential spirit of the legends that they recreate so vividly, even as they take liberties with many traditional elements. Thus in Closs' novel, Iseult of the White Hands recalls the tale of the Fair Maid of Astolat and Tristan remembers the story of Parzival and the Grail; Hunter's Percival, for his part, searches in vain for Arthur, and wonders whether he is any more than legend!

That the novels in this group should owe so much of whatever success they achieve to their exploration of the ironic interplay between illusion and reality is only to be expected. The world of Arthurian romance created in the High Middle Ages is, after all, a literary illusion, and to approach it with the techniques of the realistic novel is to present the reader with a paradox. Those authors who can pierce through this illusion to the profound human truth that it represents, who can ironically reverse our expectations of illusion and reality, find that their subject matter and their literary techniques are most in harmony, and the results can prove striking.

Since they lack this advantage, the sentimental romances have less inherent impact, but this does not prevent them from exploring the theme of illusion and reality, as Clemence Housman, the sister of A. E. Housman, demonstrates in *The Life of Sir Aglovale de Galis* (1905).[16] Starting from the details provided in Malory, whom she constantly calls "my most dear Master," Housman expands imaginatively upon his outline to construct a dramatic interpretation of the ill-starred career of Aglovale, son of King Pellinore, brother of Lamorak, Durnor and Percivale, and half-brother of Tor.

Aglovale's problem is that he places truth above personal reputation. Thus when he gives way to his own baser impulses, or when he acts with tragic consequences, he refuses to deny his failures. This brings him much dishonor and shame. Yet he is ever his own harshest critic, at one point even fighting against his friend Grifflet to maintain, in trial by combat, that he is indeed a liar and a traitor, when the latter insists that he is noble-hearted! As Ector complains, "Sir Aglovale goes not by the ways of knighthood." Launcelot responds, however, "Alas for knighthood" (p. 226).

His lament is justified. The Round Table is preoccupied, not with justice, but with the appearance of justice. Knights fight to preserve their reputation rather than acknowledge their faults, and the consequences of this hypocrisy finally prove disastrous. Confronted by evidence of the affair between Launcelot and the Queen, Arthur chooses truth in order to protect his honor, knowing full well that should the lovers escape it would be seen as a mockery of justice. Yet by refusing Launcelot the right to defend the reputations of himself and his lady, Arthur is himself guilty of an injustice, and many oppose him since "by the rule and custom he himself had established, himself would he not abide" (p. 236). Both alternatives will inevitably destroy the Round Table, as Aglovale points out to Arthur during their climactic confrontation, yet it is no more than the just punishment for such sins as his incestuous begetting of Mordred and slaying the children born on May-day. Ironically, Arthur now proposes to favor truth over honor, when earlier he condemned Aglovale for admitting the faults he might have successfully denied to preserve his honor.

Housman thoughtfully probes the paradox that lies at the heart of Arthurian society and eventually destroys it. Unfortunately, her treatment is ponderous: the plot particularly rambles with too little control over the material. This is a weakness that all the sentimental romances in this group share to varying degrees. They model themselves too closely upon the prose romances and so fall heir to faults such as a long and episodic plot that rapidly grows tedious. Edith Tatum's short story, "The Awakening of Iseult" (1913), and novels like Dorothy Senior's *The Clutch of Circumstance* (1908), Sara Hawks Sterling's *A Lady of King Arthur's Court* (1907), Chester Keith's *Queen's Knight* (1920), Lord Ernest Hamilton's *Launcelot* (1926), Warwick Deeping's *Uther and Igraine* (1903), Philip Lindsay's *The Little Wench* (1935), all contain episodes that are entertaining enough, but too often they are predictable and do little to develop theme in any meaningful direction. They are also prone to make use of contrived and improbable situations. This is most noticeable in Sterling's novel, where the heroine spends three years in her husband's company disguised as a monk, yet is never recognized by him, not even when they share the Grail vision along with Galahad and Percivale at the Grail Castle.

The other pervasive flaw in these romances is that the sentimentality not only grows tiresome, but also costs the story some of its power. Thus in *Uther and Igraine* Deeping presents Uther as a pillar of justice, who rides about under the name of Pelleas, performing deeds of solitary knight-errantry. In this guise he rescues Igraine, but nobly renounces any claim upon her affections that gratitude might have prompted. This virtuous decorum predictably allows many plot complications before the two are happily reunited, though there appears little doubt that marriage will precede Arthur's conception.

By turning Uther into a perfect gentleman, Deeping transforms his relationship with Igraine from a wild and lawless passion into a pure and virtuous love that any innocent soul might hear of without a blush. However, it robs the story of the vitality and dark power of the original version.

Hamilton commits a similar error in his *Launcelot* by tidying up the hero's love life. Launcelot falls in love with Elaine, the daughter of Earl Pelles, after rescuing her from an abductor, and the two are happily married. Gueneviere is a bored and selfish woman who tries to seduce the reluctant Launcelot with very limited success. Since little is said about Arthur's incest, either, the culpability of the main actors is reduced to the point where the tragic dimension of the story disappears.

This is not to deny all merit to these sentimental romances. Despite their fondness for inflicting suffering upon their innocent heroines, both Deeping and Sterling allow them an independence of spirit and sense of initiative that are certainly attractive. Deeping's Igraine even fights valiantly in the disguise of a knight errant for some time. And Lindsay offers some perceptive criticisms of the double standards at Arthur's court in *The Little Wench*, observing that "Mellygraunce had misbehaved, not by the act of rape, but by permitting the act to become known" (p. 172), and that while "Men were permitted to rape, to murder" (p. 179), women were expected to remain faithful to their husbands. Yet the dominant impression with which one (thankfully) leaves most of these sentimental romances remains that of their faults, particularly tediousness.

Perhaps because they thought their audience had a shorter attention span, the authors of adventure stories for juveniles gave the Arthurian legend briefer and livelier treatment. They also went to some pains to provide a moral lesson in their stories. Thus Eleanore Jewett's *The Hidden Treasure of Glaston* (1946) deals with the discovery of Arthur's tomb at Glastonbury Abbey in the twelfth century. Through his self-sacrifice the young hero earns a vision of the Holy Grail which miraculously cures his lameness. The novel also presents an informative picture of ordinary life in a medieval abbey.

These twin goals, providing moral instruction and information about life in the Middle Ages, are central to two books by Eugenia Stone, *Page Boy for King Arthur* (1949) and its sequel, *Squire for King Arthur* (1955). The books warn against the perils of self-indulgence, teaching instead the importance of honesty, generosity, courage, perseverance, and responsibility. By means of these young Tor, the son of a cowherd, achieves a station in life normally restricted to the aristocracy:[17] in the first book he saves the life of Sir Launcelot; in the second he rescues the son of King Pellinore from the Saxons. At the same time the books provide extensive information about the duties of churls and page boys in a medieval castle. The author integrates these two purposes well, as Tor is moved from task to task because of the carelessness that he must learn to overcome. This situation eventually grows contrived, but it should certainly appeal to the intended readers, children who might dream of Arthur and his knights while neglecting practical responsibilities. They might find it easy to identify with Tor when he lingers to watch squires jousting instead of tending a boring old fire—which spreads and nearly burns down the entire castle!

A similar book is Catherine Peare's *Melor, King Arthur's Page* (1963). Melor too keeps making thoughtless mistakes, but he redeems himself when he saves Arthur's life from a huge boar. Clyde Bulla's *The Sword in the Tree* (1956) and Donald Sobol's *Greta the Strong* (1970) are two imaginative tales of high adventure in an Arthurian setting. The eleven-year-old hero of the former courageously wins his inheritance from a scheming uncle with the aid of a knight of the Round Table; the latter recounts the exploits of a female knight errant, charged with the task of restoring peace and justice by Sir Porthal, last of the knights of the Round Table. Both stories show how young people can break out of the dependent role that society expects them to fill.

The Adventures of Sir Lancelot (1957) by John Paton and its sequel, *The Adventures of Sir Lancelot, Book 2* (1958) by Arthur Groom, are adaptations from a television series of the same name starring William Russell, and they are illustrated by stills of the series. Lancelot here performs a series of untraditional deeds of knight-errantry.

E.M.R. Ditmas' *Gareth of Orkney* (1956) and Francis Owen's *Tristan and Isolde* (1964) are more closely based upon Arthurian tradition. Ditmas follows Malory's tale of Sir Gareth closely, but skilfully provides credible explanations for various events. Thus the year of service in the royal kitchens is imposed upon Gareth by his mother, who wants him to become a monk as part of her penance for committing incest with Arthur. Always an amiable and attractive youth, Gareth undergoes little character development. However, because he is such a credible and sympathetic figure, the younger reader finds it easy to identify with him, particularly during his struggle to win acceptance from scornful adults, and during the difficulties that he experiences in winning the love of the heroine.

Owen retells the legend of Tristan and Isolde with extensive authorial commentary on historical and geographical details, sometimes placed in the mouths of characters such as Dinadan. He makes a number of changes in the material, including turning Gawain and Lancelot into brothers, but by far the most striking is the happy ending that he provides. The lovers are rescued by Palomides and Dinadan, who kill Mark and Andret, and they live out their lives at Joyeuse Garde, together with Lancelot and Guenevere, who join them after the death of Arthur, and Dinadan and Bragwaine, who get married. Even Palomides, who is slain during the rescue, dies happy in the knowledge he is serving his beloved Isolde! Such an ending is clearly contrived, and it offends against the tragic spirit of the original story. However, Owen tells us that tragedy was beloved in the Middle Ages because of an underlying pessimism. His preference is for comedy. Despite this disarming protestation, most people will miss the dark power of the original version.

Like the psychological novels, the juvenile adventures achieve most success when they focus upon the theme of illusion and reality. This usually involves the reversal of unrealistic ex-

pectations that becomes part of the growth of the young protagonists towards maturity and responsibility. In proving
themselves, they also reverse the unfair expectations of their
elders who consider them too young and inexperienced to meet
their challenges successfully.

Unfortunately, the didactic aims of these juvenile adventure
novels generally prove more of a hindrance than a help. Too
often the authors seem to be talking down to their audience, a
fatal mistake when writing for young people. It is no accident
that the best-written novel in this group is Ditmas' *Gareth of
Orkney*, which is most successful in establishing a true sympathy
for the hero and the difficulties he faces. Because Gareth is so
involving a figure, his learning experience is less obtrusive and,
ultimately, more effective. The novel is also the least sentimental
of these tales, for it avoids both excessive self-pity on the part
of the protagonists, and those convenient but unlikely turns of
plot that allow them to redeem themselves.

The high moral tone of many treatments of Arthurian legend,
from Tennyson on, provoked an ironic response from writers
with a satirical bent. The most important are fantasies and will
be dealt with in the appropriate chapter, but over a dozen novelettes and short stories that can be classified as historical fiction
appeared, mainly in the pages of various popular magazines.
"The Camelot Jousts" (1910) by Maurice Baring are six letters
exchanged between Arthur, Guinevere and Iseult, in which the
two ladies make catty remarks about each other in a very contemporary style. P. G. Wodehouse treats us to his special brand
of humor in "Sir Agravaine. A Blithesome and Knightly Tale
Throwing New Light upon the Mystery of Affinities" (1923).
Don Marquis pokes fun at taking life too seriously in "King
O'Meara and Queen Guinevere" (1930), a stage Irish account of
how the merry Tim O'Meara, High King of Ireland, shows Arthur and Lancelot how to beat "thim Sassenach" (p. 152).

Most prolific was the Canadian author, Theodore Goodrich
Roberts, who published no fewer than three novelettes and nine
stories in *Blue Book Magazine* (1947–52). The novelettes are "By
My Halidom," "The Merlin Touch," and "The Disputed Prin-
cess"; the stories deal with the adventures of Sir Dinadan: "A
Quarrel for a Lady," "A Purfle for a King," "A Quest of the

Saracen Beast," "The Madness of Sir Tristram," "Sir Dinadan and the Giant Taulard," "The Goose Girl," "For to Achieve Your Adventure," "A Mountain Miracle," and "Daggers in Her Garters." He wanted to publish the three novelettes, which are loosely related, as one book, and the Dinadan stories as another. Of the latter project he wrote, "Though the magazine runs them as individual stories of Sir Dinadan and his dapple-grey Garry, each takes direction at least from the preceding adventure."[18] Accordingly, he took the last eight tales, omitting "A Quarrel for a Lady," modified some of the titles as chapter headings, wrote a new story entitled "Quest's End" for a conclusion, and assembled the manuscript under the title "Good Knight! (The Romantic Exploits of Sir Dinadan)." However, he was unable to find a publisher before his death in 1953.

All the stories in this group are sentimental comedies, for the irony is affectionate rather than scathing. It does not urge reform, rather shares a gentle laugh with the reader at the foibles of its basically lovable characters. These foibles stem from an impractical sense of honor, and they are readily apparent in those traditional areas of heroic endeavor, love and war, as a scrutiny of Marquis' story and Roberts' "Sir Dinadan and the Giant Taulard" shows.

In Marquis' tale the British have honorable knights and warriors in abundance, but little concept of strategy, until King Tim comes over to instruct them in such mysteries as "circumvallyation" (p. 152). Yet they never learn how to match guile with guile. Concerned that Lancelot is "too open-hearted and aboveboard" to deal with Mordred, Tim asks, " 'what are ye doing to make Mordred kape the dacent tongue in his head these days?' 'Four days a week regular I call him into me tent and beat him up good, Tim,' says Lancelot, 'and the other three days I tell him what it's for' " (p. 119).

Tim also tries to teach Arthur and Lancelot how to enjoy themselves, but he finds their over-refined sense of honor too great an obstacle. Both are deeply depressed by their relationship with Guinevere, though, as she complains, the difficulties arise not from what they do, but from what they don't do: "And together they come, and together they kiss me hands, and together they go sighing away—sighing and sighing, full of honor and sighs!" (p. 154). Eventually "The Blameless King" and his "gentle paladin" sadly kill each other, since honor demands it: "each walked agin the other wan's sword. . .and, mingling their tears, they died" (p. 119). As Guinevere remarks, "perhaps 'tis betther so; nayther wan had the knack of being cheerful" (p. 119). This is certainly not Tim's problem, and so, singing merrily, he and Guinevere set sail together for Ireland to live life to the full.

Yet while Tim knows how to enjoy himself and give Guinevere the full-blooded love that she needs, he has limitations that suggest he is not intended to be taken seriously as a model of behavior. He is a cheerful adventurer, who takes the responsibilities of kingship very lightly. When he hears that Ulster and Connacht are at war, and "filled with widows and wakes this day," he retorts, "that's merely a habit" (p. 6). This is no cautionary tale, rather a merry celebration of youth and its freedom from responsibility. The conduct of its characters does, nevertheless, provoke some thoughtful reflections.

Roberts takes the figure of Dinadan from Malory, where he stands out from other knights because of his unconventional speeches on love and war.[19] Roberts explains these as a pose, the attempt of an impractical romantic to protect himself from needless slaughter and designing women. Dinadan is not really averse to combat, but he is too chivalrous to take advantage of a foe. When he discovers that his giant opponent in "Sir Dinadan and the Giant Taulard" is really quite ineffectual, he breaks off combat with the comment, "I'm a knight, not a butcher" (p. 104). Since he is also too proud to accept gifts from friends, he is constantly in financial distress.

However, what causes him still greater discomfort are damosels. As a sympathetic duchess observes, "They lack the brains and experience for wit and wisdom and understanding sympathy with a poet's mind and heart. So in their feckless, shallow, selfish vanity they have made a railing cynic of him" (p. 95). Despite this pose of cynicism Dinadan keeps falling in love with pretty damosels, only to lose them for one reason or another. His futile attempts to escape their charms generate humor at his expense, but it remains gentle.

Roberts considers the romantic impulse that arouses his hero's expectations, only to have them dashed yet again, to be an essentially noble quality. This is what makes him a poet whose skill on the harp is such that it restores the love of life to a dying maiden in "Mountain Miracle." In "Quest's End," the unpublished conclusion to the planned collection of Dinadan stories, the author finally rewards his hero with the love of a more appreciative damosel. Nor does he require that Dinadan change his character to merit this reward. In rejecting the Dinadan collection, the publishing house of Macmillan commented that the chapters lose novelty as they progress, and this is a fair criticism. Roberts starts off with an interesting idea, but he rests content to repeat the formula without developing it in more thoughtful directions.[20]

This lack of ambition prevents all these sentimental comedies from encouraging more than amiable laughter at the foibles of their characters. Yet they too are at their most effective when they measure the gap between appearance and reality, such as is created by Dinadan posing as a cynic to protect his romantic idealism.

There is one other short story set in the High Middle Ages, but it does not fit into any of the four categories. Maxey Brooke's "Morte D'Alain: An Unrecorded Idyll of the King" is a mystery thriller in which Merlin solves a murder at Arthur's court. Merlin is no enchanter, but an illusionist with the modern magician's bag of tricks, such as breathing fire. Thus he finds the murderer, not by supernatural arts, but by the simple device of matching bootprints. Though not particularly well written, this story too contains some interesting implications about the theme of appearance and reality: Merlin uses the pretense of sorcery to extract a confession from the murderer, though as he afterwards remarks, "There are no powers of darkness save in the minds of men" (p. 273). However, this theme is not developed.

The approach to character in all the historical fiction set in the High Middle Ages is, as one would expect, very traditional. After all, the choice of a setting created by literary tradition rather than by history indicates a respect for that tradition and an awareness of its advantages to the writer. This is particularly true of the sentimental romances and the juvenile adventure stories. This does not prevent criticism, as Housman demonstrates when Sir

Aglovale points out the error of Arthur's ways. However, these criticisms are elaborations of those found in the sources upon which they are based. Even the occasional minor departure can be traced to hints in sources. Thus Hamilton enlarges upon Malory's account of Ywain's temporary banishment from Arthur's court to turn the knight, whom he calls Ewin, into a traitor who helps his mother, Morgan le Fay, against the king. The sentimental comedies also interpret character along traditional lines so that they can point out the humor inherent in such features as the impractical preoccupation with honor.

The psychological novels show more independence in their approach to characterization. Erskine makes Galahad self-righteously arrogant, and he favors Palamede and Brangain over Tristan and Isolde; Borowsky portrays Arthur as a country oaf and surrounds him with selfish and ambitious nobles; Closs' Tristan is a poet, Hunter's Percival an existential man. By contrast Dorothy Roberts is more conventional in her character portrayal. The authors who explore the theme of illusion and reality most probingly are thus freer in their approach to character roles.

Yet the departures from tradition are more illusory than real. From the point of view of society the Galahad of medieval romance can be considered self-righteous and arrogant, and the steadfast devotion of Palamede and Brangain is more admirable than the lack of consideration that Tristan and Isolde show for others. When he first pulled the sword from the stone, Arthur was resented as a youth of low birth and he had to struggle hard against powerful and rebellious lords. Tristan was widely famed for his harping, and Percival did search at great length—in some versions without final success—to discover the meaning of the elusive Grail. These novels have discovered the paradox of similarity underlying apparent difference, of the reality of identity behind the illusion of change, and of the deeper mythic reality in which the eternal and unchanging figures continue only as long as they are constantly redefined and recreated. They excell at discovering fresh and thought-provoking possibilities in the rich body of tradition.

The problems of structure, which afflict the historical fiction set in the Dark Ages, are equally noticeable in novels set in the High Middle Ages. While less obtrusive in the sentimental comedies and juvenile adventures, which tend to be shorter, the fault is revealed in the repetition of a basic situation in the writings of Stone and Theodore Roberts. The psychological novels move at a very leisurely pace that can drag at times, and the sentimental romances sprawl expansively. The former sometimes bog down in their scrutiny of the minutiae of behavior or in prolonged conversation, the latter ramble from adventure to adventure with too little concern for developing theme.

An overview of the historical fiction reveals some interesting fluctuations in popularity. The sentimental romances, whether set in the Dark Ages or the High Middle Ages, are concentrated in the first two decades of this century. The last to appear was Lindsay's *The Little Wench* (1935) which is permeated by a healthy realism. The juvenile adventures were most popular during the decade following the Second World War. Very few historical novels set in the High Middle Ages have been published since 1958. By contrast, novels set in the Dark Ages have grown slowly but steadily in popularity.

The popularity of historical fiction about Arthur thus remains assured, but this very popularity means that the quality of this fiction is very uneven. However, the finest works, by Powys, Closs, Sutcliff, and Hunter, succeed in evoking the heroic spirit of the Arthurian story as well as giving it life and immediacy. At times they can move us as powerfully as any novelist, and give keen insights into the human condition that are as relevant to our own age as they are to Arthur's. This is particularly true when they explore the themes of compassion, and of illusion and reality.

NOTES

1. See, for example, Morris, *The Age of Arthur*, pp. 103–41; Beram Saklatvala, *Arthur: Roman Britain's Last Champion* (Newton Abbot, England: David and Charles, 1967), pp. 45–52; Richard Barber, *The Figure of Arthur* (London: Longman, 1972), pp. 11–53.

2. See Roger S. Loomis, *Celtic Myth and Arthurian Romance* (New York: Columbia University Press, 1927), and Morris, *The Age of Arthur*, p. 118.

3. The romances offer an idealized model for the aristocracy to emulate. For a discussion of their impact upon chivalric conduct, see the

various studies reviewed by Tony Hunt, "The Emergence of the Knight in France and England 1000-1200," *Forum for Modern Language Studies,* 17 (1981), 93–114.

4. Frye, *Anatomy of Criticism,* p. 33.

5. See Leslie Alcock and Geoffrey Ashe, "Cadbury: Is It Camelot?" in *The Quest for Arthur's Britain,* pp. 154-88; and Leslie Alcock, *Arthur's Britain* (Harmondsworth, Middlesex: Penguin Books, 1971), pp. 220–27.

6. See Gildas, *The Ruin of Britain and Other Works,* ed. and trans. Michael Winterbottom (London and Chichester: Phillimore, 1978), pp. 28–36.

7. See, for example, the chronicles; also the various versions of the story of Lanval and of the chastity test posed by the magic horn and mantle.

8. The exception is the third Gwenhwyfar in *The Great Captains,* who is only a child indulged by the aged Artos. With her protector's death, her rape seems imminent.

9. See the author's explanation of his use of tradition in the Postscript to *The Crimson Chalice* (p. 225). All quotations are cited from the paperback edition, *The Crimson Chalice Trilogy* (Harmondsworth, Middlesex: Penguin Books, 1980).

10. Quotations are from the Fawcett Crest Reprint [n.d.], New York.

11. Sutcliff was the first to fuse these two characters, but both Gillian Bradshaw and Mary Stewart have followed her lead.

12. This motif recurs in Sutcliff's historical novels. Thus *Dawn Wind,* set in the period after Arthur's death when the Britons have been driven into the West, also develops love and caring as a bridge between hostile peoples.

13. Like Sutcliff and Bradshaw, Stewart gives Bedwyr Lancelot's role as the queen's lover. The affair does not appear to be consummated, but their emotional attraction is evident enough to give opportunity to their enemies.

14. See Morris, *The Age of Arthur,* pp. 120–23.

15. Cf. Marion Zimmer Bradley, *The Mists of Avalon.*

16. Quotations are from the Revised Edition of 1954.

17. The stories seem inspired by Malory's account of Tor, the illegitimate son of King Pellinore. He also appears in Housman's *The Life of Sir Aglovale de Galis.*

18. Letter dated 26 August 1951, collected in the Archives of the Harriet Irving Library at the University of New Brunswick.

19. Dinadan's unconventional conduct has excited considerable discussion amongst scholars: see, for example, Eugène Vinaver, "Un chev-

alier errant à la recherche du sens du monde: Quelques remarques sur le caractère de Dinadan dans le *Tristan* en prose," in *Mélanges Delbouille*, II (Gembloux: Duculot, 1964), pp. 677–86.

20. Roberts possessed talent, but like the authors of many of the stories that appeared in pulp magazines he was under too much pressure to earn a living from the sale of his writings to spend extra time crafting them. He produced quantity, but at the cost of quality.

5

SCIENCE FICTION AND SCIENCE FANTASY

There are very few science fiction novels about King Arthur and his knights, and only one of any real merit. It is not that science fiction authors have overlooked Arthurian legend, but when they have chosen to write about it they have cast their novels in the form of fantasy. Even those writings that do qualify as science fiction often contain fantasy elements.

This situation is inherent in the focus of the genre, which is upon the consequence of human progress. Most typically this progress results from some scientific advance, such as travel faster than the speed of light, but it may also be caused by social or political developments. We find all three in a novel like Aldous Huxley's *Brave New World*. Since science fiction starts off with the premise, "what if such and such were to happen?" its eyes are on the future. Arthur, however, lived in the past.

Science fiction can respond either by moving back in time to the Dark Ages, or else recreating elements of the legend in the future. Moving back means swimming against the natural forward-flowing current of the genre, and only one author has done it: Andre Norton in *Merlin's Mirror* (1975).[1] Norton is better known as a writer of fantasy, but in this novel she explains the powers of Merlin and Nimue, the Lady of the Lake, as the product of a highly superior extra-terrestrial technology, which is viewed as magic by the people of Earth. The conflict between the supernatural powers of good and evil, which we often find in fantasy, is transformed here into one between the "Sky Lords" and the "Dark Ones." Yet these forces are not simply good and bad. Nimue convincingly argues the dangers of external intervention in mankind's development, teaching men "what they were not yet ready to know" (p. 202). Unfortunately, the merits and demerits of the accelerated progress offered by Merlin and Arthur are raised but insufficiently explored in the novel. Their courtesy, reasonableness, and care for others is so much more attractive than the intolerance of Christian priests like Gildas, and the insolence of Modred, that we cannot but regret the failure of the hope for civilization that they offer. This might have seriously prejudiced Nimue's case were it not that the author does such a poor job of winning sympathy for Merlin and Arthur as characters. Like so many of Norton's novels, *Merlin's Mirror* has interesting potential that is infuriatingly neglected. What makes this even more regrettable is that had a case been made against the ostensible benefits of Arthurian civilization it would have offered an intriguing contribution to the tradition.

As one might expect, attempts to recreate elements of the Arthurian legend in the future have been much more common in science fiction. Often this amounts to no more than borrowing quotations and drawing analogies. Thus the young protagonist of Gordon R. Dickson's juvenile novel, *Secret under the Caribbean* (1964), rallies his courage by recalling the words of Bleoberis, from a retelling of Malory for younger readers, "I dread no Cornish Knight"; another character quotes from Tennyson's *Idylls of the King*, "The old order changeth giving way to new." In his forthcoming novel, *The Final Encyclopedia*, Dickson uses not only quotations but specific analogies, comparing the passing of the splinter cultures like the Dorsai, with all their ideals and aspirations, to the fading dream of the Round Table.

Other novelists borrow names and minor details or the vaguely "Arthurian" setting found in medieval romances of chivalry. This is best seen in the trilogy of Arthur H. Landis, *A World Called Camelot* (1976),[2] *Camelot in Orbit* (1978), and *The Majick of Camelot* (1981). The code of feudal chivalry that pervades this world recalls that of Arthurian romance, just as the hero's role as savior recalls that of King Arthur. The second novel even includes a brief vision of the Grail, scientifically projected to warn the hero of deception. Another novel by Landis, *Home—*

To Avalon (1982), places some mysterious viewing devices called Merlin's Eyes on another feudal world called Avalon. More specifically Arthurian are the handful of writings that use characters from the legend. The earliest is Theodore Sturgeon's "Excalibur and the Atom" (1951), in which a private detective encounters various reincarnated Arthurian characters before he eventually discovers that he is himself Galahad. However, these reincarnations bear but superficial resemblance to the original characters. This is in keeping with the general clumsiness of the story which fails to integrate plot, character, and theme, and stretches plausibility with sketchy "scientific" explanations.

The remainder all place their characters in the roles of Arthurian heroes for various purposes. The hero of Vladimir Nabokov's "Lance" (1952) is named after Lancelot, and his voyage in space is compared to crossing the "Bridge of the Sword, leading to the Other World ('dont nus estranges ne retorne'). Lancelot crawls over in great pain, in ineffable anguish" (p. 23). The story deals with the problem of explaining the space age to an uncomprehending older generation, but it gets tied up in its own self-conscious complexity. The bumbling hero of John Phillifent's *Life with Lancelot* (1973) is also named Lancelot, and he finds himself on another world called Avalon, where the culture is "based on Arthurian legend" (p. 8). Some humor is generated by his attempts to live up to the prestige of his name, and by the foibles of the people whom he meets, but these are not explored further. In his short story "Merlin" (1960) J. F. McIntosh also places a feudal culture on a planet named Avalon. The characters are named after figures in Arthurian legend, but they do not always behave as did their predecessors. The potential for exploring class conflict in the story is neglected in favor of casually asserting the superiority of progress generated by free enterprise over mindless adherence to tradition.

Partly because they are written with insufficient care, and partly because all except the Nabokov story focus upon adventure for its own sake, these works neglect the opportunity to explore the gap between illusion and reality inherent in their material. Fortunately for the reputation of science fiction, however, this challenge was taken up by C. J. Cherryh in *Port Eternity*

(1982). Cherryh is an award-winning author with a talent for portraying the effects of stress upon personality. She typically takes a small group of characters, disrupts their familiar routine by placing them in a crisis situation, then examines how they react under pressure. This is precisely what she does in *Port Eternity*: a private space craft is marooned in another dimension where its occupants find themselves threatened by aliens.

Their anxiety is heightened by the nature of the staff and crew of the vessel. They are "made people," cloned from special genetic combinations, then conditioned with "deepteach" tapes to create a special "psych-set." These "made people" are "sold out" to "born people" when ready at sixteen or eighteen, and "put down" when they pass forty years of age. The sole reason for their existence is to serve their owners, and their programming is so tight that they have very little freedom of choice. Thus when confronted with a crisis that is outside their limited range of experience, they have great difficulty in handling it. However, in this it turns out that they are not so different from the born people, who experience equal difficulty in coping with the unexpected. Cherryh thus reveals the extent to which we are all the product of our innate tendencies, developed in certain directions by our specific experience of life. We have little real freedom of choice, because we react as our personalities dictate: "They made us out of born-man material, and perhaps...somewhere at base they and we were not so different...born-men would do things because it leapt into their minds to do them, like instincts inherent in the flesh" (p. 169).

What serves to throw this scrutiny of human conditioning into focus is the Arthurian element. Influenced by Tennyson's *Idylls of the King*, Dela, the wealthy owner of the craft which she named "Maid of Astolat," has decorated the interior "in a strange mix of old fables and shipboard modern" (p. 10): old-looking beams mask structural joins, lamps mimic live flame, banners and swords hang on the walls of the dining hall. But her fantasy extends beyond furnishings to the made people who serve her. There are seven of them, and all have been modeled upon characters in Tennyson's poem: the pilots are Gawain and Lynette; the engineers are Percivale and Modred; the accountant is Vivien; the household is run by Lancelot; and Lady Dela's personal servant, and the narrator of the novel, is Elaine (of Astolat). On this journey, as on so many others, they "play out the old game" (p. 12), the familiar and comfortable Arthurian fantasy created by their owner. But this escapist fantasy entangles her as well, so that Elaine wonders at "Dela, who lived stories that were long ago and only maybe so, whose life came down to tapes, just like mine. . . . the greatest joy in her life was to pretend. All my existence was pretense, the pretense of the tapes which fed into my skull what my makers and my owner wanted me to know and believe" (pp. 10–11). Even her born-men guests are drawn into the fantasy. Thus Dela behaves often like an imperious Queen Guenevere, while Griffin, her lover and prospective husband, fills the role of an aggressive Arthur: even his name recalls Pendragon.

This familiar pattern is irrevocably shattered when they find themselves marooned in another dimension, and the crisis is complicated by the made people's discovery of their Arthurian personae. This exerts conscious pressure upon them to act out their traditional roles: "Percy talking about God and Modred turning on us—and Lance and Gawain at odds. . . We're all lost in Dela's dream" (p. 148). Much of this pressure comes because they begin to react to each other as to their legendary namesakes. Thus when Modred advises that they supply the aliens with complete information about themselves, they suspect that he wishes to betray them. He had "a name that had stopped being a joke. He was Modred" (p. 158). And because we tend to become what other people expect us to be, forced into the role by their attitude toward us, the illusion becomes the reality, the Arthurian persona takes over the original person. To survive, the humans need all their resources, but find instead that they are hindered by mistrust of one another, uncertain what to expect. Starting out as illusion, a game, an escapist fantasy, the Arthurian pattern gradually enmeshes the characters, becoming the reality.

Cherryh borrows not only characters from Tennyson's *Idylls of the King*, however, but the quotations that head each chapter also. These help to reveal that the plot structure is based upon an Arthurian pattern. Like Arthur and his court, the humans have achieved success in their world, and settled into a comfortable way of life; this ends abruptly, and they find themselves threatened by external invasion; but their resistance is weakened by internal dissension; they are overwhelmed in the last battle, which ends when their leader is carried off to the other world; he does not die there, but recovers. In this science-fictional Avalon, peopled with creatures "strange as any heraldic beasts of our dream" (p. 189), the humans live out their Arthurian roles: Modred always devising new ideas; Vivien compiling careful records of what she finds out; Percivale discussing philosophy; Gawain and Lynette traveling widely throughout the land; Griffin and Dela (Arthur and Guenevere) living together in their Camelot; Lancelot, who loves them both, living finally with Elaine in a tower by the lake (del Lac?): "Whether we dream, still falling forever, or whether the dream has shaped itself about us, we love...at least we dream we do" (p. 191).

This conclusion underlines the final paradox of loss and gain in the novel. On one hand we witness the descent into complete illusion, into another world from which there is no return. Failure to return from the other world bearing the treasure of knowledge is a traditional signal of defeat in legend and folklore, a symbolic death.[3] Thus despite the contentment of being with those one loves, there is also a lack of intensity about life in this other world. The fierce emotions of the struggle for survival prior to entry are gone, replaced by a dream-like detachment in a world outside time where nobody ages—or develops.

Yet Arthurian legend teaches us that this defeat is also a triumph. The aching loss of Arthur's glorious realm is balanced by the heroic achievement of those who strive against all odds to hold back the dark for a while. Their lives become an inspiration to those who follow, "something brighter and more vivid than ourselves" (p. 141). In *Port Eternity* the humans rise above their limitations. Armed with only swords and their courage, they resist valiantly to the end, struggling against overwhelming odds and their own weaknesses. What Elaine says of Modred, she might equally say of all, including herself: "He did the best he knew" (p. 183). When the battered human survivors, with what little strength they have left, limp painfully forward toward their mighty enemies, they are stepping into legend. Moreover, by conquering fear and doubt, they triumph. Their enemies become friends. From this point of view they have, in fact, become their heroic predecessors, resting in Avalon, the home of legend. Here they remain, waiting to inspire others by their example: "And whenever the call goes out, echoing clear and brazen through the air, we take up our arms again and go" (p. 191). This is a complex novel that can be confusing at times, but its achievements are impressive, particularly the tight interdependence of setting, character, plot and theme, and the skilful use of Arthurian legend.

To these few Arthurian works of science fiction, we can add another half dozen novels of science fantasy. Science fantasy is a curious blend of science fiction and fantasy. On the one hand it creates a secondary world where magic operates; on the other it offers a scientific explanation, however cursory, for the existence of this secondary world, though not of the magic. Magic and science are thus integrated in a functional manner.[4]

Five of the novels use the familiar device of parallel universes to account for their secondary world of magic. In *Witch World* (1963), another novel by Andre Norton, the hero sits upon the Siege Perilous in order to gain entry into the Witch World of the title. Here he encounters numerous lively adventures that proved so popular with readers that the novel became the first of a series. The Siege Perilous is here a stone of power, like the Lia Fail which acknowledges the true king of Ireland. "Arthur was supposed to have discovered its power through the Seer Merlin and incorporated it among the seats of the Round Table" (p. 11).

The other four novels borrow characters rather than objects. The hero of Poul Anderson's *Three Hearts and Three Lions* (1953) finds himself in an alternate universe after receiving a head wound. His adventures help him to progress along the path to self-discovery, until he finally emerges as the reincarnated Ogier the Dane. His valor at a time of crisis turns back the tide of Chaos in its struggle against Law in both universes. Anderson draws upon the legend of Ogier the Dane, not upon that of Arthur, but Morgan le Fay belongs to both. Moreover, the role that she plays as the servant of Chaos is closer to that of Arthur's arch-enemy than to that of Ogier's mistress. The conflict between her impulses to love and to destroy does, in fact, recall the ambivalent role that Morgan plays in Arthurian tradition. Unfortunately it is not a direction that the author chooses to explore.

Roger Zelazny's popular saga of Corwin, Prince of Amber, borrows widely from various legends, including the Arthurian. In the second novel of the series, *The Guns of Avalon* (1972), Sir Lancelot du Lac appears as a valiant knight fighting against the demons of Chaos. However he is detached from his Arthurian milieu and plays a minor role in the novel. The fifth and concluding novel, *The Courts of Chaos* (1978), introduces us to Merlin, the son of Corwin and a shape-shifting demoness from Chaos. He plays no significant role in events, nor does he have any Arthurian connection other than his name, except perhaps that like his namesake he is connected with demons.

Clive Endersby's *Read All About It!* (1981) is a juvenile adventure story based upon a T.V. Ontario program. It blends science fiction, fantasy and realism in a series of episodic adventures that teach the children some valuable lessons. Merlin makes a brief appearance so that he can use his magic to send the children to another world.

John Brunner's *Father of Lies* (1968) differs from the other science fantasies in that it explains the magical secondary world as the creation of a mad child with mutant powers. These transform his immediate environment into an Arthurian fantasy world, complete with ogres, dragons, and Merlin imprisoned in an oak tree. He himself adopts the role of Arthur. Unfortunately this is not one of Brunner's better novels, and he neglects the chance to examine role-playing except at its most superficial level. He prefers to have his characters concentrate upon uncovering the explanation for this bizarre world.

In point of fact, none of these science fantasy novels uses the Arthurian borrowings as more than a convenient device to advance the plot. Their focus is upon other matters. Only Anderson offers interesting insight into the borrowed feature, and this but a brief glimpse of undeveloped possibilities.

What most of the science fiction and science fantasy novels have in common is the potential to explore the theme of illusion and reality. *Merlin's Mirror* disputes the merits of accelerating civilization through external intervention by arguing that the loss of independence and initiative outweighs the apparent benefits. More typical is the ironic effect created by characters playing legendary roles with varied results. This approach has yielded one novel of merit in Cherryh's *Port Eternity*. Treatment of the Arthurian legend has otherwise been disappointing.

One result of this has been a widespread failure of science fiction and science fantasy to contribute more than perfunctory insight into Arthurian tradition. We are afforded tantalizing glimpses of possibilities, but little more. What are the implications for the legend of making the Siege Perilous an entry into an alternate universe? of Morgan's dual nature? of a reincarnated Galahad? of latter-day attempts to play the role of Merlin? or Lancelot? or Arthur himself? Only Cherryh satisfactorily answers such questions, and her perceptions reveal the power of legend to move us in ways both perilous and glorious. Indeed there can be no glory without the peril. We learn, too, about traditional characters: the essential innocence of Elaine, the cold rationality of Modred, and about Lancelot who lost when he seemed to win. Our understanding of them grows as we watch their reactions to new experiences. The experiences seem radically different from those that first shaped the traditional characters, yet ultimately they test the very same qualities that first distinguished them. This is as it should be. Science fiction, like all fiction, is concerned with enlarging our understanding of ourselves, and human nature remains basically the same, no matter how unusual the experiences it encounters.

Thus, despite inherent difficulties in dealing with Arthurian material, science fiction and science fantasy have the potential to develop the legend in challenging directions. Where the tension between the conservative tradition of the legend and the innovative point of view implied in the literary forms can be harnessed, the results can be striking. However, the task will take superior literary talents.

NOTES

1. I have chosen to include Mark Twain's *A Connecticut Yankee in King Arthur's Court* among the fantasies. See Chapter 6, note 4.
2. Using the pseudonym James R. Keaveny, the author published

an earlier and somewhat different version of this novel under the title, "Let There Be Magick" (1969).

3. See Joseph Campbell, *The Hero with a Thousand Faces* (Cleveland and New York: World Publishing, 1956), pp. 193–243. (First published New York: Bollingen Foundation, 1949.)

4. See Tymn, Zahorski, and Boyer, *Fantasy Literature*, pp. 17–19.

6

FANTASY

Of all the literary genres which deal with the Arthurian legend, modern fantasy has demonstrated the most dramatic growth. By the end of the 1920s, Arthurian fantasies were appearing at the rate of one every two years, and this continued until the mid-1950s, when the rate doubled. During the early 1970s, the rate doubled again to two books annually, then rose to three during the second half of the decade. This rate has been maintained into the 1980s, and it reflects the vigor and popularity of fantasy in general, despite the recession that has hit the publishing industry.

Indeed the economic recession may actually have contributed to the popularity of fantasy, which offers escape from a bleak reality, much as did Hollywood in the 1930s. Moreover, in a world of increasing complexity, where it is difficult to recognize the causes of misery, much less fasten blame and make corrections, fantasy seems to offer a world where good can confront and defeat evil. Intrepid heroes undertake daunting quests and overcome dark lords, cleansing the land and restoring a reign of love and justice.

The escapist label long precluded fantasy from serious critical attention by scholars trained to appreciate a more realistic tradition of fiction. However, since J.R.R. Tolkien argued the case for escapism as a potentially constructive and reinvigorating process,[1] scholarly acceptance of fantasy has been widening, albeit slowly and grudgingly. Serious study demonstrates that the apparently simplistic world of fantasy can, in fact, prove to be very sophisticated indeed, as capable of probing the truths of the human condition as the most introspective of psychological novels.[2] While it remains true that much fantasy is of inferior standard, in this it differs little from other literary genres, and it at least manages to avoid the pretentiousness of some.

Fantasy is distinguished from other literary genres in that the element of the marvelous is crucial. Moreover, the way in which the marvelous is used distinguishes between the two major classifications: high and low. The world depicted in low fantasy is the primary world with which we are familiar, and no explanation is offered for non-rational phenomena. Their impact, thus, tends to be mysterious and frightening, which is why they often figure in horror novels. By contrast, high fantasy creates a secondary world where non-rational events are accounted for by some supernatural agency that is acceptable in that world.

All but a handful of Arthurian fantasies belong to this latter category. They can be divided into three generally recognizable groups: mythopoeic, heroic, and ironic.[3] In mythopoeic fantasy the conflict that we witness is but a part of the larger struggle between the forces of good and evil, or light and darkness as they are frequently called. This struggle takes place primarily at a supernatural level, between beings wielding awesome powers, yet its outcome often hinges upon the contribution of human protagonists, despite their relative weakness. As they rise to meet the challenge posed, these apparently ordinary characters discover extraordinary resources within themselves, learning valuable lessons as a result.

In heroic fantasy this process of self-discovery is equally important, but it is not part of a broader supernatural struggle. Supernatural beings have faded from the picture, although their power remains as magic. Occasionally we may catch glimpses of them as fays and demons, but power is generally wielded by human magic workers, like Merlin, Morgan le Fay, and the Lady of the Lake.[4] Moreover, this power is clearly circumscribed, sometimes amounting to little more than mere illusion or prescience. As a result the contribution of the human heroes stands out as more significant, and their stature grows accordingly.

Ironic fantasy, by contrast, measures the human achievements, not against the high odds, but against the even higher expectations of the characters, to reveal a comical gap. The results can range from devastating satire to affectionate humor, from high comedy to low buffoonery. We are invited to relish the ridiculousness of it all, and thus to ponder the folly of all human pretensions.

It should be reiterated that these groups represent a general direction within the fantasies, rather than rigid and exclusive categories. Many works not examined in the ironic group make very effective use of irony, notably T. H. White's *The Once and Future King* and Godwin's *Firelord*. Although the first two novels of Gillian Bradshaw's Arthurian trilogy are mythopoeic, the supernatural conflict fades from sight in the conclusion. Robert Newman's first Arthurian fantasy for juveniles could be considered as either heroic or ironic, while its sequel is mythopoeic. Strong arguments can be advanced for including Richard Monaco's Grail trilogy in any one of the three groups. Authors, after all, are more concerned with their artistic vision than with the categories drawn up by scholars. I shall discuss these debatable novels in the categories wherein I perceive their main thrust places them.

LOW FANTASY

There are very few works of low fantasy that use the Arthurian legend. Nor are the reasons difficult to perceive. In low fantasy the supernatural inexplicably intrudes upon our ordinary world with often frightening effect. However, supernatural elements are not only an integral part of Arthurian tradition, but also are more freely accepted in it. We perhaps flatter ourselves when we assume that our forebears were more credulous than we are, but it is certainly true that their scientific knowledge was more limited. Less had been passed down to them. Consequently, a whole range of what are now recognized as natural phenomena might be accorded supernatural explanations. Since apparently supernatural phenomena were more familiar, they had less shock impact. Indeed the knights of Arthurian medieval romance usually confront shape-shifters, giants, and fays with as much courage as they confront their human adversaries. The distant past then, has not proved as attractive to low fantasy as one might expect, except as the origin of non-rational phenomena, such as ancient curses, that intrude upon the present. Thus the Arthurian element in low fantasy appears as a non-rational and unexplained intrusion into our contemporary world.

Several of the novels examined in Chapter 3 have some claim to be considered low fantasy. St. John's *Guinever's Gift* uses supernatural overtones to build an atmosphere of brooding mystery, but it eventually provides a rational explanation for events. Novels by Powys, Machen, and others include a vision of the Grail, but these are part of a spiritual perception of life that the reader is not expected to find unacceptable. There are elements of low fantasy also in some of the high fantasies, notably mythopoeic works by authors like Susan Cooper, Alan Garner, and Penelope Lively. Here the conflict between good and evil spills over into our primary world with bewildering effect. However, an explanation for the supernatural acts is eventually offered. Since all these novels are considered elsewhere, five works of low fantasy remain.

The earliest is Mary Mitchell's *Birth of a Legend* (1956), a historical novel that tells the story of Lohengrin, the son of Perceval. The inexplicable arrival of the Swan Knight in a Swan-like vessel, just in time to defend a maiden in trial by combat, is used to reveal human frailty. The trouble is that most people are too suspicious to accept an apparently miraculous event with simple faith. Their minds are swayed by doubt, by ambition, and by self-delusion. Even the noble emperor believes that God intervenes through natural, rather than supernatural, means. The result, finally, is the betrayal of trust, and the departure of the Swan Knight from a world that is not innocent enough to accept him without doubt. The challenge of discerning illusion and reality serves thus to probe human nature.

The only short story in this category is "Lancelot Returned" (1957) by Irving Cox. Here an ugly and neglected idiot girl conjures up a fantasy that takes on reality: that Lancelot has come to take her off to Camelot. Although the flat characterization is relieved by a sardonic humor, the possibilities of exploring the theme of illusion and reality are not developed.

Much more impressive are the three juvenile novels. William Mayne's *Earthfasts* (1966) incorporates the legend of Arthur and his knights sleeping in a cave under a mountain.[5] Time passes so quickly in this cave that a drummer boy who enters in the eighteenth century finds that over two hundred years have elapsed when he returns to the surface. Unfortunately, he takes with him a candle that he found burning, and this theft arouses the slumbering supernatural powers. They resume their long sleep when the candle is finally returned. In Nancy Bond's *A String in the Harp* (1976) three American children find themselves unwillingly transplanted to Wales for a year. One of them finds the ancient harp-tuning key of Taliesin which enables him to see with an inner eye events from the bard's life. *Raven* (1977), by Jeremy Burnham and Trevor Ray, is based upon a television series written by the same authors. A rebellious youth emerges as reluctant leader of a conservationist movement to preserve an ancient network of caves with religious significance. These caves too are linked with the cave-legend of Arthur, and there are suggestions that the hero is the king reborn, and that his mentor, an archeology professor, is Merlin.

What distinguishes all three is the way in which the supernatural is used. Not only does its intrusion into the ordinary world heighten the oppressive sense of danger and build tension, but, even more important, it develops character. In *Earthfasts*, thus, the aroused supernatural powers pose a physical threat that demands courage and resourcefulness from the young protagonists. Furthermore, the supernatural also challenges the conventional view of reality. Confused people desperately seek rational explanations for non-rational phenomena. Thus one father, "having reasoned everything tidy,"[6] retires to bed; another, a scientifically minded medical doctor faced by the return of a son declared dead, first tries to avoid the facts, then "looked at the pupils of his own eyes, to see whether he was normal or concussed or had done something that would alter his memory" (p. 185). Meanwhile creatures out of legend, like giants and boggarts ("slightly touchy house spirits," p. 88), begin to stir from their long sleep, for rejection of the supernatural as impossible superstition is a form of psychological repression that merely strengthens its power.[7] Only those who have the courage and open mind to accept the validity of the non-rational, and to deal with it on its own terms, even at the risk of public ridicule, can respond to the threat and restore the proper order. Thus Keith returns the candle to the cave, so that "the lock in time" may "be set again, and bind the King to the end of his sleep" (p. 174). The story thus teaches the importance of preserving an open mind if one is to grow in understanding and win peace.

A String in the Harp offers the same lesson. The children have recently lost their mother and this trauma has left the entire family grief-stricken. However, much of their grief stems from self-pity, from resentment at enforced domestic change. This psychological change is mirrored externally by their removal from the comfortable surroundings of New England to the unfamiliar bleakness of northwest Wales in winter. Initially, each is blind to everything but his or her own misery. To escape this trap of self-pity, each must learn to look beyond such selfish concerns. Thus the key that they find proves invaluable as a key to freedom. The visions allow them to escape from their present unhappiness into another world. Yet, paradoxically, this is not an escape from responsibility. Events are viewed through the eyes of others, so that the dreamers inevitably share the others' point of view. They learn thereby to look beyond the differences, and so discover the beauty of this unfamiliar land and the warmth of its people. This broader perspective leads to growth and acceptance, which in turn enable the family to reconcile itself to its loss and resume living once again.[8] Now, however, it has learned to appreciate things that it once took for granted.

Raven is also about growing up. The rebellious young hero reluctantly accepts the mantle of leadership, discarding in the process his cynicism and mistrust of society. He remains hostile to authority, but he discovers that he can influence its conduct by skilful and courageous use of its own rules. Insensitive politicians and bureaucrats are, he discovers, shy of adverse publicity. His energy and idealism are thus harnessed for constructive purposes. Instead of plaguing society as a juvenile delinquent, Raven sets about rebuilding it with truer values. The use of visual devices, such as television monitors and interviewers, betrays the novel's origin as a television series, but it offers thoughtful observations upon the relationship of the individual to society.

The Arthurian figures occupy traditional roles in low fantasy: Lancelot and Lohengrin rescue maidens in distress; Taliesin is a wandering bard; Arthur will return to save Britain. However, since they are also used to heighten the sense of mystery and danger, their more sinister and threatening aspects are emphasized. Lohengrin is inflexible in the conditions that he imposes; Lancelot will brook no interference with his rescue; the visions of Taliesin's life seem at first an unhealthy withdrawal from contact with reality; both the Merlin and Arthur figures in *Raven* seem hostile and anti-social; the prematurely awakened Arthur in *Earthfasts* not only threatens to violently disrupt the ordinary world, but even attacks one of the young protagonists for hindering his return.

In each novel Arthurian tradition supplies the supernatural element that leads to character growth. Moreover, the supernatural has the paradoxical effect of bringing the protagonists into contact with a deeper reality. In *Earthfasts* and *Birth of a Legend* they must reject the limited vision of convention in order to deal with new experiences provided by the appearance of Arthur and Lohengrin; in *A String in the Harp* Taliesin's key helps them escape the subjective world of self-pity and discover a wider world beyond; in *Raven* the awareness of his Arthurian heritage liberates the young hero from the prison of his own hostility, so that he realizes his own ability to function effectively within society. The Arthurian low fantasies thus use the apparent illusion of non-rational phenomena to bring their characters and readers to awareness of true reality. Those who ignore or reject the non-rational are, by contrast, most firmly in the grip of their preconceptions—in other words, their illusions. The novels thus warn people not to rest content with knowledge based upon limited experience. They must be prepared to accept new ideas if they wish to grow into the fuller understanding that maturity brings. Failure brings loss, as experienced in Mitchell's novel, where the Swan Knight withdraws from the world he had enriched with his vision of love and justice.

MYTHOPOEIC FANTASY

Among the various groups into which Arthurian high fantasy can be divided, the most interesting and thoughtful is the mythopoeic. Here the struggle between good and evil is waged between supernatural powers. What we witness in these novels is but one often minor skirmish in an eternal conflict, though to its human participants it takes on great importance. Indeed the fate of the human race may well lie in the balance, even if its significance is dwarfed by the scale of the forces that war together.

Three of the novels belong to a rare sub-category, known as didactic fantasy.[9] Coningsby Dawson's *The Road to Avalon* (1911) is an allegorical novel that contains Arthurian characters.[10] Under the pseudonym of Geoffrey Junior, William Courthope wrote *The Marvellous History of King Arthur in Avalon* (1904), a pseudo-chronicle in archaic diction. Morgan la Faye here carries Arthur and the knights of the Round Table to Avalon, where she beguiles them with her spells into forgetful pleasure. Eventually they are roused and establish a more just and equitable society. This is really a political allegory attacking the abuse of the parliamentary system in Britain, with its lack of true representation and accountability, and its preoccupation with narrow party politics at the expense of the nation's needs. John Cowper Powys' *Morwyn or the Vengeance of God* (1937) is largely a vehicle for condemning religious and scientific fanaticism, particularly the vivisection of animals. Powys argues, "More will perish because of science than will live because of it" (p. 205). The bard Taliesin appears as a guide and helper for the young couple as they wander through a strange underworld filled with dead souls. Here they find Merlin asleep in his *esplumeoir*. When his sanctuary is invaded by rapacious vivisectors, he wakens to transform them briefly into their suffering victims, but he returns to sleep as soon as they flee.

The Arthurian element in these didactic fantasies is totally subordinate to the central purpose of condemning excess. As a result it remains very general or peripheral. Characters fulfil their traditional roles: Arthur returns to establish a just kingdom; Merlin and Taliesin give help and guidance. As a group it is not without interest, but it contributes little to Arthurian tradition.

Most of the truly mythopoeic novels are placed in a contemporary, or at least post-medieval, setting, as Arthurian characters are revived by various means to participate in new struggles. The earliest is Charles Williams' *War in Heaven* (1930), a gripping story of spiritual conflict in a disbelieving world. The only Ar-

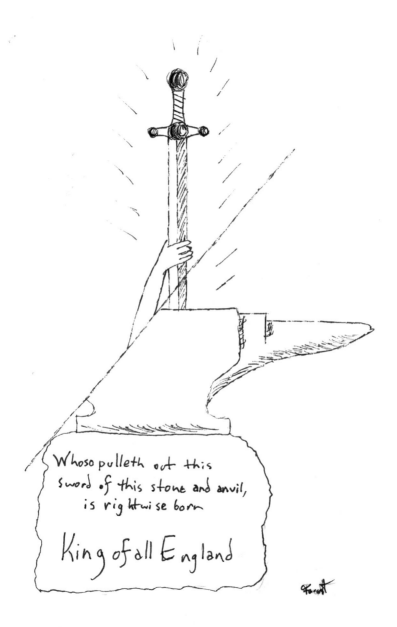

Whoso pulleth out this
sword of this stone and anvil,
is rightwise born

King of all England

thurian borrowing is the Holy Grail, although its keeper, Prester John, is linked with Galahad. The search for the relic does, however, recall traditional elements of Arthurian Grail quests: the torment and despair of the Archdeacon on the very eve of triumph is the same as that experienced by Perceval in the Perilous Chapel before his vision. The war between good and evil for possession of the Grail takes place on both the physical and spiritual planes, and it reveals the limitations of mere human reason. The focus upon Christian mysticism in the modern world, however, precludes attention to aspects of the Arthurian legend outside the Grail.

In *That Hideous Strength* (1945), the third novel of his Space Trilogy,[11] C. S. Lewis borrows more extensively from Arthurian tradition. Here good and evil are characterized as the spirit of Logres and the spirit of Britain, respectively. The handful of the faithful who fight for the former are led by Ransom, the Pendragon and thus heir to the authority of King Arthur. He is also known as Mr. Fisher-King, and like the figure out of Grail legend he suffers grievously from an unhealed wound, in the foot in his case. Among his enemies is "Fairy" Hardcastle, a cruel woman whose name and personality recall Morgan le Fay. Both sides in the struggle seek the aid of Merlin, who is awakened from the underground chamber in which he has slept through the ages.

The Arthurian elements serve to evoke the eternal quality of the struggle between good and evil which is here waged at a cosmic level. The war between Logres and Britain has endured, like the legend, through the centuries. Now it is being fought between those who cherish natural harmony, beauty, love, and responsibility, and an organization named N.I.C.E. (National Institute of Co-ordinated Experiments) which seeks to destroy these in the name of progress towards a dehumanized and totalitarian world order, inspired by short-sighted self-interest. The negative impulses within N.I.C.E. contribute significantly to its own downfall, but the principal agent of destruction is Merlin. He agrees to serve the supernatural spirits of good, known as the Oyéresu, and serves as a channel for their awesome powers.

Merlin belongs to an earlier age when the division between

good and evil was less clear-cut. He could manipulate the so-called "Neutral" spirits of the world, though at a spiritual cost, for "They sort of withered the man who dealt with them."[12] Thus he can serve as "A tool...good enough to be so used and not too good" (p. 343). Yet just as contact with the neutral powers withers a man, so wielding the still greater powers of good consumes: "you could see in his face that he was a man used up to the last drop...that he'd fall to pieces the moment the powers let him go" (p. 432). Merlin realizes his peril, yet despite an understandable reluctance, he accepts the necessity of his task. His action demonstrates the commitment to love and responsibility for other people that alone can overcome the selfishness of N.I.C.E.

Anne Saunders Laubenthal is indebted to both Williams and Lewis for many of the ideas in *Excalibur* (1973), as she herself acknowledges (p. xi): from the former she takes the idea of assuming another's burden, from the latter the concept of the hereditary Pendragonship. The struggle between good and evil to secure the Grail and Arthur's sword is set in modern Mobile, Alabama, and the Welsh legend of the twelfth-century voyage of Madoc is invoked to account for their presence in so unlikely a spot. Laubenthal succeeds in integrating these disparate ingredients into a suspenseful tale that builds toward a satisfying climax, as good and evil race to find the Grail and Excalibur. Her particular contribution to Arthurian tradition lies in her convincing characterization of Morgause and Morgan le Fay, both of whom return to participate in the struggle. The former has been consumed by revenge and ambition until she has become a mighty power of evil, the Queen of Air and Darkness; but Morgan is depicted as an ambivalent character, torn between resentment for past wrongs and yearnings to serve the mother goddess to whom she has dedicated herself. The perspective which this pair provides to events, both in the present and in the past, permits sympathetic insight into how their enmity to Arthur arose out of Uther's high-handed treatment of their family.

Tim Powers' *The Drawing of the Dark* (1979) is unique among Arthurian high fantasies in that it is set in the post-Arthurian past,[13] in this instance the Turkish siege of Vienna in the sixteenth century. This historical crisis is transformed into an encounter between good and evil, this time as West and East. The former are led by the Fisher King and by Merlin, who brings back from Avalon the spirit of King Arthur, temporarily resurrected as Brian Duffy, an Irish soldier of fortune. Duffy is unaware of his submerged identity, and reluctant to accept that he might be anyone other than himself. Indeed he regards Merlin's assurances with a mixture of irreverent cynicism and genuine alarm at what he conceives to be a threat to his own identity. The humanity of this reaction makes the fantasy all the more acceptable: we sympathize with his skepticism at the incredible events; we share his rueful recognition that he had more enjoyment and relaxation as Duffy than he ever did as Arthur; and we understand his complaint that Excalibur is too ponderous for contemporary swordplay, even if we are no more willing than Merlin to have it reforged to the new style.

What all four novels share is the process of self-discovery and growth on the part of the protagonists. The Archdeacon in Williams' work discovers the Christ-like potential that lies within each of us when he undergoes a form of crucifixion, resurrection and transfiguration; Ransom, Merlin, and their followers in Lewis' work draw upon formidable powers to destroy the evil embodied in N.I.C.E.; in their quest for Excalibur and the Grail the various protagonists of Laubenthal's novel find the inner resources to successfully defy the oppressive powers of evil, and Morgan le Fay develops a deeper understanding of the mother goddess whom she serves; Duffy in Powers' novel accepts his role as a reborn Arthur in time to turn back the Turkish invasion that threatens Europe. In each instance the heroes discover that their true selves possess god-like potential to frustrate apparently overwhelming evil.

Yet they achieve this insight only at great personal cost. Like Christ, the Archdeacon must endure despair at feeling abandoned by God in his hour of darkest torment; the powers unleashed to destroy the center of the enemy's hideous strength also consume Merlin who wields them; after their anguish the young people must leave behind the glory won by their brief contact with sword and Grail, for as the Pendragon laments, "There is an emptiness in my hands because I have touched it and will never touch it again" (p. 233), and after Morgan glimpses

the true face of the mother goddess, she is destroyed by puri-
fying flames; Duffy must risk the annihilation of his identity in
order to allow Arthur's return. Moreover, the Arthurian borrowings are central to each novel because they help to define
both the power and its cost: the Holy Grail is achieved only after
the doubt and despair of the quest; the Fisher King expiates his
former sins through suffering from his wound; Merlin gains
power, but must eventually sacrifice himself and leave this world;
Arthur preserves civilization for a while longer, but only by
giving up his own personal happiness; Morgause and Morgan
gain power from their dealings with darkness, but it consumes
the former who destroys Arthur through her son, and it confuses
the latter so that her attitude to Arthur is ambiguous, sometimes
supportive, at other times hostile.

This pattern of growth achieved only at great personal cost is
the basis of the best of the mythopoeic novels for juveniles. Here
the discovery of supernatural powers serves as a paradigm for
progress toward maturity, and it is a path that brings pain as
well as joy. Thus Alan Garner allows the young protagonists to
acquire power only at the price of lost innocence in his Alderley
books, *The Wierdstone of Brisingamen* (1960) and its sequel *The
Moon of Gomrath* (1963).

Garner does not name the mighty king who sleeps with his
warriors in a chamber below the ground, awaiting the land's
hour of direst peril, but the Alderley Edge legend upon which
his stories are based identifies him as Arthur; and in "The Edge
of the Ceiling" Garner himself says, "we accepted that King
Arthur lay asleep behind a rock we called The Iron Gates."[14]
This identification is reinforced by the information that the Lady
of the Lake, who also appears in Garner's books, is married to
one of the sleeping knights. In Arthurian legend the Lady of the
Lake is married to Pelleas, one of the knights of the Round Table.
Traditionally the sleepers are watched over by Merlin, and though
Garner calls the enchanter Cadellin Silverbrow, this latter epithet
recalls Silvester, one of Merlin's names.[15] His principal antagonist is the Morrigan, one of whose manifestations is Morgan
le Fay, the traditional enemy of Merlin and Arthur. Celemon,
leader of the Shining Ones in the second novel, is called the
daughter of Cei, one of Arthur's chief knights. These various

clues reveal the Arthurian link, but they raise the question of why the author chose to mute it. The answer may be a wish to integrate the borrowings into the world of primitive forces and wild magic that Garner creates in his novels. The supernatural features so common in early Welsh tradition were often rationalized in later romances. Since Garner is concerned to give a personal coloring to existing themes, as he himself points out in his note at the end of *The Moon of Gomrath*, he may have wished to avoid association with the more sophisticated world of Arthurian romance.[16]

In his role as enchanter and guardian of the sleeping warriors, Cadellin leads the forces of good in their struggle against evil, but the story focuses upon the adventures of two children, Susan and Colin, who assist him in the fight. In the first novel, against all odds they rescue and deliver the magical stone of the title to Cadellin who uses its power to defeat the enemy. This is Garner's first published novel and it is little more than exciting adventure fantasy, though involving and well paced. The sequel, however, probes much more deeply. Here the children, particularly Susan, draw upon unsuspected sources of supernatural power within themselves to frustrate their foe. This development marks a growth in the children, a movement toward independence and responsibility that involves a loss of innocence as well as the acquisition of power. As Cadellin observes, the bracelet which Susan uses to focus power is both "her blessing and her curse. For it guards her against the evil that would crush her, and it leads her ever further from the ways of human life. The more she wears it, the more need there is to do so. And it is too late now to take it off" (p. 70). There is no turning back from the road to maturity, nor any avoiding the choice between good and evil that awaits those who have earned the freedom to choose.

Yet, the children's growth is emotional rather than intellectual. They work the "Old Magic" which is "of the heart, not of the head" (p. 69). Because it is so difficult to control, Cadellin mistrusts the Old Magic. He prefers the High Magic which can be mastered with knowledge, and his reasoned approach is revealed in his decision to remain behind when Susan and her companions set out to rescue Colin: "My duty is here, guarding the Sleepers. Only I can wake them. If I were killed, I should have betrayed my trust, and only in Fuldindelve can I be certain of life" (p. 126). This is wisdom as all acknowledge, but Susan has "too much emotion" (p. 127) in her own nature to make such a decision herself. She has much to learn yet, for as the Lady of the Lake perceives, "She is but green in power!" (p. 155). At the end of the novel, therefore, when the Wild Hunt and the Shining Ones ride forth "free for ever" (p. 156), Susan cannot join them despite her yearning. " 'It is not yet! It will be! But not yet!' And the fire died in Susan and she was alone on the moor, the night wind in her face, joy and anguish in her heart" (p. 155).[17] Colin, too, shares in the growth that brings pain as well as joy, thrilling to the sound of a horn, "so beautiful that he never found rest again" (p. 156).

The children have plumbed new emotional depths, far beyond those they dreamed of before, but they have still to learn the lessons that the wisdom of Cadellin can teach. In *The Moon of Gomrath*, however, this wisdom seems cold and calculating compared to the impetuous heroism and self-sacrifice of Susan as she confronts and defeats the Morrigan. This effect is heightened by the truly "magical" beauty that Garner weaves into his description of the Old Magic. The ride of the Wild Hunt and the Shining ones is told with an imaginative power that outshines anything Cadellin can offer. Despite its real achievements, *The Moon of Gomrath* is an early novel that lacks the control over material that Garner reveals in his later works.

The other novelist who exacts a heavy price for wisdom and power is Susan Cooper in her series, The Dark Is Rising. The first novel, *Over Sea, Under Stone* (1965), seems little more than a well written children's adventure story in the tradition that Enid Blyton made popular. However, when the series resumed in 1973 with *The Dark Is Rising* it became apparent that the author had developed a more profound vision than readers of the first book might have anticipated. *Greenwitch* (1975) seems closer in spirit to the first book, but *The Grey King* (1975) and *Silver on the Tree* (1977), which conclude the series, fulfil that vision marvelously.[18]

The early books only hint that Professor Merriman Lyon is really Merlin, but the last two novels are explicit. These also introduce the figure of King Arthur, and Taliesin appears in *Silver on the Tree*. Merriman is a senior member of an immortal race known as the Old Ones, who are gifted with supernatural powers. They are engaged in a struggle against the forces of evil, here known as the Dark, and the battlefield is human nature itself, torn between base and noble impulses. As the series title proclaims, the Dark is rising for a last major assault, and the books describe how various talismans of power are collected to aid the Light in the imminent struggle. These tasks are performed by several young people: the three Drew children find the Grail; Will Stanton, last-born of the Old Ones, gathers the six signs of power; with the aid of Bran, the son of King Arthur and Queen Guinevere, he goes on to win first the golden harp that awakens the Six Riders, and finally, the crystal sword.

The young people are afforded some protection and guidance by Merriman, but they are forced to draw heavily upon their own resources to accomplish the various quests in the face of grave danger. The school of experience is a rigorous one and mistakes can cost dear. Thus in *The Dark Is Rising* Will revels in his awakening powers as an Old One by lighting a fire, only to find that it draws the attention of the Dark. He is fortunate to be rescued by Merriman from the consequences of his indiscretion: "in your state of untrained power, you would have made yourself so vulnerable that all the things of the Dark that are in this land would have been drawn towards you" (p. 58).

Just as adults are busy with pressing affairs necessary to earn a living, so must the Old Ones strive to save the world from the Dark. In both cases the struggle may be so close that it leaves little room for acts of charity and mercy, or for protecting a wayward child, as Will grows to understand in *The Grey King*: " 'Sometimes,' Will said slowly, 'in this sort of a war, it is not possible to pause, to smoothe the way for one human being, because even that one small thing could mean an end of the world for all the rest' " (p. 147). And he recalls "the strong, bony face of Merriman his master, first of the Old Ones, cold in judgment of a much-loved figure who, through the frailty of being no more than a man, had once betrayed the cause of the Light" (p. 146).[19]

Left largely to make their own decisions and abide the consequences, the young people learn quickly. Yet the growth in maturity and understanding brings still heavier responsibilities, particularly the agony of choice. In *Silver on the Tree*, just as Merriman must abandon Will at a time of crisis in order to rescue Simon Drew from drowning, so Bran must choose whether to join his father, Arthur, or to remain with his stepfather. Bran chooses to stay with the humans amongst whom he has been reared, recognizing that "Loving bonds...are the strongest thing on the earth" (p. 263). It is a brave and wise decision, yet the cost is high, as Merriman warns: "If you give up your place in the High Magic, your identity in the time that is outside Time, then you will be no more than mortal.... You will remember nothing that has happened, you will live and die as all men do.... you will never see your high father again" (pp. 263–64).

Growth in power brings not only harder decisions but also isolation and loss, as one grows away from the companions of one's childhood. In *The Dark Is Rising* Will uses his power to drive back an assault of the Dark upon himself and others, including his older brother, Paul. Then he finds "his brother looking at him with a kind of fearful remoteness that bit into him with the pain of a whiplash" (p. 130). He is obliged to erase Paul's memory of the experience to dispel this alienation, and to repeat this step later when another brother discovers his power in *Silver on the Tree* (pp. 14–16). Bran's special powers mark him out as different also, and in the latter novel he recalls bitterly "the years of people sneering and muttering" (p. 81).

For Cooper's final message is that adulthood is not an escape from the tiresome restrictions of childhood, but a shouldering of responsibilities: "the world will still be imperfect, because men are imperfect. Good men will still be killed by bad, or sometimes by other good men, and there will still be pain and disease and famine, anger and hate. But if you work and care and are watchful,...then in the long run the worse will never, ever, triumph over the better" (p. 267).

Of the remaining mythopoeic fantasies for juveniles, only Penelope Lively's *The Whispering Knights* (1971) teaches the young protagonists the bitter lesson that power costs dearly. Three children thoughtlessly concoct a magic brew that raises Morgan le Fay. Morgan represents the powers of darkness, "the bad side of things,"[20] and her favorite weapon is despair. By refusing to give in, despite their enemy's fearful strength, the children eventually triumph, but the struggle is a hard one they will not forget. Here too experience proves a harsh teacher. This is a perceptive novel, though it lacks the mythic resonance and depth that distinguish the work of Garner and Cooper.

The other three juvenile novels also teach a lesson, but the young people do not learn by their own mistakes. *Merlin's Magic* (1953) by Helen Clare tells the story of a treasure hunt organized by a young man named Merlin. He turns out to be the Arthurian enchanter himself, and he sends a group of children upon some magical adventures. One of them meets an absent-minded Lady of the Lake and an unpleasant Morgan Le Fay, before she finds Excalibur and returns it to King Arthur. The treasure turns out to be the human imagination, and with the aid of such imaginative creations as King Arthur and Excalibur, it is found and preserved from machines that seek to destroy it. The story argues the value of the imagination, which gives a glory to life in the shape of figures such as Arthur, and warns that it must be protected from destruction by a dehumanized and mechanical system. Unfortunately, the author values imagination too highly to control it properly, with the result that she rambles from one adventure to the next with too little sense of purpose to prevent boredom. Moreover, the treasure is won and the imagination preserved at little cost. It is all too easy.

Andre Norton has dealt with the Arthurian legend not only as science fiction and science fantasy, but also as mythopoeic fantasy. In *Steel Magic* (1965) three children accidentally enter the Otherworld of Avalon where each regains a stolen talisman of power: Huon's horn, Merlin's ring, and Arthur's sword Excalibur. The success of each is made dependent upon his or her ability to conquer secret fears: of spiders and insects, of water, and of darkness. This is a thoughtful and well-structured novel, but it lacks imaginative power.

Jane Curry, in *The Sleepers* (1968), is another author who makes use of the cave-legend. Arthur and his knights are discovered sleeping underground by four children following archeological excavations in the Eildon Hills of south Scotland.[21] The four find and release Myrddin from the spell with which Nimiane (Lady of the Lake) imprisoned him. Then they help him to foil a plot by Morgan le Fay and Medraut to destroy the Sleepers and capture the thirteen Treasures of Prydein (Britain). The novel reveals the short-sightedness of hard-headed realism that hinders the imagination. By their obstinate refusal to acknowledge the non-rational, the adults imperil the safety of their own world, did they but know it: "I'm not interested in things that don't have a logical explanation" (p. 31), one grumbles. However, Curry is more interested in developing mystery and suspense than theme. The result, after a slow start, is a generally exciting adventure story that neglects its broader implications.

In these four juvenile fantasies, the young protagonists all develop their potential, but they discover no supernatural talents of their own. Thus while they demonstrate courage and resourcefulness under adverse conditions, their growth in insight is less dramatic, less intense. Without an awakening of supernatural talents of their own, they view non-rational elements with greater detachment. Nor do they learn through harsh experience that added power brings added responsibility. The primary function of the marvelous shifts thus from developing character to furthering plot. This distinction is apparent in the novels of Garner and Cooper. *The Wierdstone of Brisingamen* is less successful than *The Moon of Gomrath* where Susan discovers her supernatural powers; *Over Sea, Under Stone* is less successful than the later novels, largely because the basically ordinary Drew children interest us less than do Will Stanton and Bran, who gradually discover their supernatural talents. Significantly, our attention is aroused by Jane Drew's ability to establish an empathetic bond with beings who do wield supernatural power— the Greenwitch in *Greenwitch* and the Lady in *Silver on the Tree*.

Where most authors of mythopoeic fantasy choose a contemporary setting for their action, two do prefer Arthur's day. Robert Newman uses the High Middle Ages for the setting of his two juvenile novels, *Merlin's Mistake* (1970) and its sequel, *The Testing of Tertius* (1973). The former is an ironic fantasy, and will be dealt with later. In the latter, however, the supernatural conflict between good and evil intrudes into human affairs. Merlin and his former master, Blaise, work for good, and they are opposed by Nimue and by Urlik, a very powerful black wizard, perhaps even "the present manifestation of *the* Dark Power" (p. 12). The young protagonists again learn some important lessons, but this time about themselves rather than others. Before they can combat evil they must combat and banish their own deep-rooted feelings of fear and guilt, the former by courage, the latter by self-sacrifice. The Arthurian borrowings are used to reinforce the lessons, for Arthur is himself willing to die rather than submit to the powers of evil. The humor of the earlier novel is replaced in the sequel by a more serious tone befitting the grimmer struggle we must wage with our own failings. *The Testing of Tertius* continues to teach the importance of courage and love, and it too succeeds in subordinating action to theme, particularly that of illusion and reality. Thus in one scene set in the Otherworld Brian must find his beloved amidst a confusing array of imitations, all in the guise of an old crone. He identifies her by her tears.

The two novels together thus mark stages in the growth to maturity. But where the first deepens understanding of the world around us, the sequel reveals our own selves. Consequently, when Brian and two of his companions venture into the Otherworld, the terrors that they encounter represent our subconscious fears: of nightmare monsters, of supplanting a mother, of trying to kill a father. The supernatural conflict between good and evil takes its place beside these Freudian symbols as part of our internal moral struggle. Only when we have conquered the fear and guilt that make us despair of attaining virtue can we master our evil impulses and work effectively toward good ends.

Unlike Newman, Gillian Bradshaw chooses the Dark Ages as the setting for Arthur's court. Her trilogy opens with *Hawk of May* (1980) which describes the struggle of Gwalchmai (Gawain) to win the trust of his uncle, King Arthur; it continues in *Kingdom of Summer* (1981) with the account of his ill-fated love affair; and it concludes with the fall of Arthur's kingdom in *In Winter's Shadow* (1982). The human conflict reflects a broader supernatural struggle, between the forces of Light and Dark: the former are led by Lugh of the Long Hand and the Sidhe who dwell on the Isle of the Blessed; the latter by the queen of Darkness. In *Hawk of May* we learn that the queen stalks the earth as Morgawse, "a Power wrapped in human flesh, long ago consuming the mind that had invoked it" (p. 61). She tries to shape her son Gwalchmai to her purpose, but he chooses to serve the Light instead.

Bradshaw creates sympathy for her narrators by exposing them to unfair harassment in the form of bullying and mistrust. This experience provides a series of trials and tribulations over which they must triumph in order to gain wisdom and acceptance. However, since we can see no really good reason to excuse the treatment they receive, we tend to dislike their persecutors. Gwalchmai, his servant Rhys, the Queen Gwynhwyfar, the narrators of the three novels, all win our sympathy, but only at the cost of turning Agravain and Cei into bullies, Lot and Rhuawn into fools, Elidan and Arthur into obstinate fanatics. This can sometimes lead to inconsistencies in their behavior that subsequent explanations do not always satisfy. Agravain's bullying of Gwalchmai may be understandable in the insecure youth in the Orcades, but not in the famous warrior who greets his brother with such warmth when they meet near Camlann. Arthur's initial mistrust of Gwalchmai is explained by his guilt over incest with his nephew's mother, Morgawse, but it persists to unwarranted lengths.

Yet this apparent confusion is integral to Bradshaw's vision of the Arthurian legend. She sees the fall of Arthur's realm and the promise that it offered as the failure of those who strove to create and uphold it. Thus a distraught Gwynhwyfar bitterly laments in *In Winter's Shadow*:

"An emperor commits incest with his sister and begets his own ruin in the person of a treacherous, malicious son; and an empress divides the realm at the critical time by playing whore with the emperor's best friend!...Not only is it all lost, it was we who lost it, we who by our own stupidity and weakness allowed ourselves to be divided and break, like a pot flawed in the firing that spills everything put into it." (P. 370)

The pettiness and folly into which people fall, especially those who should know better, is a measure of the limitations that doom their aspirations.

The aspirations that build Arthur's kingdom are most clearly demonstrated in the figure of Gwalchmai, his nephew. Sickened at his mother's cruel sorcery, he rejects the power that she offers, turning instead to the Light. At great personal peril he thus conquers the evil side of his own nature, and this victory is signaled by his journey to the Isle of the Blessed where he receives from Lugh his magical sword, Caledvwlch, and later Ceincaled, one of the horses of the Sidhe. Thereafter he bears about him the sign of that contact with the Otherworld, a look of "haunted brilliance" (*In Winter's Shadow*, p. 344) that leads some to wonder whether he might not be "one of the Fair Ones" (*Hawk of May*, p. 141). In place of the injured pride and thirst for revenge that prompted his turning to Morgawse, he displays true humility and charity.

In *Hawk of May* when his brother Agravain begs his forgiveness, he takes the blame upon himself: "I was a fool then, and took things over-much to heart" (p. 167). Similarly, when he later learns of Arthur's incest, he responds with pity, ignoring the injustices that he himself has suffered at Arthur's hands: "I had divided the Family, and killed, and made your victories bitter for you. Forgive me" (p. 270).

In this first novel forgiveness is won, and Gwalchmai is reconciled with both his brother and uncle. However, the victory is only partial in *Kingdom of Summer*, where his face "was already marked by pain and disappointment" (p. 15). Morgawse's plot to kill Arthur is foiled and she herself slain, but Medraut sets out for Arthur's court to accomplish the destruction; angered at Gwalchmai's betrayal of a promise, Elidan, his beloved and mother of their child Gwyn, refuses to be reconciled with him, despite his humble plea for forgiveness: "The children of Caw accounted it a dishonor to forgive" (p. 182). Only on her deathbed in *In Winter's Shadow* does she recognize that love and mercy are more important than pride and honor: "things which once seemed great to me seem less now. . . .I forgive you now for the way in which you wronged me; forgive me also for the pain I have caused you" (p. 145). Her failure to forgive until it is too late foreshadows Gwalchmai's own fate in the same novel. He who had been so noble and forgiving turns implacable in his demand for justice when Bedwyr kills his son Gwyn by mischance when rescuing Gwynhwyfar. This turning away from mercy is reflected in Gwalchmai's appearance. The glimmer of Light that has always marked him is transformed, so that he looks "like a creature from the dark Otherworld" (p. 250). Only as he too lies dying does he confess in a letter to Bedwyr, "I wished for justice with a longing greater than was just. . . . I forgive you my son's death. Forgive me my vengeance" (p. 343). At this moment the Light returns to him: "suddenly his dark eyes flooded with brilliant life" (p. 343). He prays for God's mercy on them all, even asking Gwynhwyfar to tell his brother Medraut that he loved him.

The fading of "the dream that the hearts of all men have ever longed for" (p. 377) is reinforced by the shifting point of view. In the first novel we share Gwalchmai's journey to the Otherworld, the glory of his wondrous sword and steed. In the second his activities remain central, but distance is imposed by the narrative perspective of his servant, the practical Rhys, who reports supernatural events with a skeptical eye. In the third Gwalchmai is no longer the central character, and Gwynhwyfar reports his dealings with the Otherworld as rumors only. The supernatural element thus recedes, and with it the bright hope that it represents. Gwalchmai himself bitterly reflects upon this:

Once I sailed to the Kingdom of Summer, the Otherworld. I thought then that the struggle between Light and Darkness was fought upon the Earth, and that the intentions of our spirits reflected it, and bound Earth and the Otherworld. But now that world seems unconnected and remote from here, for even the best intentions of those devoted to Light can create Darkness. (P. 291)

Gwynhwyfar ultimately learns to accept what has happened. In the Epilogue of *In Winter's Shadow* she muses, "it was worth it to have possessed that joy for a few years, and I cannot regret that we tried" (p. 377). Yet the dominant tone imposed by the thematic patterns is one of loss. The struggle is too hard, the moments of joy too fleeting, and often recalled with a nostalgia that makes the loss more bitter by contrast: "The Light has gone, and the Darkness covers Britain" (p. 370, cf. pp. 137–38).

Bradshaw draws widely upon Arthurian legend, including

some of the less familiar medieval versions: the reluctance of Arthur to accept Gwalchmai comes from the Latin *De Ortu Waluuanii*; the story of Gwalchmai's affair with Elidan from the First Continuation of Chrétien's *Percival* in the French. She also fuses characters to suit her needs. Gwyn, Gwalchmai's son, takes over the role of his beloved brother, Gareth, as well as that of the Fair Unknown; as in Sutcliff's *Sword at Sunset*, a Breton-born Bedwyr assumes Lancelot's position as the Queen's lover and the king's best friend. The author integrates these various borrowings with skill, using inconsistencies in behavior as evidence of mankind's inherently flawed nature. The result is a Dark Age world that is very credible despite the supernatural intrusions.

The unexpected credibility of the ordinary world is a feature that Bradshaw's trilogy shares with the other fantasies in this mythopoeic group. This arises from more than just attention to realistic and often homely detail, such as the aroma of wood fires, the brightness of sunlight upon new-fallen snow, the hard feel of stone or metal under the touch, the sound of children laughing and arguing. Of even more impact is the characterization. Since the mythopoeic novels present a conflict between good and evil, we should expect the characters to be clearly identified with one side or the other. To some extent this is true. The Fisher King, Merlin, and Arthur are prominent among the forces of good, leaders of the struggle to establish and preserve the dream of justice and mercy. Against them stand Morgause, Morgan le Fay, Nimue, and Mordred, figures of unredeemed evil. All the characters are measured by their contribution to the primal clash. Yet their service is marked by uneven success, as they fluctuate between valuable contribution and disastrous mistakes. Newman's young protagonists must learn to purge their feelings of despair before they can conquer evil; Cooper's Hawkin must expiate his betrayal through long and bitter years; and even so dedicated a servant of the Light as Bradshaw's Gwalchmai can lapse into unforgiving vengefulness. Indeed the foremost on both sides of the struggle can show flashes of humanizing weakness: Garner's Cadellin grieves that he must stay behind while Susan and her companions ride forth to rescue her brother; and Bradshaw's Medraut sorely laments the death of Gwalchmai, the brother whom he sought so long to destroy. These

signs of mankind's flawed nature make for highly credible characterization. We meet people who struggle with feelings and
doubts, with hopes and fears, and these encourage identification. Moreover, this process is strengthened by the Arthurian
borrowings. The fluctuation between failure and success lies at
the very heart of the legend, and the behavior of all its principal
characters reflects this humanizing duality. Mordred's sorrow
over his brother's death is part of the tradition in the English
alliterative *Morte Arthure*, just as Gawain's vengefulness is found
in the French Vulgate *Mort Artu* and later accounts based upon
it, including Malory's. Even Cadellin's subterranean confine-
ment recalls Merlin's eventual fate in the French Vulgate *Merlin*.

The Arthurian borrowings help not only to humanize the characters, but also to provide an eternal dimension to the conflict
between good and evil that takes place within all the novels in
this mythopoeic group. In Garner's Alderley books Cadellin and
the Sleepers wait through the ages for the final battle, while in
Curry's *The Sleepers* they waken to protect the Treasures of Prydein from Morgan's attack in the twentieth century. In Cooper's
Silver on the Tree Merriman reveals, "the peace of Arthur that
we shall gain for this island at Badon will be lost, before long,
and for a time the world will seem to vanish beneath the shadow
of the Dark. And emerge, and vanish again, and again emerge,
as it has done through all the length of what men call their
history" (p. 44). In Bradshaw's *In Winter's Shadow* Gwynhwyfar
also ponders the cyclical pattern: "the hopes remain in this realm,
more powerful than the spring when the sun circles round from
the dark winter. Our failure cannot put out the sun" (p. 378).

The Arthurian borrowings also heighten the sense of the supernatural. The figure of Merlin not only wields great powers
but also lives untouched by time, sometimes asleep, at other
times moving freely between this world and the next.[22] Arthur
too survives outside time, sleeping in a cave in the novels of
Garner and Curry, residing in an Otherworld in the novels of
Clare and Norton, while at the conclusion of Cooper's *Silver on
the Tree* he sails outside Time in his great ship *Pridwen*. Cooper
gives him other supernatural powers as well, for she makes him
a great lord of the High Magic in *The Grey King*, and in *Silver on
the Tree* she hints at his identity with Herne, antlered leader of

the Wild Hunt.[23] The bard Taliesin who helps the protagonists in this novel, reappears in Bradshaw's trilogy as one of the Sidhe in human guise. Arthur and his other followers remain mortal, but they do win help from the powers of Light. Gwalchmai's sword and horse, and his strength that waxes with the sun, all traditionally of supernatural origin,[24] are made gifts of Lugh to aid in the struggle against the Darkness. In Bradshaw's trilogy Morgawse is chief servant of the Darkness, and she uses its powers to destroy Arthur and his dream. Garner, Curry, and Lively, on the other hand, all choose that well-known enchant-ress and destroyer of good knights, Morgan le Fay, to lead the struggle of evil against good. Newman uses Nimue, the en-chantress who imprisoned Merlin, as an important servant of the Darkness.

One of the main weapons of evil in this struggle is deception and this theme is intensified by use of the Arthurian legend. In the novels of Williams, Lewis, Garner, Cooper, Curry, Lively, and Bradshaw, evil uses a persuasive and disarming exterior to beguile the unwary. Thus in Cooper's novels, agents of the Dark lurk behind amiable features: there appears to be "Nothing sin-ister about Maggie" (p. 55), the apple-cheeked dairy-girl in *The Dark Is Rising*, but she nearly takes the magical signs from Will; in *Silver on the Tree* Mrs. Rowland's face is "like the voice, gentle and warm and beautiful all at once, with a glow of kindliness" (p. 71), but she too "belongs to the Dark" (p. 233). The earlier betrayal that brought about the fall of Arthur's realm looms ominously behind the modern struggle, and is evoked by such details as Guinevere's trip forward in time to give birth to Bran, "because once before she had deceived her lord" (*Silver on the Tree*, p. 93). In Bradshaw's trilogy Morgawse and Medraut are adept at winning the confidence of others. The former dazzles men with her terrifying beauty, the latter presents so smooth and plausible an exterior that he wins over many of Arthur's own warband, "deluded by another's eloquence" (*Kingdom of Summer*, p. 210).

Such deceptions develop the theme of illusion and reality that is so important in the mythopoeic fantasies. Behind the ap-pearance of normal life, a supernatural struggle is taking place. When ordinary humans are caught up in it, their concepts of reality are contradicted so rudely that they experience confusion and distress. The first reaction of most people is to reject supernatural explanations, and this leaves them all the more vulnerable to the deception of evil. Because characters like Cei, Agravain, and Rhuawn in Bradshaw's trilogy disbelieve Gwalchmai's account of his visit to the Isle of the Blessed and of the demonic commitment of Morgawse and Medraut, they make the hero's task all the harder, his enemies' all the easier. The protagonists in most of the mythopoeic novels thus find themselves isolated in their fight against evil. Most people are either unaware or hostile at what they consider irrational claims and accusations. Because they are less set in their idea of what constitutes reality, the protagonists are often young people. Gwalchmai dedicates himself to the service of Light at an early age in Bradshaw's trilogy; in Curry's novel the children help Myrddin, while the adults reject non-rational phenomena; in Cooper's series the young Drews rally to the aid of the Old Ones, whereas Will's older brothers are so disturbed and alienated when they discover the supernatural conflict that he decides to protect them by erasing their memories. At the end of the series the memories of all the mortals, including the Drew family, are erased, for it is judged that some experiences are better forgotten.

We are faced, thus, with a striking paradox. In the fantasy world the concept of reality which we accept in our primary world becomes the illusion, while the supernatural element that permeates life is the reality which mankind is unable, or unwilling, to accept. In order to heighten the paradox, the world into which the supernatural intrudes is made as realistic as possible. For this reason, Bradshaw's Arthurian trilogy gains power from its very credible Dark Age setting. Conversely, the novels of Clare and Norton neglect to develop the realism of the ordinary world that their young heroes leave to venture into the Otherworld, and they are the weaker for it.

The theme of illusion and reality is also developed by the basic pattern of growth achieved at heavy cost. In *The Whispering Knights* the magic spell cast as a joke releases a power for evil that threatens to destroy the young protagonists. In *The Testing of*

Tertius, as in *Steel Magic*, they must painfully learn to master their own weaknesses before they can gain the strength to defeat evil.

Moreover, in many of these mythopoeic fantasies power brings, not freedom as one might expect, but a heavier burden of responsibility. In *That Hideous Strength* Merlin must expend himself to destroy the enemy, while in *The Drawing of the Dark* Duffy discovers how little happiness he enjoyed as Arthur. In *The Moon of Gomrath* Susan is no more free to follow heedless impulse than are Will and Bran in Cooper's series: the former is still "green in her power" (p. 155); the latter pair have special responsibilities and, as Will reminds his friend after an angry outburst in *Silver on the Tree*, "you and I may not forget it for a moment. And you may not. . .let go, like that" (p. 81). In *Kingdom of Summer* Rhys is shocked at how worn is Gwalchmai by the demands that he makes upon himself: "Not what I'd expected for so glorious a warrior" (p. 15).

An important ingredient in this sense of responsibility is compassion. This concern for others often prompts acts of self-sacrifice. Thus it is that Susan sets out to rescue her brother in Garner's *The Moon of Gomrath*; that the Stantons help a dark-skinned child being bullied by racists in Cooper's *Silver on the Tree*; that Gwalchmai wins Arthur's trust in *Hawk of May* by struggling to save the life of a stranger; that Merlin expends himself against evil to redeem mankind in Lewis' *That Hideous Strength*. The reality of power is often personal loss—a loss that may seem to outweigh the gain.

The pervasive pattern of illusion and reality, whereby our expectations are constantly reversed, gives thematic expression to one of the essential features of the fantasy form, as discerned by J.R.R. Tolkien. Fantasy allows us to discover the fullness of evil, so that we can combat it more readily in real life.[25] So it is that the protagonists of these mythopoeic novels discover the supernatural power of evil and learn to fight against it. Without this imaginative acceptance of fantasy and the world of good and evil that it reveals, we cannot truly appreciate the possibilities for good and evil within ourselves. Like so many adults in these novels, we reject this awareness at our peril, helping the cause of evil by default. The challenge of the supernatural is the challenge of fantasy: to know ourselves and the world about us better.

HEROIC FANTASY

By far the most popular of the groups into which Arthurian fantasy can be divided is the heroic. Like the medieval romances that they so closely resemble, the novels of heroic fantasy follow the adventures of one or more heroes, usually warriors, as they pursue some dangerous quest, or engage in battle against the enemy. The struggle is not part of a larger supernatural conflict as in the mythopoeic fantasies. However, it does test the extent to which the protagonists are prepared to follow the standards of conduct that they hold dear. Consequently they too learn to know themselves and the world about them.

Many fantasies owe a minor debt to Arthurian legend, but they separate the borrowings from their Arthurian context. Thus in *The Box of Delights* (1935) John Masefield has one character make use of the names of Arthur's knights during a conversation with the young protagonist who is called Kay. In Ruth Nichols' *The Marrow of the World* (1972) a cruel witch named Morgan adopts the guise of a beautiful young maiden to seduce unsuspecting men; she holds them captive in her castle on the shores of Lake Evraine, where she lives with her daughter, Ygerna; the names recall those of Morgan le Fay, her mother Igraine, and her son Ywain. At the conclusion of Michael Moorcock's *Gloriana or the Unfulfill'd Queen* (1978), the unscrupulous hero, Captain Arturus Quire, is revealed to be Prince Arthur of Valentia, and despite striking differences from his noble namesake, he does recall the Prince Arthur of Edmund Spenser's sixteenth-century poem, *The Faerie Queene*. Jack Vance's *Lyonesse* (1983) is set in the lands from which Arthur's ancestors fled.

Yet although such borrowings are largely removed from their Arthurian context, they do retain some of their traditional associations, and these associations do enrich the novels. In Masefield's novel they extend the imaginative range of material revealed by the magical box; in Nichols' novel the associations with Morgan le Fay make the forces that threaten the young protagonists still more sinister and threatening; in Moorcock's novel the hero's Arthurian antecedents prepare us for his transformation from unscrupulous self-seeker to savior of his country and restorer of chivalry in a renewed golden age; in Vance's novel Arthurian legend foreshadows the structural pattern in which a young prince succeeds in enforcing his disputed claim to the throne, despite formidable opposition.

While some authors choose to distance their Arthurian borrowing from its sources and so mute the echoes, others prefer to evoke the tradition more explicitly. Unlike the mythopoeic fantasies, most of the heroic fantasies that borrow from Arthurian legend are set in the Arthurian past. A few, however, are set in the contemporary world, and three achieve this feat by bringing back Merlin. In Peter Dickinson's *The Weathermonger* (1968) the enchanter is aroused from his long sleep and responds by turning the people of Britain against machinery.[26] Attention is focused not upon Merlin, but upon the human reaction to the situation that his magic has created. Dickinson poses some interesting questions about the price of progress, for despite its bigotry the anti-machine culture created by Merlin offers the benefits of social stability and an unpolluted environment, which a civilization bent on ruthless exploitation ignores. Merlin remains a mysterious figure whom we glimpse but briefly. His conversations are conducted in Latin and are usually reported by others.

Linda Haldeman's *The Lastborn of Elvinwood* (1978) again makes use of Merlin's talents as an enchanter, this time to provide the magical spell that will enable an exchange between a fairy and a human. Here too, however, Merlin remains in the background so that the focus falls upon the central characters. They must learn for themselves, without any magical help, that happiness can only be won through self-sacrifice.

In Roger Zelazny's short story, "The Last Defender of Camelot" (1979), Merlin wakens from his sleep, eager to set about righting wrongs and punishing the wicked. He has magically preserved Lancelot from aging so that the latter can give him aid at the moment of reawakening. Over the centuries, however, Lancelot has learned that right and wrong are not so easy to determine, and that people should not be forced to adhere to values that they do not share. He strikes up an untraditional alliance with Morgan le Fay, and together they destroy Merlin, albeit at the cost of their own lives.

These fantasies all show Merlin in an imperious role. To preserve their independence people are forced to oppose him and a conflict of wills ensues. In Haldeman's novel this is resolved amicably, so that Merlin and the protagonist learn mutual respect. In the other two works Merlin either disappears or is destroyed. The message in all three cases is that we need to learn our own lessons, bitter though they may be. External regulation, no matter how well intentioned, hinders and warps our natural development.

Another small group of fantasies uses time travel to link the contemporary world to the Arthurian. The most famous of these is Mark Twain's *A Connecticut Yankee in King Arthur's Court*, which is dealt with later.[27] Rupert Holland's "The Knight of the Golden Spur" (1911) is a typical boys' adventure story in which the young hero travels back in time aided by an amulet and magic spell. He acts as Lancelot's squire and helps him to rescue a damsel.

Will Bradley is more ambitious in *Launcelot and the Ladies* (1927), where the protagonist relives scenes from the Arthurian past, first by burning, then by rubbing together, English yew chips. He witnesses the love triangle formed by Launcelot, Guenevere, and Elaine, here a fusion of the Maid of Astolat and Elaine of Corbenek, mother of Galahad. Between these visions he manages to get involved in a similar triangle in his own time. He, however, chooses to marry the younger woman, a charming lass named Eileen, and thus he discovers a happiness never found by Launcelot. The author is commenting upon what he considers Launcelot's mistake in choosing the wrong woman, but he shows too little sympathy for either Guenevere or her modern counterpart to generate any real conflict. This is a sentimental romance that comes to life only when it touches a genuine human emotion, as in Guenevere's jealous reaction to a maid's comment upon Launcelot's lack of wife: "Thoughtful words, these, and kind, for a maid to be saying to a man, and he a bachelor; and they two, alone, riding the sunny glades of the wildwood, with birds mating and nest-building all about and he knowing it for spring. The bold piece!" (p. 68).

Where these two fantasies return to the world of the High Middle Ages, Meriol Trevor sends her protagonist back to a Dark Age setting in her juvenile fantasy, *Merlin's Ring* (1957). Felix, the thirteen-year-old son of an archeologist, finds Merlin's ring by a mosaic on the site of a Roman villa, and he uses its power to change places with an ailing namesake in the days leading up to Arthur's victory at Badon. During his visit he witnesses the plotting and political divisions that ultimately destroy Arthur's realm: "danger to Christian men, the defenders of civilization, is not so much from the enemy without, whom all can see, but from the enemy within: their own divisions, their selfish passion for wealth and ease and power, when love is forgotten and grows cold. This is the invisible sickness of the soul" (pp. 179–80), Merlin pronounces. Felix himself learns by hard experience not to trust first impressions, for initially he prefers the friendly Aurelius Caninus over his stern uncle Constantine. However, the amiable manners of the former mask cruel ambition, whereas the harshness of the latter conceals an honest and noble nature that spares the life of a slave who tries to assassinate him. As in most didactic novels, the characters are sharply divided into good and bad, but Arthurian legend fortunately lends itself to such an approach. Thus Guenevera is proud and selfish, while Arthur is generous and trusting, qualities that ultimately cause his downfall: "his own goodness...destroyed him, for he would not look at the evil in other men and that can be a weakness" (p. 183). Felix finally concludes, "the only real defeat is to give in to evil, to ambition and spite and greed. I hope I never will! I don't want to be like Aurelius and Mordred and those who destroyed unity" (p. 191).

In Andre Norton's *Here Abide Monsters* (1973), two young people find themselves not in the past, but in an alternate world called Avalon, which is filled with creatures out of legend. Merlin makes a brief appearance at the end of this juvenile novel that demonstrates the importance of adjusting to changing conditions.

Padraic Colum also includes Merlin amongst the many fabulous creatures in *The Boy Apprenticed to an Enchanter* (1920). He and Vivien find true love, retiring from the world to dwell together on a magical island. The young hero is helpfully transformed into a variety of shapes by Merlin, yet he must return to his own form before he can prevail in his struggle against a wicked magician.

Like the first three, these fantasies also emphasize the need to learn through personal experience. The protagonists all get involved in the Arthurian world, and most of them profit from the experience. Unfortunately, this experience is too often acquired in the course of an episodic series of adventures that obscure rather than clarify the point. Trevor exercises better control over his material, and this enables him to probe more keenly into his various themes, amongst which that of illusion and reality looms large, as in the mythopoeic fantasies. This he develops not only by examining the perils caused by deception, but also through his use of form. The Dark Age setting, with its attention to detail of dress and custom and to the intricacies of the political scheming that lost Britain, is created with a realism that stands in contrast to the supernatural means of time travel. This is underlined by the characterization, which divides people into good and bad in the way of romance, even while it individualizes them as does the realistic novel.

The other authors also show interest in the theme of illusion and reality. Where Trevor shows the need to fight evil, Zelazny warns that the demand for virtue can turn into intolerance and oppression. Where Zelazny advocates freedom, Dickinson reminds us of the dangers of pursuing it for selfish ends. Both Haldeman and Colum show that supernatural power cannot protect one from hard decisions. Norton invites us to look for the advantages in a change that seems for the worse. Bradley suggests that we should be warned by Launcelot's delusion that he could find happiness with the wife of his best friend.

Of those heroic fantasies that are placed entirely in an Arthurian setting, some half dozen belong to the category popularly known as sword and sorcery.[28] These novels feature a barbaric superhero—Robert Howard's Conan the Barbarian is the most famous example—who fights his way through a series of savage adventures. Theme and character are ignored in favor of action which emphasizes gratuitous and even sadistic violence.

The earliest Arthurian works in this vein were written by H. Warner Munn. *King of the World's Edge* first appeared in magazine form in 1939 before it was published as a novel in 1966, to be followed a year later by a sequel, *The Ship from Atlantis*. The two were bound together as *Merlin's Godson* in 1976, two years after the publication of a third novel in the series, *Merlin's Ring*. The first novel describes how a shipload of refugees from Arthur's last battle at Camlan sail to North America, led by a Romano-British centurion and Myrdhinn (Merlin). There they forge an alliance between the Aztecs and Iroquois to overthrow the cruel empire of the Mians. Unfortunately, the values of the victors differ little from those of their predecessors, apart from a slightly greater respect for the independence of others. Arthurian tradition provides both a starting point for the voyage and a magician to help the Britons, but the novel owes more to tales of Lost Civilizations by authors like H. Rider Haggard.[29]

The Ship from Atlantis is linked to Arthurian tradition only in that the hero, Gwalchmai, is the son of Arthur's former centurion and the godson of Myrdhinn, both of whom train him to honor their own customs. From the enchanter he inherits a magic ring whose power helps him defy various enemies and even the passage of time itself in this novel and in *Merlin's Ring*. In the latter he reaches Britain where he finds Arthur's sword in a faery mound. He returns it to the king who lies sleeping in a cavern beneath St. Michael's Mount in Cornwall. Like the composers of many late medieval romances, Munn uses Arthurian legend as a vague general background to what are essentially independent and episodic adventures.

Like Gwalchmai, the hero of Chris Carlsen's Berserker series also endures through time. In the second book, *Berserker: The Bull Chief* (1977), he is reborn in Ireland, which he leaves, after many adventures, to help Arthur win his victories over the Saxons. The novel's confused moral values and its preoccupation with bloodshed and violence affect the presentation of Arthur, who kills the hero despite his services. The king is possessed at the time by a supernatural being, but he shows little regret for the betrayal afterwards. Guenevere is transformed into a savage Irish warrior queen named Grania.

The hero of David Drake's *The Dragon Lord* (1979) is another

Irish warrior who fights for Arthur against the Saxons. The king here is driven by ambition to become a mighty conqueror, whatever the cost, and he treats his followers with a sadistic callousness that hardly warrants their loyalty. Mind you, these followers are so bloodthirsty themselves that they hardly notice.

The hero of Keith Taylor's *Bard* (1981) is also Irish, but he is a warrior bard who performs magic with his harp music. In the course of his wanderings through southeast Britain two years after the battle at Badon, where he fought for Artorius, Count of Britain, he finds himself involved in a feud with a werewolf.[30] On one adventure he has a brief affair with Vivayn, here the British daughter-in-law of Cerdic of the West Saxons; and he shares another adventure with ten of Artorius' warband, led by Palamides. In this novel the brutality is muted by some pleasant touches of humor.

The superhero and the extreme violence found in sword and sorcery fantasy both have a predictable impact upon Arthurian tradition. In order to assert the superiority of the superhero and to win sympathy for him, enemies are made more cruel, no easy task given the protagonist's own savagery. Whenever Arthur or his followers are among these enemies, as in the novels of Carlsen and Drake, they are portrayed as cruel oppressors. Yet even when they are on the same side, the need to enhance the hero's prestige requires that his deeds overshadow those of traditional champions and of Arthur himself, as in the later medieval romances. Thus Arthur is kept very much in the background in the novels of Munn and Taylor. In order to accommodate the brutality of this subgenre, events are set, not in the High Middle Ages of romance, but in the Dark Ages as pictured in the anti-romantic historical novels. Moreover, the aimlessness of the violence is reflected in the episodic structure of these fantasies.

Although it avoids this violence Allen French's *Sir Marrok: A Tale of the Days of King Arthur* (1902) also keeps Arthur and his followers in the background in order to focus upon the adventures of a new hero. Set in the High Middle Ages, this tells the story of a knight's struggle against evil-doers. After initial success against brigands, he is deceived by a witch who masks her evil behind an attractive appearance, and she transforms him into a werewolf.[31] Nevertheless he continues to oppose her and to protect his vassals until he destroys the enchantment. Uther, Merlin, Pellinor, and Tristram all make brief appearances in this didactic story for juveniles that extols the virtues of gratitude, discretion, and, most especially, fortitude in adversity on the one hand, while it warns against being deceived by appearances on the other. Thus the werewolf who harasses the beautiful lady is really a transformed knight protecting the innocent against the oppression of a cruel witch. As in sword and sorcery fantasy, the Arthurian setting serves primarily to indicate a remote time when wonders occurred, much as in Chaucer's tales of the Wife of Bath and the Franklin in the fourteenth-century *Canterbury Tales*.

The remaining heroic fantasies deal with the activities, not of newcomers, but of traditional Arthurian figures, and most choose to develop one episode from the legend as the basis of their story. Two of this group are short illustrated books for children. Errol Le Cain's *King Arthur's Sword* (1968) tells the story of Excalibur, the magical sword given to Arthur by the Lady of the Lake, then stolen by Morgana le Fay. In Ruth Robbins' *Taliesin and King Arthur* (1970) the young Taliesin relates the riddle of his own magical transformation from two individuals, an ugly infant and a little shepherd boy, into one beautiful and talented child. Both books make imaginative use of beautiful illustrations to enhance the element of the marvelous.

Of the other stories in this group, the earliest is Arthur Machen's "Guinevere and Lancelot" (1909). This version of their love follows tradition, except that Guinevere uses a sorcerer's magic spell on a wych-elm branch to bind Lancelot to her. Their conduct is condemned as wantonness, though magic serves to explain Lancelot's betrayal of his lord and subsequent repentance when the spell is broken.

Another early story is *Perronik the Fool* (1926) by George Moore.[32] This is a version of Perceval's quest for the Grail, but most details have been changed in this "Breton tale." Like Perceval, Perronik is a simple-minded youth, and it is this innocence that preserves him from the attractions of the beautiful guardian of a Diamond Spear and Golden Bowl. The Spear destroys all at whom it is cast, the Bowl feeds all who eat from it, and their recovery releases the land from drought, features that clearly identify them as the Lance and Cup of Grail legend.

A sentimental and romantic spirit colors Vera Chapman's trilogy of The Three Damosels. *The Green Knight* (1975) is based upon the great fourteenth-century poem, *Sir Gawain and the Green Knight*, and it inevitably suffers by contrast. *The King's Damosel* (1976) continues the story of Lynett, who guided Gareth to rescue her sister in Malory's *Le Morte Darthur*. *King Arthur's Daughter* (1976) invents a child for Arthur and Guenevere, and describes her futile attempt to claim the throne after her father's departure for Avalon.

All three demonstrate that love must be won by forgiveness and self-sacrifice, but the lessons and the changes in character that they cause come too easily to the various protagonists. The result is that the situations seem romantically contrived. Nevertheless, the trilogy offers a valuable feminine perspective on the predominantly masculine world of Arthurian chivalry. This enables it to develop a deeper insight into such traditional knightly qualities as courage, loyalty, and courtesy to others. Lynett serves Arthur as bravely as any knight errant; she loves as devotedly as any courtly lover; and she sacrifices herself as utterly as any Grail knight, so that she too ultimately achieves the Grail quest.[33] The trilogy also affords insight into adolescent yearnings for an idealized love, and this provides some unity to the narrative structure of each novel. Too often, however, the adventures seem merely episodic, much as in the later medieval prose romances.

These novels are all set in the High Middle Ages, but the next two move back to the Dark Ages. According to Andrew Greeley, his novel, *The Magic Cup: An Irish Legend* (1979), is based upon an Irish version of the old Celtic myth from which the story of the Holy Grail evolved. He enlarges upon the Arthurian parallels in his Notes (p. 241), but the differences are marked. The hero does indeed set forth on a quest to find a magic cup and a magic princess, but what he really finds is true love. This is achieved through a steady growth in wisdom, under the tutelage of the witty and spirited heroine. The effect is a story that is both charming and well-wrought, and it provides another level of meaning to the mystery of the Grail legend.

In *Guinevere* (1981) Sharan Newman tells the story of her heroine's youth, concluding with her marriage to Arthur. As one might expect, women play a key role in the novel. We know that the Saxons are villainous because they abduct Guinevere and are unkind to their own women. By contrast the British men are devoted to their women—with good cause as it happens, because their wives are invariably much better at efficient organization than they are themselves. Unfortunately, this method of characterization seems contrived and sentimental. More interesting is the use of the faery world to indicate alienation within a character. Geraldus, Alswytha, and Guinevere alone can see or hear the faery folk and they are all outsiders in society. Geraldus is more interested in culture than war; Alswytha is a Saxon hostage, resented by both her own people and the British; Guinevere is rapt in her own self-centered dreams, symbolized by her bond with a unicorn. However, these disparate elements are not sufficiently integrated, and so the novel remains disjointed.

In *Idylls of the Queen* (1982) Phyllis Ann Karr returns to the High Middle Ages when she borrows from Malory the story of the poisoning of Sir Patrise by an apple at a banquet given by Guenevere. Suspicion falls upon the Queen, until the truth finally emerges, thanks largely to Kay. Like the traditional detective, the sharp-minded seneschal unravels the mystery, though others win the praise: Lancelot, who defends the Queen in trial by combat, and Nimue, the Lady of the Lake, whose magic enables her to confirm the true murderer's guilt. This resolution comments upon the Arthurian world, where valor and sorcery are more highly prized than intelligence. Kay is the narrator and his acerbic wit provides a point of view that is both entertaining and refreshing. Since he judges people by the criteria of intelligence and loyalty, he is impatient with such traditional heroes as Lancelot and Gareth: the former he considers a "valorous hypocrite" (p. 30), concerned only with the irresponsible pursuit of glory, the latter a sanctimonious, hero-worshipping innocent. By contrast, despite his suspicions he grows to understand and even sympathize with some traditional villains. Mordred emerges as an intelligent man, shocked and embittered by the discovery of his incestuous birth and the prophecy that he will eventually destroy the Round Table. Morgan le Fay also appears to advantage as one genuinely concerned with the well-being of the realm. Karr succeeds in making her characters credible by allowing them to speak for themselves, and to explain their motives. This leads to fascinating reinterpretations of Arthurian tradition, as when Dame Iblis concludes her version of one chivalric adventure with the observation "that justice is one thing for men and another for women" (p. 115).[34] Unfortunately such reinterpretations often prove to be digressions that slow the pace and complicate the plot unduly. The novel thus intrigues those familiar with Malory, but fails to integrate the complex material into its own structure.

Although the two early fantasies view women in one of their traditional romance roles as the destroyers of good knights,[35] the more recent novels present attractive heroines who encourage us to look at Arthurian legend from a different point of view. The women appear as sympathetic figures, while the men are often defined by their relationship to them. Thus the Britons win our approval because they treat women with greater respect than do the Saxons in Newman's *Guinevere*, whereas Gaheris forfeits that approval because he mistreats women in the novels of both Chapman and Karr. In Greeley's fantasy the hero's progress toward the wisdom necessary to achieve his quest is measured by his growing appreciation of the keen-witted heroine. This interest in character development can create problems, however, when character is insufficiently integrated into the overall structure of the novel. Other elements also tend to be neglected, notably plot which is usually far too loose.

The remaining heroic fantasies deal, not with episodes from Arthurian legend, but with the story in its entirety. Of these Andrew Davies' *The Legend of King Arthur* (1979) is an illustrated account for juveniles, based upon a BBC television series. It consists of eleven episodes and an epilogue in a Dark Age setting, beginning with Arthur's conception, concluding with the last meeting of Lancelot and Guinevere after his death. The series might justifiably have been called the revenge of Morgan le Fay

because this motif supplies a link between otherwise independent episodes. She embraces evil in order to avenge the death
of her beloved father, Gorlois, but learns to mask her hatred to
accomplish her purpose more readily. Arthur, by contrast, is
brave but naive, and this proves his downfall.

The Tristan legend has been largely neglected by fantasy,
though the lovers sometimes make a brief appearance at Arthur's
court and Tristram hunts the werewolf in French's *Sir Marrok*.
The one full treatment of the Tristan legend, however, is perhaps
the most singular in modern fiction, for it places it in a discon-
certingly anachronistic setting. Thus early in Ruth Collier Sharpe's
Tristram of Lyonesse (1949) the hero sits drinking tea with his
cousin while they discuss poetry, astronomical experiments, and
philosophy. Meanwhile Arthur Pendragon, King of *England* no
less, "raised his elegant brows" (p. 76) as he leads his elegant
court in elegant repartee. Noblemen duel with foils and go fox-
hunting, villains brandish a green eyeglass mounted on a gold
and jeweled stick, and court intrigue abounds everywhere. This
is gothic melodrama, the Tristan legend rewritten by Alexandre
Dumas! It might have been fun, but the novel is unrelentingly
humorless, as well as far too long and convoluted. It is also
weakened by vapid characterization and by sentimentality. Indeed such is the mutual admiration between Morholt and Tristram that the former is wounded because he hesitates to strike
a death blow at the latter. However, he recovers from his wound,
as is only fitting for a knight so noble as to personally sympathize
with the Cornish wish to be free of Irish oppression. Doubtless
inspired by this unselfish example, Tristram later deliberately
loses a duel with the betrothed of Ysolt of Brittany, though it is
true that he does not love the lady. She, of course, had fallen
in love with him while he was gloomily occupying his exile by
doing a sculpture of her; to complicate an already complicated
situation he finds a mysteriously long-lost cousin serving as her
tutor, who, of course, had loved her long and hum-
bly.... Fortunately, Ysolt of Ireland arrives in time to heal her
lover, despite the mix-up over the black and white sails; Mark
generously gives her another divorce (in case the first one proves
insufficient); and the two marry and rule Lyonesse. As a treatment of the Tristan legend this book is... different.

Probably the best-known and best-loved modern version of the Arthurian legend is that of T. H. White. This starts with *The Sword in the Stone* (1938) which describes the boyhood of Arthur, affectionately known as Wart. *The Witch in the Wood* (1939) continues with the childhood experiences of Gawaine and his brothers in far-off Orkney, and the early struggle of Arthur against the rebel kings. *The Ill-Made Knight* (1940) concludes with the love of Lancelot and Guenever and its tragic conclusion. In 1958 these were collected together and revised: the second volume was retitled "The Queen of Air and Darkness," a fourth section entitled "The Candle in the Wind" was added, and the whole published as *The Once and Future King*. A final section called *The Book of Merlyn*, written originally 1940–41, was published posthumously in 1977, but this will be considered with the ironic fantasies. The setting is that of the High Middle Ages, with Saxon serfs and Norman masters. White's ingenious solution to the anachronism is to reverse history and legend: "Look at the Norman myths about legendary figures like the Angevin kings," he tells us.[36]

The most enchanting part is *The Sword in the Stone*. Here the author creates a wondrous world where childhood dreams of high adventure are fulfilled in deeds such as the rescue of Friar Tuck from a fairy castle. He peoples this world with comical yet kindly characters, like Arthur's foster-father Sir Ector, who is portrayed as a bluff English country squire; his friend, the bumbling King Pellinore, whose combat with Sir Grummore and whose pursuit of the Questing Beast delightfully reveal the comedy inherent in chivalric romance; and his well-meaning but absent-minded tutor Merlyn, who transforms him into various creatures: "Education is experience, and the essence of experience is self-reliance" (p. 41), his tutor pronounces, settling down for a nap as he sends his pupil off. As fish, hawk, goose, and ant, Arthur learns the dangerous lessons of life, the realities of power.

When he becomes king, he decides to oppose the unprincipled use of power, the idea that Might is Right. Instead he founds an order of chivalry sworn to ensure "that Might is only to be used for Right... turning a bad thing into a good" (pp. 254–55). With the aid of the knights of the Round Table, led by Lancelot,

Arthur achieves remarkable success, yet ultimately his efforts are doomed by mankind's flawed nature. All his knights, even Lancelot, fail to live up to their vows. Moreover, there is an inherent contradiction in the king's plan: "in the effort to impose a world of peace, he found himself up to the elbows in blood.... He often thought that it might have been better for all his dead soldiers to be alive—even if they had lived under tyranny and madness—rather than be quite dead" (p. 380). At the end, as the aged Arthur sits in his tent on the eve of the last battle at Camlann, amidst the ruin of all that he so painstakingly built, he ponders the extent of his failure and its tragic implications: "He was only a man who had meant well, who had been spurred along that course of thinking by an eccentric necromancer with a weakness for humanity. Justice had been his last attempt—to do nothing which was not just. But it had ended in failure" (p. 671).

The mood of the books grows increasingly sombre and disillusioned as they move towards their tragic conclusion, and the culminating vision of *The Book of Merlyn* is clouded by bitterness and political railing. Yet this bitterness is in part a measure of the early hope that transfigured *The Sword in the Stone*. Like Malory, whose romance forms the basis of his series, White succeeds in creating a true sense of tragedy because he is able to impart an aching sense that something precious has been lost. It is not just the dream of peace, justice, reason, and respect for the rights of all living things that perishes with Arthur, but also the bright hopes of childhood for a beautiful and golden world of love. Ector's castle, where Arthur grows to manhood, is a rural idyl, "a paradise for a boy to be in.... For every season he had the best place, like a cat, and he yelled and ran and fought and upset people and snoozed and daydreamed and pretended he was a Knight, without stopping" (p. 38). The castle is depicted as a farming community where "Everybody was happy" (p. 130). Under the benevolent protection of the kindly Sir Ector, the villeins thrive: "They were healthy, free of an air with no factory smoke in it, and, which was most of all to them, their heart's interest was bound up with their skill in labour" (p. 131). This world of security and kindness gradually recedes as the series develops, replaced by the harsher realities of human conflict and betrayal. Such good-natured characters as Pellinore and Grummore, whose comical misadventures delight the reader of the first two books, fade from sight in the third, the former a victim of the feud with the Orkney faction. In their place sinister figures like Mordred and Agravaine stalk, "*Homo ferox* instead of *Homo sapiens*" (p. 667). The magical world of fantasy to which Merlin introduces us also recedes, replaced by the cold realities of human folly. What White laments is the loss of innocence, and it gives his story a heart-breaking power.

The second major account of the entire legend in heroic fantasy is Parke Godwin's *Firelord* (1980). Godwin makes Arthur the narrator of the story, which is set in the Dark Ages. He also makes him into one of the most vigorous and attractive characterizations of the king in modern fiction, balancing idealism with pragmatism, romanticism with humor, compassion with heroic self-sacrifice. The result is a leader whom most would gladly follow to the gates of death and beyond.[37]

Arthur is, first and foremost, a dreamer inspired by the vision of "bright tomorrows you carved out of wishes and painted with dreams" (p. 7; cf. p. 390). Indeed, the figure of Merlin here is a projection of Arthur himself, speaking to him out of his dreams. Dreams, however, cannot be attained without sacrifice, as Ambrosius teaches him. In order to restore order and preserve what is left of Britain from feuding princes and marauding Saxons, Arthur must seize imperial power. But in order to achieve, then maintain, this power, he will have to compromise his honor. It is a lesson that he absorbs during the brutal campaign to clear the midlands of Saxon settlers, leading his men against not only warriors, but also women and children. Only thus can the land be secured for its British inhabitants. He also learns to use people if need be. Thus he deceives the loyal Gawain so that he can out-maneuver Agrivaine and win the throne. For these are the realities of power, and "this was how it was done, not with honor but betrayal, not flags but flies" (p. 189).

Arthur's romantic impulse is evident in his imaginative and appreciative response to people: to Trystan, the graceful poet; to Geraint, the flamboyant warrior; to Peredur, the gentle, thoughtful prince; and to Drost, beloved child of the Prydn, for Arthur recognizes that never will he "find a greater treasure or truth than this small, shining life" (p. 69). Yet this romantic perception is balanced by a keen sense of humor. He is aware of Trystan's self-indulgence, of Geraint's impetuousness, of Peredur's impracticality. Thus he paints a comical picture of the reckless Prince Geraint pursued by his harried ministers as he charges from one place to the next, a "volcano of changing mood, innocent wonder, ignorant ire" (p. 237). His assessment of the self-righteous Eleyne of Astolat is still more sardonic; while of her child, the young Galahalt, he observes that his "complacent stare looked from birth on a fixed cosmos where God sat ringed about with the house of Astolat, the archangels somewhere below the salt" (p. 238).[38] Nor does he spare the fond paternal pride of his oldest and dearest friend, Bedivere, when he shows off his beloved infant daughter: " 'Say da, love. Who do you love best?' 'Ging,' burbled the child. 'There, will you listen to her!' " (p. 212).

Most important of all, Arthur is able to laugh at himself. At the very outset of the novel, as he lies in Avalon swathed in bandages, he perceives what a ridiculous figure he cuts, "like a silly Yule pudding" (p. 1). The more exalted one's rank, he recognizes, the greater the need not to take oneself too seriously. Hearing the Saxon story that Cerdic was born with a sword in his hand, Arthur quips, "Symbolic, of course, but awkward for his mother. God help a king without a sense of humor. He may stand close to his legend, but he should never lean on it" (p. 111).

Despite his keen sense of humor the dominant note in Arthur's attitude toward others is compassion. He excuses their errors with understanding, praises their virtues with sincere admiration. This is particularly striking in his dealings with his enemies. He wryly appreciates the scheming talents of such reprobates as his father-in-law, Prince Cador; he openly admires the genius of Cerdic, leader of the Saxons, much to the amazement of his own men at Badon; he genuinely regrets the circumstances that antagonize former friends, such as Gawain, Peredur and Lancelot; and despite her betrayal, Guenevere remains his soulmate, the hard-working queen without whose help so much that he achieved would have been impossible. Ultimately his love grows to embrace all his people, most passionately on the hill at Badon when his exhausted and outnumbered warriors sing in the face of the enemy "with a beauty to burst the heart" (p. 325).

The growth of Arthur's compassion and understanding provides a structure for the novel. As a youth he is carelessly arrogant despite his bright ideals, so that he gives needless offense to others, such as Geraint. From Morgana and the Prydn he learns the value of love, realizing "we're human because we care" (p. 89). This knowledge sets him free to return to his own people. He has now learned to love those comrades who follow him, and on the eve of the battle at Eburacum confides to Guenevere, "these people pull at my heart" (p. 109).

Yet this compassion still has its limits. When Guenevere arranges the murder of Morgana and her party of Prydn, he is outraged at this betrayal and throws her in prison. He has good cause for his action, but it is an ill return for the Queen's invaluable service as co-ruler. Moreover, the consequences are a rebellion that threatens to destroy all they had so carefully built. Only when he hears his men singing on Badon does he finally realize that he loves all his people, both the "flowers" and the "fruit" (p. 391). This awareness leads him to seek a reconciliation with Guenevere, to place the good of others above his own personal feelings. Typically he accomplishes the task with masterly skill and irrepressible humor. His concern for the dying Peredur is such that he allows this important captive to seek the Grail (suitably escorted of course!) and prays for his success with typical skepticism: "Someone who heeded fallen sparrows might take a moment for Peredur" (p. 352; cf. p. 113). Nor does he neglect to instruct the escort to ensure that the impractical prince wrap his chest against the cold. Even on his own deathbed, his care for others leads him to think of the small details as well as important matters, instructing the scribe to write larger in the letter with which he sends Trystan's son to Yseult, because her eyesight is no longer so keen, and enjoining Guenevere to dress warmly, eat regularly, and take sufficient rest, as well as heed the good advice of Bedivere and Gareth. For they, like all his close friends, mirror his concern for others.

The price of compassion, however, is heroic self-sacrifice, though it is a price that Arthur willingly accepts: "To be a king, to wear a crown, is to know how apart and lonely we are and still exist and *dare* to love in the face of that void. To crown your brow with knowledge sharp as thorns, bright and hard as gold" (p. 91). Because he cares, he suffers when good friends die: "they weigh on my heart, all the good-byes" (p. 242). In order to save Eburacum he leaves behind the personal happiness he has found with Morgana and the Prydn, and this sets in motion the cruel train of events that leads to Morgana's murder and the consequent hatred of Mordred. Mortally wounded in the ambush laid by his son, Arthur still tries to save him, though the effort proves unavailing. Blinded with tears, he tenderly cradles the head of the dying parricide in his arms. Mordred's last response is to spit in his father's face. Arthur gives unstintingly of himself for his subjects, yet they "take everything and give nothing back" (p. 342). To them he becomes virtually a god, yet this requires that he fulfil the traditional pattern: first they hail and love, then betray, then "feel remorse with the twice-crowing cock" (p. 342). Yet finally, the god must die for them, a need reflected in the novel's recurrent image of the crown of thorns.

Nevertheless, the dominant mood is not tragic but heroic. Like Canning's Crimson Chalice trilogy, *Firelord* focuses upon valiant struggle and positive achievement rather than failure. The cruel campaign in the midlands is passed over quickly (even lightened at points by bitter humor such as Arthur's jest over his scribe's squeamishness) in order to recount at length the heroic ride north to claim the crown. Even the conclusion looks forward to Arthur's glorious career in history and literature with typical humor. In the voices of his men singing at Badon the king hears, "The sound of love.... That's when I knew how needed the flowers are. The dreamers. They give reason to all the rest. They grab life by the collar, make it shine and boot it into tomorrow" (p. 391). There could be no more fitting description of Arthur himself. He is a hero to make the spirit soar and the heart ache: "ready to dare as well as dream" (p. 341), ready to love all mankind until he declares, "it's not death I fear so much as leaving something so beautiful as life" (p. 115); ready to warm us with his laughter at the human follies he himself shares.

As a novel *Firelord* may have its faults, for like all versions of the life of Arthur its structure is not always as tidy as it might be. However, it offers the reader one of the most exuberant and enjoyable stories in all Arthurian literature, and, like Sutcliff's Arthur, a hero who is indeed worthy of dreams.

The most recent heroic fantasy is Marion Zimmer Bradley's *The Mists of Avalon* (1983), and it too is set in the Dark Ages. Here, however, the principal actors are the women whose lives affect Arthur, and it is their point of view that we share: occasionally the successive Ladies of the Lake, hereditary high priestesses of the Mother Goddess, or Arthur's aunt Morgause; more often his mother, Igraine, and wife, Gwenhwyfar; usually his sister Morgaine, whose progress toward wisdom and enlightenment as servant of the Goddess unifies the novel.[39] As a result the focus shifts from the battlefield to the political and domestic conflicts that raise Arthur to power, then destroy him.

The author's primary concern is to explore the psychology of her characters as they interact with each other. We share with them the experiences that develop self-awareness and maturity. Moreover, their struggle to reconcile the conflicting elements within their own personalities both influences and mirrors the broader political conflict in which they are involved. Ultimately their failure to achieve this internal reconciliation prevents the external reconciliation between opposing political factions, and thus spells the doom of Arthur's kingdom.

The basic conflict is waged between tolerance and intolerance, the former reasonable, understanding, generous, and forgiving, the latter emotional, ignorant, selfish, and vengeful. On the political level, the older religions centered in Avalon—Druids, Early Christians, and worshipers of the Mother Goddess—all of whom believe that there are many paths to truth, that all Gods are One God—must struggle against persecution by a more narrow-minded Christianity that condemns those who will not share its beliefs. On the personal level, the characters face the same challenge: Morgause is kindly and easy-going at times, malicious and ambitious at others; Gwynhwyfar's periods of perception and generosity are interspersed with bouts of religious prejudice, jealousy, and recrimination against both herself and others; even Morgaine, as she struggles up the long path to wisdom, looks back with anguish on her mistakes and their tragic consequences, before she finally accepts the inevitability of fate.

This acceptance is the ultimate goal toward which all must move if they wish to achieve wisdom and peace. However their human impulse to be independent and control their own fate wars against this acceptance. Thus Viviane, the reigning Lady of the Lake during the first part of the novel, antagonizes her half-sister Igraine by ordering that she marry Gorlois of Cornwall for political purposes, then betray him with Uther in order to produce a new heir who will honor the Mother Goddess. Viviane later tricks Morgaine and her half-brother Arthur into producing yet another heir by bringing them together in the ritual marriage of the Goddess and King Stag. These actions are necessary to accomplish the will of the Goddess, and as Viviane tells Morgaine, "the hope of Britain is more important than your feelings" (p. 191). However, they breed anger and lasting resentment. Like her mother before her Morgaine is appalled at the apparent insensitivity with which human beings are manipulated, as if they were "puppets to serve you" (p. 190). Because of their resentment, both Igraine and Morgaine choose to avoid Avalon. Yet the choice of independence is really an assertion of selfish egoism, and it brings happiness to neither. On her deathbed Igraine confesses the price that she paid for staying in Tintagel rather than returning to Viviane in her beloved Avalon: "I could not forget it was she who had married me to Gorlois. . . . Beyond that garden wall lies Tintagel, like a prison. . . a prison it was to me, indeed. Yet it was the only place I could call my own" (p. 358). Similarly, obstinate self-assertion in defiance of common sense causes Gwenhwyfar to walk into Meleagrant's trap. As a result she is taken captive and raped.

However, the cost of struggling against reason and acceptance of fate is most visible when the characters seek revenge for what they perceive to be injustice. Balin wrong-headedly avenges the mercy killing of his dying mother upon Viviane, killing her in Arthur's court. He pays the price of his own life and that of his beloved foster-brother Balan, for the latter is Viviane's son (as is Lancelot), and he too avenges his mother's death. Jealousy and ambition lead Morgause and Mordred (or Gwydion as he is also called) to trap Lancelot and Gwenhwyfar in adultery. The cost is the life of Gareth, whom Mordred loves beyond all others: "Gareth was the best of us, and I would not have sacrificed him for a dozen kings!...I should have died first" (pp. 858–59). In anguish Mordred turns against Morgause, whose spite against Arthur urged him on. Her plots thus ruined, Morgause is left to count her losses: "I am an old woman. And I have lost my son Gareth, and I have lost Gwydion, and I will never now be Queen in Camelot. I have lived too long" (p. 860).

Even those who act from what they consider to be noble and selfless motives can find that their deeds exact a high price. Gwenhwyfar, Balin, and Archbishop Patricius oppose other religions from a genuine sense of the rectitude of their own Christianity. Yet the cost of their intolerance is the fall of Britain. Viviane works tirelessly "to save this land and its people from rapine and destruction, a reversion to barbarism" (p. 191), but she alienates those she loves best. "She thought of Morgaine with a sorrowful hope that one day the young woman would understand" (p. 192). Morgaine does indeed discover the cost of serving the Mother Goddess, but only through bitter personal experience. To protect North Wales against intolerant Christianity, she arranges the death of Uriens' oldest son, but when her complicity is revealed she loses the love of both Uriens and his youngest son Uwaine; to punish Arthur for neglecting his oath to Avalon in favor of Christianity, she sets her lover, Accolon, to kill him, but it is Accolon who dies instead; to punish Kevin, the Merlin of Britain, for planning to desecrate the Holy Regalia of spear, cup, and dish, she sets Nimue to seduce him, but her scheme claims the life not only of Kevin, who was always a dear friend, but also of Nimue, her designated successor as Lady of the Lake.

Faced with the miscarriage of her best laid plans and the triumph of Christianity, Morgaine despairingly wonders why the Mother Goddess seems so determined to destroy Avalon. Only at the end does she realize that the Goddess does endure "in the hearts of all men and women" (p. 876). The passing of Her worship, as the island of Avalon recedes into the mists, is but Her transformation from one phase to another. "I did the Mother's work in Avalon until at last those who came after us might bring her into this world. I did not fail. I did what she had given me to do. It was not she but I in my pride who thought I should have done more" (p. 876, cf. p. 752).

Ironically, by opposing the new Christianity with such intransigence, Morgaine betrays the understanding and tolerance so essential to her faith in the Mother Goddess. Instead she adopts the tactics of her enemies. Only at the end does she gain true wisdom and insight.

Yet insight and tranquility come too late, and as in Bradshaw's trilogy the focus falls upon the frustration of effort, the fading of a cherished world as fate rolls inexorably over all that men and women have so lovingly built. This sense of loss gains strength from the feminine perspective; the heroism that wins victories on the battlefield is replaced by the grief of those who must count the cost. Its sombre vision balances the heroic optimism of *Firelord*.

All three heroic fantasies that deal with Arthur's entire career are concerned with illusion and reality. This is particularly noticeable in their treatment of the Grail quest. White follows Malory in using the quest to expose the spiritual limitations and instability that lie behind the worldly achievements of the Round Table. Godwin has Peredur return with a battered cup which may be the one brought over by Joseph of Arimathea: the gap between this humble reality and the Grail of legend must be bridged by faith. Bradley has Morgaine transformed briefly into a manifestation of the Mother Goddess herself to bear the Grail through Arthur's hall. The mystical experience that all present undergo is subjectively interpreted in the light of their own particular religious beliefs. Each author thus adapts the Grail legend to suit his or her own purpose: White shows the failings that doom the bright hopes; Godwin shows the splendor that can be created by faith in a dream; Bradley shows the common yearning in the hearts of all, despite the apparent differences that cause such destructive conflict.

The theme of illusion and reality is developed by the learning experience that the protagonist undergoes in each novel. White and Bradley make this experience essentially tragic, involving as it does the fading from sight of the bright and innocent world of youth. For White's Arthur the bitter wisdom gained cannot compensate for the loss of innocence, as *The Book of Merlyn* reveals in all its bleakness, and though Bradley's Morgaine achieves final acceptance, the novel stresses the cost rather than the achievement. Godwin's Arthur, by contrast, strikes the positive notes of heroic endeavor. As Guenevere points out at the end, "We didn't win it all, but we gave it a fine try" (p. 394).

What strikes one most forcefully about descriptions of the Arthurian world in heroic fantasy is the sheer variety. The Arthurian element may constitute no more than a minor borrowing, like a name or an evocative situation; or it may extend into an exhaustive recreation, such as those offered by Godwin and Marion Zimmer Bradley, both of whom demonstrate impressive skill at reinterpreting a wide range of traditional material and at integrating it into the structure of their novels. It may be the bright and loving vision of childhood, as created by Le Cain, Robbins, and White in his earlier books; or it may be the dark and cynical world of cruelty and betrayal, pictured in sword and sorcery fantasy. The dominant mood may be tragic as in Marion Zimmer Bradley's novel; or it may be sentimental as in Chapman's trilogy and Sharon Newman's novel; or heroic as in Godwin's. The purpose may be pure entertainment as in Holland's story or Taylor's; or strongly didactic as in Trevor's.

The same variety marks the treatment of character. Arthur may be a compassionate hero to Godwin and White, a wise and noble ruler to Chapman but Trevor recognizes that "his own goodness...destroyed him, for he would not look at the evil in other men and that can be a weakness" (p. 183), while Bradley's Morgaine perceives that because of Arthur's desire "to see everyone happy,...He is not ruthless enough to be High King" (p. 621); in Carlsen's novel he betrays his friend, in Drake's he is a capricious tyrant. To Dickinson, Zelazny, and Drake, Merlin is sinister and threatening, whereas to Chapman, Colum, and Trevor, he is wise and benevolent. Morgan le Fay is an evil figure in White's work, but Karr, Godwin, and Marion Zimmer Bradley view her with understanding and sympathy.

Unfortunately, this variety of approach is too often accompanied by structural weaknesses in organizing material. Plots become episodic as digressions are pursued and adventures are needlessly multiplied. Characters may be thinly drawn and behave without due consideration for consistency. Nevertheless, a pattern does exist, and it is provided by the learning process that takes place in almost all the heroic fantasies. The protagonists discover the realities that lie behind their illusions, and they grow in wisdom and maturity as a result. In juvenile novels, like Trevor's *Merlin's Ring*, this is part of the experience of growing up, but it is equally important in the novels written for adults. Even in the sword and sorcery fantasies where this pattern is less noticeable, the learning process continues to take place, although the lesson seems to amount to little more than not to trust others too readily. The lesson may be bitter, as in White and Marion Zimmer Bradley, or joyful as in Godwin; it may be serious and cautionary, as in French and Trevor, or humorous, as in Greeley. But whether it is sobering or heart-warming, the lesson is taught, and it dictates the approach to Arthurian tradition.

The most important lesson is to care for others, and this criterion usually determines how a character is viewed. Even in the brutal world of sword and sorcery the hero is distinguished from more savage figures by his affection for a loyal sword-companion and a devoted mistress, and the help that the latter provides in return is often crucial to his success. Thus we have the insensitive Merlin of Dickinson, Drake, and Zelazny, as opposed to the helpful magician of Munn, Norton, and Colum. Haldeman's ambivalent Merlin is both helpful and insensitive, mirroring the dual impulses within the protagonist himself. Guenevere is usually selfish, and thus serves as an object lesson in the novels of Trevor, Machen, and Will Bradley. Both T. H. White and Marion Zimmer Bradley develop this selfishness into part of the inherent contradictions in the Queen's character, and her failure to control it mirrors the larger political failure of Arthur's kingdom. However, she emerges as a warm and caring person in the novels of Karr and Godwin, both of whom reverse the usual pattern by making Lancelot the less sympathetic of the two. Karr criticizes the knight for seeking glory regardless of the cost to others; Godwin notes a lack of humor and perception that are ultimately self-centered. White's Tristram is selfish because he loves without thought for the consequences, whereas Sharpe's hero is conscience-driven to a fault; in French's tale he is generous enough to spare the werewolf hero when he sees the villagers gather to protect the animal that has so long protected them; and in Godwin's story he holds silent during his trial for murder rather than offer an explanation that would imperil Arthur's plans to protect Britain. Agravaine is driven by pride and ambition, regardless of the cost, in Karr, White, and Godwin; Gaheris treats women callously in Karr and Chapman.

The Arthurian borrowing thus fulfils two major functions in heroic fantasy. The first is to provide a setting where the intrusion of the marvelous is more acceptable than might otherwise be the case. Should the plot require a magic spell, a prescient vision, or a supernatural visitation, then the long traditions associated with Merlin, Morgan le Fay, Morgause, the Lady of the Lake, and the Grail invite our suspension of disbelief. So strong are these traditions that the mere choice of the Arthurian world as a general setting encourages us to accept such magical phenomena as the transformation of a human into a werewolf in the novels of French and Taylor. In this the heroic fantasies follow the pattern established by medieval romance, which also uses Arthurian legend as a remote setting where marvels may occur.

The second function of the Arthurian borrowing is to facilitate the exploration of theme, most frequently that of illusion and reality. As in mythopoeic fantasy this may involve discovering the limitations of supernatural power. This encourages heroic self-reliance, particularly in the novels which borrow only a few elements of the legend. Paradoxically, however, those works that explore the legend more fully discover that beneath the glorious achievements of the surface runs a dark current of inexorable fate, from Arthur's conception outside marriage, through his own conception of Mordred in unwitting incest, to his final death in reluctant battle against this unsought-for son. Despite all his best intentions, Arthur's tragic destruction must be accomplished. The illusion thus lies in the human hope of escaping the reality of our doom. And since the legend already decrees the basic outline of the plot, it adds to the power of the tragic pattern, just as does the legend of Oedipus. In these novels, resistance to fate provides the heroic stature. Some choose to emphasize what is lost, so that the mood is sombre and tragic, as in White and Marion Zimmer Bradley. Others stress the glorious achievement, so that the mood is positive and romantic, as in Greeley and Godwin (and even the early White). Significantly, humor is a vital ingredient in these works. In their exploration of the contradictions inherent in Arthur's kingdom, these fantasies thus span the complete spectrum of the heroic mood, from the tragic to the romantic.

IRONIC FANTASY

As authors like Godwin so keenly appreciate, the noble aspirations and high-minded ideals of Arthur and his knights, although they inspire heroic endeavor, do have their comic aspect. When this perception dominates the approach to the legend, then it creates a category that we may call ironic fantasy. Here we are invited to consider, not the heroic achievements, but the gap between expectations and results. This ironic gap is the source of humor, be it dark and bitter, or light and affectionate.

Irony has, in fact, a long and venerable tradition in Arthurian literature. It has yielded some of the finest achievements of medieval romance, notably Chrétien de Troyes' *Lancelot* in the twelfth century, Raoul de Houdenc's *La Vengeance Raguidel* in the thirteenth, and *Sir Gawain and the Green Knight* in the fourteenth, to say nothing of the many lesser poems such as the thirteenth-century *Le Chevalier à l' Epée* and the fifteenth-century *Sir Gawain and the Carle of Carlisle*; in the eighteenth century Henry Fielding composed his entertaining farce about Tom Thumb; and James Merriman has praised John Hookham Frere's unfinished *The Monks and the Giants* (1817–18) for its humor.[40] The most memorable comic treatment of King Arthur in the nineteenth century is Mark Twain's *A Connecticut Yankee in King Arthur's Court* (1889), the earliest of the ironic fantasies.

In this novel Hank Morgan travels back in time to the days of King Arthur, and he uses his technological expertise to gain power. The author encourages us to identify with Hank's humorously cynical observations about the naive and unsophisticated society of the period, here the High Middle Ages. Hank is, after all, like us a product of a technologically advanced society, and when he fixes the Holy Fountain in the Valley of Holiness by simply mending the crack through which the waters have been leaking away, it is easy to share his derisive attitude toward the monks for their reliance upon supernatural forces to restore the flow.

Hank uses his relentless practicality to reveal the follies of those who surround him, be they the exaggerations of the knights of the Round Table boasting over their exploits; or the prejudices of the Examining Board which appoints officers on the basis of birth rather than military knowledge; or the naive delusion of Sandy rescuing a herd of pigs which she believes to be nobly born ladies. Not content with rescue, she assembles the pigs the following morning and gives them breakfast, "waiting upon them personally and manifesting in every way the deep reverence which the natives of her island, ancient and modern, have always felt for rank, let its outward casket and the mental and moral contents be what they may" (p. 237).[41]

Indeed, Hank is barred from joining the august company for breakfast because he is not of aristocratic birth. By contrast, Sandy earlier refuses to eat breakfast with a group of freemen, observing that "she would as soon think of eating with the other cattle" (p. 155). Such farcical episodes contrive to win our approval of Hank's sardonic reactions.

However, the humor which colors Hank's attitude is a manifestation of his own lack of imagination and it prevents him from sympathizing with others. After a tournament, while the physicians are amputating limbs from the injured, he grumbles, "They ruined an uncommon good old cross-cut saw for me, and broke the saw-buck, too, but I let it pass. And as for my ax— well, I made up my mind that the next time I lent an ax to a surgeon I would pick my century" (p. 120). The satiric technique of making an outrageous statement (complaining about ruining a saw without any concern for the agony of the cripple) under a pretense of generosity ("let it pass"), only to proceed to an even more outrageous statement (complaining about ruining an ax, an even more brutal instrument for a surgeon), generates a grisly black humor whose very extravagance distracts attention from the inhumanity of the reaction, much like Swift's "Modest Proposal." Ironically this passage follows Hank's complaint about the bloodthirstiness of the ladies watching the tournament.

Because Hank's callousness is vital to his sense of humor, providing the detachment necessary for comedy, it is easy to excuse. Thus when he decides to allow Morgan le Fay to hang not only the composer of a tune which he happens to dislike, but the whole band that played it as well, he observes, "This little relaxation of sternness had a good effect upon the queen," and he concludes that "A little concession, now and then, where it can do no harm, is the wiser policy" (p. 198). In this case an act of callous self-interest is humorously presented as a humane concession; its very audacity distracts from our awareness of the implications of his action.

Hank's lack of compassion is less excusable, however, when he blows up two knights with a dynamite bomb. It is true that the device saves both his own life and that of the king, but the relish with which he watches the gruesome effects of modern weapons upon his unprepared victims is chilling: "Yes, it was a neat thing, very neat and pretty to see. It resembled a steamboat explosion on the Mississippi; and during the next fifteen minutes we stood under a steady drizzle of microscopic fragments of knights and hardware and horseflesh" (p. 318). The comparison to a steamboat explosion reveals the distance between the narrator and Twain, a former riverboat pilot to whom such a sight would have been particularly distressing.

The deployment of modern weapons against medieval knights culminates in the massive slaughter of Hank's foes in their thousands, electrocuted by wire, mowed down by Gatling machine guns, and drowned in a flooded ditch. Insensitivity to the feelings of others, which gives Hank's humor such pungency, finally reveals its fatal shortcomings, and the course of action which we have endorsed by our laughter has led inexorably to this final monstrous act. Insofar as we have shared Hank's feelings of superiority over medieval society, we have allowed the author's satiric techniques to blind us to the fact that the technological progress of modern society has done little to change man's essential nature. This sense of superiority arises from a lack of imagination and human understanding, and it is a lack which costs us dearer than we realize until it is too late. What Twain has done is to use the technique of satiric betrayal, luring us into endorsing an attitude, then revealing the errors of that attitude so that we may learn from our mistakes.[42]

Despite the criticism of the ignorance and callousness of both

medieval and modern society, and the comedy of the exaggerations of the world of romance, there remain in the novel an
underlying admiration and affection for Arthurian legend itself.
The heroism of Arthur when he carries a child dying of smallpox
to its mother, and the generosity of Lancelot when he offers to
help Hank after the latter has defeated him in a tournament, are
qualities that the self-centered protagonist lacks, and they reveal
that the legend possesses an imaginative power absent from
Hank's view of life. As Hank himself admits he is "nearly barren
of sentiment, . . . or poetry in other words"(p. 50).

In Twain's work are thus found the three major strands of the
ironic fantasies that deal with Arthurian legend: satire of mankind's self-destructive impulses, comedy at the expense of his
foolish pretensions, and a poignant affection for the aspirations
of high romance.[43] Of the three, least common is the satire.
Interestingly, the six novels in which this dominates have all
appeared very recently. The earliest is John Steinbeck's *The Acts
of King Arthur and his Noble Knights* (1976), which is based upon
"The Tale of King Arthur" and "The Noble Tale of Sir Launcelot
du Lake" in Malory's *Le Morte Darthur*. Although he starts off
with a simplified retelling of Malory's tale, Steinbeck makes significant changes in the second half of the novel. This allows him
to develop perspectives on the characters and their experiences
that are not found in the source.

This process begins early, when the author stresses the playful
aspect of Merlin's habit of appearing to others in various guises:
"Merlin was as happy as a child at the success of his game" (p.
31). However, it becomes really noticeable in the triple quest of
Gawain, Ewain, and Marhalt. Gawain emerges as more selfish
than ever from his involvement in the relationship between Pelleas and Ettarde.[44] It is here that the darker notes of disillusionment intrude, for Gawain, despite his own misconduct, feels ill-
used by the pair, and he concludes, "A man must look after
himself" (p. 150). Marhalt conducts himself with much greater
wisdom and maturity, yet even this does not protect him from
disillusionment. He attacks the giant Taulurd with reluctance,
aware that although the creature is a danger to innocent people,
he is really no more than "a big strong baby" (p. 168).[45] He kills
the giant, but "his triumph was a sad and ugly feeling in his

throat" (p. 169). Nor does his friendship with the damsel who leads him in search of adventure live up to its early promise. The initial compatibility of two sensible and experienced people gradually dissolves as the damsel tries to make Marhalt change his way of life as a wandering knight errant and settle down instead to rule his lands. Ewain fares better in many ways, learning the skill of arms from the older damsel, and crowning the lesson with success against numerous enemies.[46] Yet he too must shed many illusions, for victory goes not to the most valiant or most deserving, but to the most skilful, especially if their weapons are superior.

The process of disillusionment culminates in the quest of Lancelot. The tale opens with Arthur's realization that all is not well at court, since "the longed-for peace, so bitterly achieved, created more bitterness than ever did the anguish of achieving it" (p. 207). In an effort to escape the malaise, Lancelot sets out adventuring, but his experiences do little to restore his spirits. In trying to escape his problems with one woman, Guinevere, he runs into difficulties with others. First of all four queens cast him into a dungeon, insisting that he choose one of them as a paramour. From this predicament he is rescued by a damsel, but she, like the others who give him help, does so only for a price. "Damsels," he concludes in exasperation, "I find the sharpest bargainers" (p. 260). Perhaps most chilling of all is the abbess who criticizes knight-errantry because it interferes with the repression of more traditional authority: "We are quite capable of hanging our own people," this pillar of the Church protests, and she goes on to grumble because "the collection of tithes, dues, and privileges is upset on the grounds of justice" (p. 252).

In Steinbeck's world heroic effort thus proves futile. Ewain witnesses the power of the longbow that is destined to kill men at a distance, no matter how brave and skilled they are; Arthur sees his hard-earned peace foster the corruption of all that he has built; Lancelot encounters only cynical self-interest when he rides forth as a knight errant. His frustration in dealing with damsel after damsel mirrors his failure to escape his love for Guinevere, despite his reluctance to betray his king and friend. For all his efforts he finds himself in the queen's arms, "Their bodies locked together as though a trap had sprung" (p. 293). At the end he blunders off, "weeping bitterly" (p. 293) at the knowledge that he, the best knight of the world, has failed. Arthur and his court cannot escape the doom of their own weakness.

Thus despite touches of playful humor at the expense of such incongruities in medieval romance as Merlin's shape-changing, the impracticality of chivalry learned by Ewain, and the irresponsibility of knight-errantry demonstrated by Marhalt, the dominant mood of Steinbeck's novel is one of disillusionment that grows increasingly bitter and hopeless. This sense of futility may account for Steinbeck's inability to continue his work. Amidst the malaise of Arthurian society, Lancelot sets out on a quest to achieve something of a positive value. Yet his adventures serve but to take him from one frustrating experience to the next, until his long, weary, and increasingly hopeless struggle to escape or sublimate his love for the Queen culminates in their lustful embrace. Lancelot's fall means the fall of the Round Table, for the failure of its finest knight seals its fate, in moral terms as well as in terms of plot development. For those who know the legend the novel is complete as it stands. The lovers' embrace is already an anti-climax, the inevitable result of Lancelot's earlier failures. To add more would merely drag out the anti-climax into what the author himself, in a letter dated September 10, 1959, calls, "a repetition of things I have written before" (p. 361).

Although it was not published until 1976, Steinbeck in fact wrote the novel in 1958–59. However, T. H. White's *The Book of Merlyn*, which appeared the next year, 1977, had been waiting for publication since 1942.[47] Here White takes Arthur, on the eve of his last battle against Mordred, and places him underground to participate in a long and bitter dialogue with Merlyn and the animals whom he met in the first book. Despite Arthur's attempts to defend at least some of man's achievements, the follies and failures of humanity are castigated stridently. The comparison of mankind to the mindless ant is particularly odious, for White uses it to attack totalitarianism, which seeks "to deny the rights of the individual" (p. 66).

Arthur himself is spared criticism, however. In the form of an ant, he stands with desperate courage between the two opposing armies, willing to die rather than acquiesce to "the callous wickedness" that "had killed the joy of life" (p. 62). It is an act that foreshadows his own final attempts to prevent bloodshed between his army and that of Mordred. Arthur realizes that the important thing is "to mean well" (p. 112). Even when people are wrong, as, cruelly, is too often the case, "here and there, oh so seldom, oh so rare, oh so glorious, there were those all the same who would face the rack, the executioner, and even utter extinction, in the cause of something greater than themselves" (p. 112).

Nevertheless, this glimpse of the heroic spirit does not balance the bitter attack upon warfare and the stupidity of mankind that allows it to happen. Moreover, White's focus shifts from the legend itself to a one-sided argument in which his narrative thread is lost. Despite the damage caused by this intrusive didacticism, the arguments do derive logically from the earlier novels to which this is intended as the conclusion. White's anguish is a measure of his love for the world of beauty and hope that the novels reveal, and of his recognition that this world has been lost through our own folly. He is bitter because he cares so deeply.

For his Grail trilogy Richard Monaco draws material from the thirteenth-century *Parzival* of Wolfram von Eschenbach. Parsival's quest for the Holy Grail starts in *Parsival or a Knight's Tale* (1977). *The Grail War* (1979) describes the apocalyptic struggle between followers of the demonic Clinschor and defenders of the Grail Castle; *The Final Quest* (1980) follows the fate of the survivors as they wander through a waste land. The novels present a world of often shocking brutality and destruction. The impact is felt more cruelly by the peasants, and the suffering they endure, especially during the wars fought by the aristocracy, is vividly captured in scenes of callous slaughter and savage rape. The aristocracy are almost all portrayed as little better than foul-mouthed bandits in their dealings with one another as well as with their social inferiors. Both Lancelot and Lohengrin stoop to assassination without a qualm.

This brutality recalls the world of sword and sorcery fantasy, but here it provides an ironic contrast to the high-minded ideals of chivalric romance and the Holy Grail. This is underlined when a minstrel in *Parsival* narrates part of a decorous romance of knightly adventure shortly before he and most of his audience are slaughtered or taken prisoner during an unprovoked attack by knights. The minstrel tells of Gawain's encounter with the sister of the King of Ascalun, a story drawn from the Grail romance of Wolfram, like the novel itself. However, the irony does not end there, for Gawain later recalls hearing the same story himself:

"I was drinking in a stew with the whores and some fellow was telling a tale of great feats and astounding achievements so that I was amazed to hear it. Later I learned it was Sir Gawain himself who had done these things." He chuckled. "I was glad to learn of them." (P. 161)

His own version of the encounter reveals that his overtures to the damsel were prompted by mere lust, not high-minded courtesy.[48] Indeed Gawain, like all the characters in the trilogy, displays a much sharper talent for insults than for polite conversation, as is witnessed by his comment on the slow-witted Lancelot: "What he has for brains makes the flowers grow" (*Parsival*, p. 174).

Beauty and happiness are found only in vision. Thus Gawain, his mind affected by a drug, "dimly recalled another world of pain, confusion, darkness and terrible sorrows back in the mists that were Gawain the knight....he was the whole now" (*The Final Quest*, p. 333). The central vision that all pursue is the Holy Grail, but the corruption of the world enmires them. As Parsival loses his innocence, so he finds his quest for the Grail all the more futile, until he realizes that it is less a physical object to be sought than a spiritual state. One must learn to look below "all the ugliness...on the surface" (*Parsival*, p. 332) in order to see the wonder of the soul's potential. In *The Final Quest* he gives up this hard-earned vision with reluctance: "Let it go this time knowing it. You cannot lose forever. You have passed through the door and now go back and do what is hardest, Grail Child" (p. 332). The problems of the world, he realizes, drag one down: "This is the most difficult of births, Lord, to enter the world knowing what awaits....No more dreaming" (p. 332).

However, vision, too, proves destructive. Galahad is slain

when he lays aside his weapons to till the soil; Gawain drowns in a shallow pool, his mind lost in hallucination; both Broaditch and Parsival are absent when their families stand in dire need of their protection. The pursuit of the dream is also an evasion of responsibility, an escape from tedious domestic burdens. Its destructiveness is demonstrated by figures like Clinschor, who devastates the country in pursuit of the Grail, and John, leader of a religious sect that practices cannibalism. Their followers share their dreams with horrifying fanaticism.

Thus neither illusion nor reality offers much hope in this dark world. Unfortunately, the scenes of brutality grow tiresome through repetition, for the glimpses of beauty are too rare, as well as undercut ironically. Moreover, the sprawling canvas with its interlacing plot lines, as characters wander here and there, encountering strange adventures, vainly seeking one another, is better suited to medieval prose romance than to modern fantasy. Although the confusion reflects the state of the world in the trilogy, it does create problems for the reader.

Robert Nye's *Merlin* (1978) focuses upon the Devil's role in the Merlin tradition. To avenge the harrowing of hell by Christ, here in the guise of an ape, Lucifer attempts to father the Antichrist on a virgin, but the plot miscarries when the child, Merlin, is christened. Merlin seeks to create a better world and he establishes the Round Table in the image of Christ's table. Yet Lucifer contrives to bring these hopes to nought, leaving his son trapped in his *esplumeoir*.

The story provides a sardonic and scurrilous comment upon mankind's predicament, caught between impulses toward good and evil. The frustration of attempts to find peace in either direction are shown not only by the plot pattern, but also by such recurring images as "the tree that is one side flames and the other side green leaves growing" (p. 210).[49]

This duality undermines the glory of Camelot, "Where, by day, . . . there is no one gentler than Arthur, no knight or baron more kind and courteous, more shiveringly chivalrous, and none so quick to come to the defending of a maiden's honour" (p. 175). Yet it is "Built upon a secret cesspool," for in the darkness of night the king gives rein to erotic fantasies, "Revelling in incest with his sister" (p. 175).

This betrayal is but one in a whole series: Uther betrays Gorlois with Igrayne; Igrayne betrays Uther with Lot of Orkney; Lot betrays Igrayne with her daughter, Morgan le Fay; Morgan betrays Lot with her half-brother, Arthur. The pattern of deepening incest culminates in Merlin's seduction by Nimue, who is no other than himself in the female form he adopted to help Uther seduce Igrayne. This pattern suggests our fascination with our own baser drives, with the dark side of our own nature, and it is this ultimately that traps and destroys us. The futility of striving for self-improvement is emphasized not only by the fates of Merlin and of Arthur, who is stabbed by Mordred when he seeks to comfort his dying son, but also by that of Gawain whose spiritual yearnings for the Grail are debased by the vulgar joke about the Sleeve Job. All three are stripped of dignity and made foolish. Others do not even aspire to something better: Igrayne, Lancelot, Guinevere, and even Perceval, the traditionally innocent Grail quester, are all reduced to shameless and self-indulgent adulterers. As the demon Astarot remarks indignantly, "some of these knights would do incubi out of a job" (p. 208). Nuns and priests, meanwhile, masturbate frenetically, possessed it is true by devils, but devils who take advantage of their own secret longings.

The action unfolds in an impressionistic series of scenes whose shock value lends them immediacy. The overall effect can be confusing and self-consciously clever at times, but both do help create a world where good is frustrated, where behind the illusion of chivalric ideals there abounds the reality of licentious perversity.

All the books in this group where satire dominates paint a dark anti-romantic picture of the world. This influences characterization. Wicked figures who play minor roles in Arthurian tradition, like Monaco's Clinschor and Nye's Lucifer, rise to prominence, along with more traditional villains like Morgan le Fay and Mordred. We are shown the less attractive side of characters such as Steinbeck's Gawain, Monaco's Lancelot, and virtually everyone in Nye's *Merlin*. White is gentler, but he stresses the futility of heroic action just as forcefully as do the other three. Since this requires the frustration of purposeful endeavor on the part of the protagonists, the plots in all the novels tend to be confused and disjointed. Although this is appropriate to the vision of these novels, it does present special problems for the reader that are exacerbated by insufficient control of the plot structure and the use of impressionistic techniques. All stress the bitter reality behind the bright illusions that inspire the Arthurian dream. They mock the hypocrisy and self-delusion that underlie such pretensions, though they preserve a note of regret that such nobility cannot survive. This, however, but adds to the sense of bitter loss and anger against the causes of failure, particularly human stupidity and selfishness.

Despite the recent surge in popularity of these satirical fantasies, those that blend high comedy with warm affection for their subject to create a more sentimental vision remain much more numerous, especially when we include historical fiction in the ironic vein. Five of these fantasies have been written specifically for younger readers, and all have appeared since the war.

In Edward Eager's *Half Magic* (1954) four children find a magic talisman that grants only half a wish at a time. They use its power to travel back in time, and on one occasion visit Arthur's court. Here one of the children uses magic to defeat Launcelot, to the general joy of all the villains and the despondency of the noble-hearted. Merlin, however, puts everything right at once by using the talisman to unwish events. Since the children are protected from the consequences of their ill-considered actions by adult intervention, the warning against the careless use of power is blurred, and attention shifts from character development to the adventures themselves. These grow tedious.

Rosemary Manning also incorporates Arthurian tradition into her series about a Cornish dragon. In *Green Smoke* (1957) the 1,500-year-old dragon tells the story of Uther and Merlin among others; *The Dragon's Quest* (1961) provides the full-length account of his adventures at Camelot, where he works in the kitchens until he proves his loyalty and worth on a quest, much like his friend Gareth. Most of the humor is generated by the contrast between appearance and reality. Despite his fearsome size and power, the dragon is really very civilized and kindly, as he proves by trying to convert some friendly giants to a vegetarian diet. By contrast, his good friend Sir Gryfflet is timorous despite

his warlike bearing, while Morgan le Fay masks implacable enmity for King Arthur beneath a sisterly affection. What is important, we are told, is to have a true heart.

Tom McGowen's *Sir MacHinery* (1971) is a lively, if episodic,
tale set in Scotland. The demons are preparing to attack mankind, but the brownies rally to the defense, enlisting the aid of
Merlin, a hippie scientist named Arthur, a veritable menagerie
of creatures, and a robot whom they mistake for a knight. Good
finally triumphs.

Although its sequel is a mythopoeic fantasy, Robert Newman's *Merlin's Mistake* (1971) is an ironic fantasy in which a
young squire fulfils his quest to save a city from bandits, and
in the process finds his missing father, discovers true love, and
wins knighthood. Brian is a likeable hero, kind, loyal, valiant,
and modest, yet very naive, and his experiences teach him to
look below the surface of things. Thus he discovers that enemies
may be less formidable than they seem at first, and that a pretty
face is less important than more practical qualities such as initiative and common sense. This process of education is accomplished by humorously exposing the impractical side of such
cherished romance figures and motifs as giants and dragons,
magicians and enchantresses, knights guarding fords against all
comers and quests to win the hand of a beautiful princess. Thus
while the adventures may ramble at times, they do manage to
generate suspense and to fit into the broad comic pattern that
is essential to the shedding of illusions.

Although the lesson that they teach lacks the bitterness of the
satiric fantasies, these sentimental ironic fantasies for younger
readers continue to warn against the dangers of illusion. Errors
lead to comical misadventures, but good inevitably triumphs,
especially if one can learn from mistakes. What is important is
to have a good heart.

Of the nine adult fantasies the earliest is James Branch Cabell's
classic *Jurgen* (1919). Jurgen is an aging pawnbroker who retains
his love for life. In the course of a series of comical adventures
he encounters many exciting and beautiful women, only to conclude ruefully that his unattractive, scolding wife is a more comfortable companion for his advancing years. One learns to
appreciate the realities of love that endures the daily irritations

of life: "when I consider steadfastly the depth and the intensity of that devotion which, for so many years, has tended me, and has endured the society of that person whom I peculiarly know to be the most tedious and irritating of companions, I stand aghast, before a miracle" (pp. 359–60).[50] The fascinating women whom he encounters also grow tiresome in their own way, nor do they understand him any better than his own wife. Thus he rejects the opportunity to accompany Helen, the vision of ideal beauty, lest she turn out to be no different from all the others. He cannot bear the thought that her perfection, too, may eventually prove less than he dreams: "I shudder at the thought of living day-in and day-out with my vision!" (p. 347).

Just as Helen represents vision and Anaïtis desire, so Guenevere symbolizes faith: "In approaching me men thought of God, because in me, they said, His splendor was incarnate," she tells Jurgen (p. 338). She inspires knights to deeds of valor so that they may prove themselves worthy of the Creator who wrought such beauty. To this end, she commands unquestioning devotion from her admirers: "That which I willed was neither right nor wrong: it was divine" (p. 338). Guenevere's sole constraint is the need to ensure that her beauty remain untainted by any hint of impropriety in her behavior, but since her will is above morality, appearance suffices. As her father warns Jurgen, "I would have you lie like a gentleman" (p. 92). This is a perceptive assessment of her role in Arthurian romance. Jurgen, however, finds this gap between appearance and reality uncomfortable, so that after some adventures, including an affair that recalls that between Gawain and Ettarde, he is ready for new discoveries in the company of Anaïtis, the Lady of the Lake and much else besides.

Heywood Broun's "The Fifty-First Dragon" is a light-hearted magazine story like those by Marquis and Roberts. A young fellow in "knight school" believes that he is protected from dragons by a magic word until he discovers that the magic was all in his own mind. His confidence evaporates despite his slaughter of fifty dragons, and he is devoured during his next encounter. The only Arthurian connection is the name of the hero, Gawaine le Coeur-Hardy.

Gwyn Jones' "Gwydion Mathrafal" (1945) is another short

story, though of greater literary merit. The hero is a Welshman who is searching for Arthur's grave. He puts to flight an insolent Englishman, who makes insulting remarks about Wales, and is rewarded by a vision of Arthur and a glorious company riding from a ruined fortress across a bridge of mist to go hunting.[51] The contrast between the shabby reality and glorious aspirations of the protagonist creates a sense of poignancy in the tale.

Like *Jurgen*, John Myers Myers' *Silverlock* is a fantasy classic, a glorious romp through literary tradition. The hero learns a fuller appreciation of the wonders of life in the course of his picaresque wanderings through a realm peopled by memorable characters from literature. Unsurprisingly, several figures from Arthurian legend assist this development, most notably Nimue and Gawain. He learns to appreciate his brief tempestuous affair with the former, here a fairy queen who takes a succession of lovers, recalling the pleasure they shared, rather than allowing the bitterness of rejection to infect his mind. Gawain he witnesses honoring his pledge to allow the Green Knight to strike off his head, and he is so moved by the hero's steadfast courage and loyalty that he is himself inspired to more honorable and considerate conduct: "I sighed wearily, cursed Gawain, and rose. What had come between me and the comforts of rationalization was the recollection of that man taking off his helmet and throwing it on the ground at the conclusion of a long search for peril. If he could do that where death had been promised him, I could take a chance."[52]

Naomi Mitchison's *To The Chapel Perilous* (1955) was the first ironic fantasy of novel length in an exclusively Arthurian setting to appear after Twain's *A Connecticut Yankee in King Arthur's Court*. She achieves comic effect by introducing the press into the Arthurian world, then sending reporters with modern professional standards to try to uncover the truth behind some of the stories that comprise the often contradictory body of Arthurian legend. Mitchison displays many deft touches, such as employing the conventional damsel and dwarf of romance as a reporter and photographer team, and making Merlin the publisher of the Camelot Chronicle newspaper. After all, newspapers, mergers, and such like come "from a fantastic world"

(p. 154), as Merlin himself gleefullly recognizes. He is, of course, fascinated by the paper's Paris correspondent, Nimue.

Modern journalism, we discover, is not as impartial as we might like to think. Powerful interest groups exert pressure without scruple, as when the Church agrees to release Lienors, the Chronicle reporter, only in return for coverage to their liking of certain events. Publishers seek to further their own political ambitions by launching campaigns and "angling" the news. The "subs" exercise ruthless censorship to avoid antagonizing advertisers and others with influence. Even the reporters have their biases based upon local loyalties or personality. The unfortunate Sir Kay receives a bad press because he once rebuked a reporter who was "snooping round the kitchens" (p. 84). He is a good administrator, trying to control expenditure and ensure honesty, "But he was tactless, and the newspapers teased him so that he would go down to posterity as a stupid and unsympathetic character" (p. 84).

Yet even those who try to guard against human bias in pursuit of the truth find that it is more complex than they suspect. Thus when Lienors and Dalyn, her colleague from the Northern Pict, delve into the conflicting claims of having found the Holy Grail, they discover that each is true in its own way: Gawain finds a Celtic Cauldron of Plenty, once the property of Ceridwen, and he uses it to feed people whatsoever they desire; Lancelot finds a Spear that drips Blood, by whose power he heals the sick and injured; Peredur/Perceval finds a Stone that spills forth gold coins; Bors the Dish of the Last Supper, which is carried forth in the procession to bless the harvest festival; Galahad, however, finds the Cup full of Blood, and it is this that the Church endorses as the true Grail.[53] As the successful knights ride off amidst the flowering Waste Land, a bemused Dalyn ponders, "we always supposed—there was only one Grail," to which a hermit answers, "Yes, indeed, . . . and each knight won it" (p. 15).

The reporters can only discover the meaning behind his words when they abandon their professional detachment to experience life themselves. Dalyn early recognizes that "he only knew the outsides of things," because if he were to see deeper, "well then, he would be out of touch. Not simply a good reporter: as he

wanted to be. But more like, well, a Grail quester" (p. 19). Yet,
paradoxically, these externals but mystify and confuse. The reporters must probe more deeply, must involve themselves in
the activities going on around them, must themselves live life,
not just observe it. When Dalyn and Lienors fall in love and
learn personal grief and suffering, then they gain wisdom. The
conflicting reports that they receive

are different patterns that people can make themselves into. Or be made
into if they aren't strong and knowledgeable. And each pattern uncovers a different aspect of the heart: a different means of wisdom. . . . And each pattern is dangerous to the other patterns and must
seem hateful to their followers. Unless to the very wise and tolerant
people. . . . Most people are much too frightened to be tolerant. And at
any one time and place there's always one pattern on top. (P. 159)

Truth turns out to be multi-faceted, but beneath the apparent
confusion lies a universal pattern, as we each discover our own
truth: "The wound is healed, the secret told, the riddle becomes
plain, the reconciliation is made between man and what surrounds him" (p. 170). Yet this discovery does not preclude others: "It would be sad beyond all telling if the finding of the Grail
were to happen once for all. Because then it could not happen
again for anyone" (pp. 170–71). Ultimately we must each forsake
detachment and make our own journey, for others cannot do it
on our behalf. Thus at the end Dalyn and Lienors set forth to
find their own Grail. And around them the Waste Land blooms
yet again, "the whole of spring rushing on and summer after
it" (p. 172).

This exploration of truth, of the reality that lies behind appearance, offers a thoughtful comment upon Arthurian tradition
where a basic pattern underlies the complexity and contradiction. The legend must be rediscovered by each of us, its meaning
experienced once again, the Waste Land revitalized by our imagination. What we discover is that those who created the legend
are, after all, human beings with human weaknesses. Yet their
aspirations for something nobler cast a heroic aura about them.
Thus the humor is balanced by affection and admiration for
characters such as Gareth, Gawain, and Lancelot, and by epi-

sodes, such as Bors' celebration of the harvest festival, that evoke images of a lost golden age.

Mitchison's novel was followed by two light-hearted comedies, both of which bring the Arthurian world into contact with modern society. Leonard Wibberley's *The Quest of Excalibur* (1959) pokes gentle fun at over-regulation in the British welfare state, which robs people of the freedom to enjoy themselves. King Arthur returns briefly, to discover that he is comically out of joint with the times, and Merlin gleefully contributes to the confusion in the guise of a Royal Automobile Club patrolman. The hero and the royal heroine are reincarnations of Lancelot and Guenevere, and they too must face a choice between love and duty. However, the parallels are not otherwise close, and a happy resolution is achieved when the lovers choose the path of duty. J. B. Priestley's *The Thirty-First of June* (1962) comically deflates the world of advertising by bringing it into contact with an alternate universe of Arthurian fantasy. Arthur and his court remain very much in the background, however, in order to focus upon magic. The literary technique is appropriate to its good-humored warning against taking oneself too seriously, whether one be an officious business executive or a grumpy monarch. However, neither novel offers more than very light entertainment, and both have become badly outdated.

Unfortunately, the same is true of Matt Cohen's *Too Bad Galahad* (1972), which is a series of very short burlesque accounts of Galahad's discovery of the Holy Grail. These are self-consciously clever, so that though they do deflate the sententiousness of some versions of the Grail quest, they grow tedious as the novelty palls.

The most recent ironic fantasy, and in many ways the most impressive, is Thomas Berger's *Arthur Rex* (1978). The novel is loosely based upon Malory, occasionally supplemented by material from independent English poems such as *Sir Gawain and the Green Knight* and *The Wedding of Sir Gawain and Dame Ragnell*. However, the author adopts a very free approach to his material, reinterpreting and even significantly changing events in order to explore their comic potential.

Like Twain, Berger has a keen eye for the ridiculousness inherent in so many romance conventions. Thus he observes that

whereas churls "died from the plague and other mala-
dies...knights did perish only in battles and ladies from love"
(p. 168). The rigid class distinction implied in the disparate fates
of peasant and aristocrat is underlined by the comment of Lynette to Gareth, whom she believes to be but a kitchen-boy.
"Can it be that thou dost not understand that I do not desire
thy protection, and that I find it greatly obnoxious? It is far more
shameful to be saved by a scullion than to be ravished by a
person of one's own class" (p. 242). Such dedication to a principle would be hard to match!

Equally dedicated to a principle is Elaine of Astolat, the living,
or perhaps one should say dying, proof that ladies in Arthurian
romance do indeed die from love. Gawaine loves her, but she
loves only Launcelot. Launcelot, however, cares nothing for
Elaine though he is concerned at the distress of his good friend
Gawaine.

"What are we to do with poor Elaine, if I can not love her, and she can
not love thee, and thou canst love no other?" He frowned in compassion
and said, "I do not speak in intentional absurdity."

"Yet, of course 'tis absurd," said Gawaine sorrowfully, "the which
is proved merely by hearing it said. And thou and I have better things
to do, no doubt." (P. 184)

It is also true that the knights of medieval romance seem to
perish only in battles, but they certainly go out in style! At
Camlann the 148 knights of the Round Table account for 20,000
of their foes.

And Sir Launcelot, with but his left hand, skewered ten Saxons at a
time on the end of his lance, and then he hurled them all away dead
and he pierced ten more....And Sir Percival...drew his sword and
holding it at the level of the neck he rode along the Saxon ranks lopping
off heads as if he were in a wheat field with a scythe. (P. 481)

The technique of such passages is that of *reductio ad absurdum*,
and it serves as a delightful parody upon the exaggeration found
in medieval romance.[54] However, Berger is equally fond of using
ironic reversal for comic purpose, as the sorry tale of Meliagrant

demonstrates. As a villain Meliagrant achieves tremendous success, abducting Guinevere, and imprisoning both Kay and the invincible Launcelot when they ride to her rescue. His plans go astray, however, when he falls in love with the Queen and attempts to win her approval by reforming. His first virtuous deed is to give alms to a beggar, who responds by crawling to a nearby shop, buying a crossbow with the money, then threatening to kill his benefactor if he does not hand over the rest of his possessions. Even after he robs Meliagrant the beggar shoots him anyway! Fortunately, Meliagrant is only wounded, and he bashes in the rogue's brains. His second virtuous deed proves equally futile. He liberates Kay in return for a promise that the latter will recommend him to the Queen. Instead Kay attacks him with his own sword, then sets off to free the Queen. Meliagrant thus discovers that "whereas he had been fearsome when vile, he was but a booby when he did other than ill" (p. 174).

His conclusion is echoed at the end of the novel by Arthur, as he lies wounded to the death by the treacherous Mordred. He despairs at "the triumph of perfect evil over imperfect virtue, which is to say, of tragedy over comedy. For have I not been a buffoon?" He is comforted, however, by the ghost of Gawaine: "For can we not say, without the excessive pride which is sinful, that we lived with a certain gallantry?" (p. 483).

What redeems, and indeed glorifies, this folly of struggling to achieve an impossible virtue is this certain gallantry, in other words the heroic self-sacrifice that the struggle produces. When Gawaine earlier complains, "Surely there is some limit to mercy towards the deceitful," the Lady of the Lake responds, "Nay,... there is no limit to mercy, and the treacherous need it most of all" (p. 106). Thus Arthur's generosity toward Mordred at Camlann, though foolish by the standards of worldly wisdom, is the sign of his worth in a higher scale. To Guinevere Arthur is "the most innocent of men though the greatest king of all, and perhaps there was some connection" (p. 459). Yet after she receives his forgiveness for her adultery and its disastrous consequences, she is wise enough to look deeper, to recognize that her husband is "not so innocent after all" (p. 459). His innocence

is like that of Percival who "believed himself to be greatly ignorant of all important matters, and therefore he was anything
but a fool, for the only truth is that of God" (p. 420).

Moreover, despite its ultimate vulnerability to evil, innocence
does provide considerable protection, and the subtlety of evil
often confounds itself. As Merlin observes, "greatness consists
not in having no weaknesses, which is impossible, but rather
in using them as strengths" (p. 75), and this is certainly the case
during the comically unsuccessful attempts upon Arthur's life
by his two half-sisters. Unaware that Margawse seeks to assassinate him, Arthur descends a winding staircase with such "boy-
ish vigor" (p. 51) that the lady is too overcome by the dizziness
of her spiral pursuit to stab her intended victim. And Morgan
la Fey, disgusted by repeated failure of her plots against the
King, finally decides to reform, "for after a long career in the
service of evil she had come to believe that corruption were
sooner brought amongst humankind by the forces of virtue, and
from this moment on she was notable for her piety" (p. 453).

Furthermore, generous self-sacrifice brings rich reward as well
as grief and loss, as the career of Gawaine demonstrates. Initially
a merry lecher, preoccupied with what the Lady of the Lake
terms the "simple philosophy of groins" (p. 105), Gawaine learns
the sorrow of a lost love at the hands of Elaine of Astolat, before
he eventually finds happiness in marriage to Dame Ragnell. Yet
it is a happiness that he earns by putting consideration for the
lady before personal feelings: "thou art not an object which I
possess like unto a suit of armor," he protests when she asks
him whether he would have her beautiful by night or day. "Thou
art one of God's creatures, and in all fundamental matters thou
must answer only to Him. This choice therefore must be thine
alone" (p. 325). Gawaine must wrestle with envy of stronger
champions like Tristram and Launcelot, and he laments that the
vanity that prompts it is not conquered once and for all, "but
must every day be fought and brought down" (p. 182). Yet he
masters it well enough to call a temporary halt to his last fatal
combat with Launcelot when he sees his friend weak from loss
of blood, and to insist that his wound be bandaged (p. 465).
This may be impractical, but it is also noble. And the author
praises the dying Gawaine as "the finest man of the company

of the Round Table (for he had all the virtues and of the vices the most natural)" (p. 466).

Just as it is Gawaine's love that we remember best—of his brothers, of Launcelot, of women, of life itself—so with the other heroes as they fall at last, one by one. The bloodshed on the battlefield is distanced by exaggeration of the numbers that they slay. Instead we recall the love of Percival, who curses himself that he cannot tell "kind lies" (p. 490) more convincingly, and who weeps "hot tears" (p. 491) over the body of his dear friend Galahad; of Bedivere, "who dying himself can carry his king down a precipitous slope" (p. 495); of Arthur who wonders, "When will the world ever again know such a company as that of my incomparable knights?" (p. 495).

Although the struggle to maintain the right may be doomed, it is not through lack of effort, but rather, as Launcelot comes to realize, "because chivalry in general was more complicated than it seemed, for it is not easy always to know what is the noble thing, or what is brave and generous or even simply decent" (p. 461). The Round Table's heroic achievement is measured finally by Gawaine, the finest man of its company: "the principle was noble and we all of us did uphold it each in his own fashion, and perhaps we did well as we could, being but men" (p. 460).

This is the reason why the heroes of so many of these ironic fantasies command our respect. We do not admire them *despite* their comic mistakes and misadventures, but rather *because* of them. They have the courage to risk mistakes and to learn from them. Characters like Newman's Brian, Manning's dragon, Cabell's Jurgen, Myers' Silverlock, Mitchison's Lienors, and Wibberley's Princess Pamela are not so afraid to look foolish that they tamely submit to the tyranny of opinion or conventional wisdom. Steinbeck's Lancelot, White's Arthur, Monaco's Parsival, and even Nye's Merlin respond to the same challenge, if with gloomier results. Because they have the courage to defy convention and risk looking foolish, they earn the wisdom not only to recognize their own limitations, but to keep striving nonetheless, for that alone can create a better world where love and decency can prevail. This is heroic self-assertion, as great as any found in tragedy or epic. "We sought no easy victories," the ghost of Gawaine reminds the dying Arthur at the end of Berger's novel, "nor won any" (p. 484). This may be folly to some. But it is glorious folly, and we are the richer for it. By contrast, the ruthless practicality with which they seek power leads Twain's Hank Morgan, Monaco's Clinschor, White's Mordred, and the Church in Mitchison's novel down the path to inevitable destruction, both of themselves and of the world that they sought so selfishly to control.

This reversal of our expectations lies at the heart of the ironic fantasies that treat the Arthurian legend. The noble aspirations may be comical, but they bring life, love, and laughter into a gray world of selfish caution. They build something worthwhile, that common sense and self-interest conspire to destroy. Thus the younger knights in Steinbeck's novel, blind to the beauty of the dream because they realize the folly of striving for an unattainable perfection, mock idealists like Lancelot and so frustrate their efforts; and Hank Morgan in Twain's novel sets about transforming, at gunpoint, romantic feudalism into a ruthless capitalist system that is just as exploitative, but lacks the imagination and even humanity of the former. White's *The Book of Merlyn* fails artistically largely because Merlyn turns against his own creations with a stridency that mirrors the very destructive qualities he condemns in mankind.

In the world of ironic fantasy, reason and cold logic are the weapons of cynicism and a defeatism that ultimately proves self-fulfilling. Cabell's Jurgen laments, "we fall insensibly to common-sense as to a drug; and it dulls and kills whatever in us is rebellious and fine and unreasonable" (p. 346); and Berger's Lady of the Lake grumbles, "I am bored...by the physical application of reason. I am interested only in that which is mythical" (p. 107). When Merlin boasts to her of scientific marvels, she dismisses them as "childish sports with matter," and asks, "art thou capable of transforming Envy, Vanity, and Spite into the virtues of Self-Respect, Generosity, and Patience?" (p. 107). Better far the dream than the protagonist's shabby world in Jones' story; than the defeat of Broun's Gawaine when his belief in his invulnerability is shattered; than the brutal devastation of the Waste Land that surrounds Monaco's Grail Castle; than the mindless totalitarianism of White's ant nest. Thus in the novels of Eager, Manning, Myers, Mitchison, and Priestley the protagonists all leave behind the world of practicality and good sense to venture into a world of wonder and excitement. In all these fantasies Arthurian tradition supplies much of the wonder. Its presence signals that the protagonists of those stories which begin in a contemporary, or at least non-Arthurian, setting have entered a fabulous world. Where the setting is completely Arthurian, the legend supplies the vision that inspires the heroes with the dream of a better society. Their attempts to pursue this vision may be comically misguided, or even futile, but they do win our sympathy and admiration. Even the satires offer us a glimpse of a nobler world, be it a romantic tale on the lips of a minstrel, or a deed of desperate defiance in the face of inevitable defeat.

Encounters with the Arthurian world or attempts to pursue its dreams almost always provide a crucial learning experience for the characters (Twain's Hank Morgan is the striking exception). The wisdom that they gain, however, is sometimes disillusioning. To their discomfort they discover that their expectations are but illusions which shatter upon contact with reality. Not least among these discoveries is awareness of their own limitations, for their good opinion of themselves is revealed to be self-conceit, as Nye's Merlin learns to his cost.

As a consequence of this approach our traditional view of Arthurian characters is often shown to be mistaken: Nye's Perceval is a lecher, Monaco's Lancelot treacherous, Cohen's Galahad idiotic; by contrast for Steinbeck, Mitchison, and Berger, Kay is a conscientious administrator. To Twain Merlin is a charlatan, to Steinbeck he is childishly playful, to White and Newman he is absent-minded, to Berger scientific. Similarly Myers' Nimue, Mitchison's Morgan, and the Lady of the Lake in the novels of both Cabell and Berger are shown to possess powers that reach even farther than one might have been led to believe by tradition. Elsewhere the novels measure the gap between appearance and reality in the deceptions practised by figures such as Steinbeck's four queens, Cabell's Guenevere, Manning's Morgan le Fay, and Berger's Mordred.

As it explores the theme of illusion and reality, ironic fantasy develops new insights into the Arthurian characters, but as in the other fictional forms these insights are based firmly upon at least hints in tradition. Perceval does get involved with a surprisingly large number of women in Chrétien's *Perceval* and its Second Continuation, both from the late twelfth century; Lancelot does betray Arthur and destroy the realm, despite his regrets; and Galahad is unworldly. It is easy to see how a conscientious seneschal could attract the criticism of medieval poets and minstrels,[55] just as it is easy to account for the confusing actions of Merlin in many ways. And studies have probed the supernatural antecedents of the mysterious Arthurian fays.[56]

This reinterpretation of traditional character roles and situations provides impressive evidence of the vitality of Arthurian legend. Unfortunately, this imaginative vigor is too rarely matched by firm control over the material. Most ironic fantasies suffer from episodic structure, because the authors allow their comic and satiric imagination to range through Arthurian tradition with a lack of restraint that can be confusing. Nevertheless, this weakness can be turned to advantage. On the one hand, the confusion may serve as a comment upon both Arthurian romance and the modern world, while on the other, the imaginative freedom may reject the limitations imposed by dull common sense with the same intoxicating zest one finds in the medieval Welsh tale, *The Dream of Rhonabwy*.

NOTES

1. Tolkien, "On Fairy-Stories," pp. 57–69.

2. While it is not my intention to provide a bibliography of theoretical studies on fantasy any more than on other genres of Arthurian fiction, those interested should consult S. C. Fredericks, "Problems of Fantasy," *Science-Fiction Studies*, 5 (1978), 33–44, and Marshall B. Tymn, "Modern Critical Studies and Reference Works on Fantasy," in *The Aesthetics of Fantasy Literature and Art*, ed. Roger C. Schlobin (Notre Dame, Ind.: University of Notre Dame Press, 1982), pp. 262–70.

3. See above, note 8 to Chapter 1.

4. Some traditions maintain that all three are of supernatural origin, Merlin the son of a demon, the other two fays from the Otherworld: see Lucy Allen Paton, *Studies in the Fairy Mythology of Arthurian Romance*, 2nd ed. (New York: Burt Franklin, 1960), and Jean Markale, *Merlin l'Enchanteur ou l'éternelle quête magique* (Paris: Éditions Retz, 1981). While

they are often supernatural creatures in mythopoeic fantasy, in heroic fantasy they are normally human despite their powers.

5. This legend is widespread in Britain: see the various references under cave-legend in Ashe's *A Guidebook to Arthurian Britain*; see also Muriel A. Whitaker, " 'The Hollow Hills': A Celtic Motif in Modern Fantasy," *Mosaic*, 13 (1977), 165–78.

6. P. 169. All quotations are cited from the paperback edition (Harmondsworth, Middlesex: Puffin Books, 1969).

7. See C. G. Jung, *Aion*, published as Vol. 9, Part II of *The Collected Works of C. G. Jung*, trans. R.F.C. Hull (New York: Bollingen, 1958).

8. This is precisely the beneficial escape described by Tolkien in "On Fairy-Stories": see note 1, above.

9. Another novel that could have been included here is T. H. White's *The Book of Merlyn*, which is discussed with the ironic fantasies.

10. Unfortunately, I was unable to locate a copy of this novel to examine it. See Northup and Parry's bibliography, "The Arthurian Legends: Modern Retellings of the Old Stories," *Journal of English and German Philology*, 49 (1950), 184.

11. The other two novels are *Out of the Silent Planet* (1938) and *Perelandra* (1943) (also titled *Voyage to Venus*).

12. Quotations are cited from the American edition (New York: Macmillan, 1945), p. 336.

13. Cf. Seton's *Avalon*, Jewett's *The Hidden Treasure of Glaston*, and Mitchell's *Birth of a Legend*.

14. Cited by Neil Philip, *A Fine Anger* (New York: Philomel Books/ Bantam, 1981), p. 23. See also Ashe, *A Guidebook to Arthurian Britain*, pp. 2–4. Other novels that use the cave-legend include Mayne's *Earthfasts*, Chapman's *King Arthur's Daughter*, Curry's *The Sleepers*, Munn's *Merlin's Ring*, and Burnham and Ray's *Raven*.

15. Cadellin figures in the long list of names by which Culhwch invokes Arthur's assistance in the early Welsh tale *Culhwch and Olwen*.

16. Garner draws his legendary material from various sources, primarily Norse in the first novel, Celtic in the sequel: see Philip, *A Fine Anger*, pp. 35–40.

17. Susan finally emerges as one aspect of the triple moon goddess: she is the maiden whose power is strongest under the new moon; Angharad Golden-Hand (the Lady of the Lake) draws her strength from the full moon; while the Morrigan wields her power under the old moon.

18. *The Dark Is Rising* was the 1974 Newbery Honor Book; *The Grey King* was the 1976 Newbery Award Winner. See Cooper's comments upon the series in her "Newbery Award Acceptance," *Horn Book Magazine*, 52 (1976), 361–66.

19. The event is recounted in *The Dark Is Rising*, pp. 97–101, 202–3.

20. Quotations are cited from the paperback edition (London: Piccolo Pan Books, 1973), p. 17.

21. See Ashe, *A Guidebook to Arthurian Britain*, pp. 156–58; cf. above, note 14.

22. For a study of the role of Merlin in modern fantasy, see my forthcoming article, "The Enchanter Awakes: Merlin in Modern Fantasy," in *Death and the Serpent: Immortality in Science Fiction and Fantasy*, ed. Carl B. Yoke and Donald M. Hassler (Westport, Conn.: Greenwood Press, 1985). See also Charlotte Spivack, "Merlin Redivivus: The Celtic Wizard in Modern Literature," *The Centennial Review*, 22 (1978), 164–79.

23. See p. 264. This would account for Arthur's otherwise curious absence from the climactic battle. Herne also rides against the Dark at the climax of *The Dark Is Rising*. Some oral traditions identify the leader of the wild hunt as Arthur: see Whitaker, " 'The Hollow Hills': A Celtic Motif in Modern Fantasy," p. 167 and accompanying note.

24. See Roger Sherman Loomis, *Arthurian Tradition and Chrétien de Troyes* (New York and London: Columbia University Press, 1949), pp. 152–59, 421–25.

25. Tolkien, "On Fairy-Stories," pp. 58–60.

26. Along with *Heartsease* (1969) and *The Devil's Children* (1970) this comprises a trilogy for juveniles entitled *The Changes*, which was later adapted for BBC-TV. Merlin does not appear in the later novels.

27. See also Edward Eager's *Half Magic*. Both are discussed among the ironic fantasies.

28. Its limitations are castigated by Hans Joachim Alpers, "Loincloth, Double Ax, and Magic: 'Heroic Fantasy' and Related Genres," *Science-Fiction Studies*, 5 (1978), 19–32; cf. L. Sprague de Camp, *Literary Swordsmen and Sorcerers: The Makers of Heroic Fantasy* (Sauk City, Wis.: Arkham House, 1976), and Lin Carter, *Imaginary Worlds* (New York: Ballantine Books, 1973).

29. For a discussion of this subgenre, see Samuel H. Vasbinder, "Aspects of Fantasy in Literary Myths about Lost Civilizations," in *The Aesthetics of Fantasy Literature and Art*, pp. 192–210.

30. Portions of this novel first appeared in *Fantastic Stories*, published under the pseudonym Dennis More. A sequel, *Bard II*, is scheduled for publication by Ace Books in April 1984.

31. The story recalls the Breton lay *Bisclavret*, where the innocent hero is also transformed into a werewolf, but parallels are confined to general situation rather than specific detail.

32. In *Héloïse and Abélard* (1921) Moore also includes a brief scene in

which a poet describes meeting the dead Arthur and his court in a ruined hall where they sit as punishment for their sins. *Perronik the Fool* was originally conceived as part of this novel.

33. Cf. Sterling's *A Lady of King Arthur's Court* where another independent-minded heroine achieves the Grail.

34. Cf. Lindsay, *The Little Wench*.

35. Many medieval romances reflect clerical suspicion of women who were considered the cause of the Fall: see my article, " 'For quenys I myght have inow . . .': The Knight Errant's Treatment of Women in the English Arthurian Verse Romances," *Atlantis*, 4 (1979), 34–47.

36. P. 240. Quotations are cited from the British edition of *The Once and Future King* (London: Collins, 1958).

37. Cf. Sutcliff's treatment. *Firelord* is the first part of an Arthurian triptych: *Beloved Exile*, which is scheduled for publication by Bantam Books in July 1984, continues the story of Guenevere after Arthur's death; *The Last Rainbow*, which should be published in 1985, shifts forward in time to deal with St. Patrick. Ambrosius Aurelianus makes an appearance, the author informs me.

38. Godwin's Eleyne, like Will Bradley's, is a fusion of both Elaine of Astolat and Elaine of Corbenek. She marries Lancelot and bears their child Galahalt. She is also sister to Geraint, prince of Dyfneint (Devonshire).

39. The concept of Morgan le Fay as a priestess of the Mother Goddess also occurs in Laubenthal's *Excalibur*.

40. Merriman, *The Flower of Kings*, pp. 139–43; cf. Taylor and Brewer, *The Return of King Arthur*, pp. 49–53.

41. Quotations are cited from the edition published for the Iowa Center for Textual Studies by the University of California Press, at Berkeley, 1979. A case can be made for considering the novel as science fiction, since it deals with the impact of technological change upon society. However, I have preferred to consider it among the ironic fantasies because of its importance to that tradition.

42. Twain greatly admired Swift's *Gulliver's Travels*, the most famous literary example of this technique.

43. It is interesting to note that both Fielding and Frere are equally affectionate in their regard for the legend: see Merriman, *The Flower of Kings*, pp. 78, 141–42. Affection for the object of irony is evident in many medieval romances also: see my article, " 'Fors del sens': Humour and Irony in Raoul de Houdenc's *La Vengeance Raguidel*," *Thalia*, 2 (1979), 25–29.

44. Malory himself shows Gawain in a less favorable light than does his source in the French Post-Vulgate Cycle, where the young knight

is virtually seduced by the more experienced lady, and subsequently regrets his action. In *The Emperor Arthur* Turton interprets the episode from this more sympathetic point of view.

45. T. G. Roberts takes a similar attitude to this giant. He makes Dinadan the hero of this adventure in "Sir Dinadan and the Giant Taulurd," but the knight is equally reluctant to attack his incompetent giant adversary.

46. The lady turns out to be a highly skilled warrior who trains young knights, much as do the witches of Caer Loyw in the medieval Welsh tale, *Peredur Son of Efrawg*, and Scathach in the Old Irish tale, *The Training of Cuchulainn*.

47. See the letters written by Steinbeck, which are appended to his novel, pp. 297–364, and Sylvia Townsend Warner's Prologue to White's novel.

48. See pp. 162–63, 131–34. Wolfram bases his account of this episode upon Chrétien de Troyes' *Perceval*, where the realm is called Escavalon. Gawain's conduct with the damsel has attracted criticism, as evidence of a willingness to be distracted from more serious tasks by a pretty face. See, for example, Peter Haidu, *Aesthetic Distance in Chrétien de Troyes: Irony and Comedy in Cligés and Perceval* (Geneva: Librairie Droz, 1968), pp. 211–20.

49. Quotations are cited from the American edition (New York: Putnam's, 1979).

50. *Jurgen* is the most important work in Cabell's series of novels, tales and poems, entitled The Biography of the Life of Manuel. Merlin appears briefly in another novel in the series, *Something About Eve* (1927). Cabell also discusses Galahad's role in the legend in "The Eighth Letter: To Sir Galahad of the Siege Perilous," in *Ladies and Gentlemen: A Parcel of Reconsiderations* (New York: Robert M. McBride, 1934), pp. 109–21.

51. Such traditions linger in parts of Britain such as Cadbury Castle: see Ashe, *A Guidebook to Arthurian Britain*, p. 50.

52. P. 323. Quotations are cited from the paperback edition (New York: Ace Books, 1966).

53. These contradictory descriptions of the Grail are all drawn from various medieval traditions: see, for example, Jessie L. Weston, *From Ritual to Romance* (Cambridge: Cambridge University Press, 1920), Chapter VI, and Emma Jung and Marie-Louise von Franz, *The Grail Legend*, trans. Andrea Dykes (London: Hodder and Stoughton, 1971), pp. 79–160.

54. The slaughter wrought by Perceval in Berger's novel, for example, is no greater than in the fourteenth-century English poem *Sir Perceval of Gales*, where he single-handedly kills a sultan and his entire army.

55. See Christopher Dean, "Sir Kay in Medieval English Romances: An Alternative Tradition," *English Studies in Canada*, 9 (1983), 125–35.

56. See Paton, *Studies in the Fairy Mythology of Arthurian Romance*, and Loomis, *Arthurian Tradition and Chrétien de Troyes*.

7.

CONCLUSION

Modern Arthurian fiction has grown in quantity at an impressive rate during the past one hundred years. From 1884 to 1920 about a dozen novels were published, but numbers rose to eleven during the decade of the 1920s, and to fourteen during the 1930s. They declined to nine during the 1940s, rose to twenty-one during the 1950s, twenty-seven during the 1960s, and fifty-four during the 1970s. Of these, thirty-six were published from 1975 to 1979, the peak years being 1977 and 1978, when the annual output reached nine. Since then the average annual output has declined to about half a dozen. To date I have located 162 novels.[1] I have also found thirty-four short stories, most of which were written during the 1940s by John Erskine and T. G. Roberts. The only decades that did not record a growth in Arthurian fiction are the 1910s, the 1940s, and (so far) the 1980s. World wars account for the first two, and a serious recession in the publishing industry following a dramatic surge in the late 1970s accounts for the recent drop. After a low of two in 1982, numbers have risen to five in 1983. If this average is maintained, the 1980s should see between forty and fifty Arthurian novels.

The most impressive areas of growth within the prose fiction form have been in historical novels set in the Dark Ages and in fantasy, particularly the heroic. There has been a slight increase in the numbers of both realistic novels and science fiction. By contrast historical novels set in the High Middle Ages have dwindled after a surge in popularity during the decade following the Second World War. Authors attracted by the setting of the High

Middle Ages now choose to write fantasies rather than historical romances, since the historical inconsistency is less disturbing there.

Choice of setting in Arthurian fiction is usually divided between the Dark Ages, the High Middle Ages, and the Modern Age, although others are found. Thus Powers chooses the sixteenth century, Seton the tenth, while science fiction writers usually venture into the far future. The Dark Ages provide the setting in over half of the historical novels, and about a third of the heroic fantasies, including all the sword and sorcery novels. The High Middle Ages figure in the remaining historical novels and almost all the historical short stories, in about half of the heroic fantasies, and three-quarters of the ironic fantasies. The Modern Age dominates the realistic novels, low fantasy and mythopoeic fantasy.

The Dark Age setting is usually one of political turmoil following the withdrawal of Roman protection and the stability that it created. Between the internal dispute over power, and the external threat of invasion from Saxons, Picts, and Irish, there is ample opportunity for heroic defiance in the face of heavy odds. When these challenges are met and surmounted by a hero of vision who offers us a glimpse of a more compassionate way of life, then the result is an inspiring work like Sutcliff's *Sword at Sunset* or Godwin's *Firelord*. Often, however, the inevitable doom that envelops Arthur's kingdom leaves the reader with a sense of sorrow over the passing of a glorious dream, as happens in Bradshaw's trilogy and Bradley's *The Mists of Avalon*. Others see more savagery than glory in the struggle, and so works like Treece's *The Great Captains*, Frankland's *Bear of Britain*, and the sword and sorcery fantasies present a brutal world where violent men betray and kill each other with unconcealed relish. Although there are exceptions, like Taylor's *Drustan the Wanderer*, most novels set in the Dark Ages are close in spirit to both chronicle and epic, and they recall works like the alliterative *Morte Arthure*.

The High Middle Ages provide a more stable political situation which, as in the medieval romances, allows greater leisure for individual development. Where the novels set in the Dark Ages focus upon the heroic struggle to establish a better way of life, those set in the High Middle Ages are more concerned with the theme of illusion and reality. Characters typically set out with foolishly high expectations only to have these disabused. Chastened, but wiser, they can then proceed to find happiness, as in Ditmas' *Gareth of Orkney* and Mitchison's *To The Chapel Perilous*. Sometimes, however, no happy solution can be achieved, and characters and readers alike are left to ponder the implications of living in an imperfect world, as in Hunter's *Percival*, Housman's *The Life of Sir Aglovale de Galis*, and White's *The Once and Future King*.

The gap between illusion and reality makes the High Middle Ages a popular setting for humorous treatments of Arthurian legend. The high-minded aspirations of chivalry are particularly susceptible to ironic treatment since they are so clearly impractical. Some novels, like White's *The Book of Merlyn* and Steinbeck's *The Acts of King Arthur*, feel grief at our failure to live up to our ideals, and satirize the follies that prevent it. Most are more tolerant, however, and, like Berger's *Arthur Rex*, admire the heroic effort and the good it achieves, even as they enjoy the humor of the misadventures. Paradoxically, all the ironic fiction, whether historical or fantasy, ultimately takes the side of those well-meaning fools who seek a better world, for they not only display heroic defiance against insurmountable odds, as in heroic fantasy, but also they encourage others to work toward constructive ends. By contrast, realistic practical characters who scoff at such dreamers emerge as selfish and destructive cynics, as can be seen from the behavior of Hank Morgan in Twain's *A Connecticut Yankee in King Arthur's Court*, Baron Howtland in Monaco's Grail trilogy, and the devils in Nye's *Merlin*.

The concern with illusion and reality also dominates the novels in both modern and future settings. Realistic fiction and science fiction both are concerned with characters who find themselves trapped in the roles played by figures in Arthurian legend. We thus discover that mankind has changed but little over the centuries, despite technological progress. Like ironic fantasy, mythopoeic fantasy reverses our expectations about illusion and reality. Just as folly is revealed to be a higher wisdom, so the supernatural emerges as the deeper reality. Those sensible people who refuse to acknowledge it because it does not fit into their concept of the world are shown to be seriously limited. They are incapable of adapting to new conditions, and thus they fail to learn the lessons necessary to survive in a changing world.

As one might expect, modern Arthurian fiction is concerned to teach us a lesson, but that lesson seems to be contradictory. On the one hand, we are urged to look beyond appearances in order to perceive the truth of things; on the other, we are advised to ignore the reality of our own inevitable failure, to persevere with our hopes and aspirations regardless. The contradiction, however, is inherent in Arthurian legend itself. This cautions us that all our achievements are transitory, that Arthur's realm will be swept away in final ruin, leaving its enemies to triumph. Yet it also demonstrates that much can be achieved by heroic defiance in the face of overwhelming odds, that a glorious kingdom can be established, to hold back the darkness for a while. And that, after all, is what life is, a brief burst of light between the darkness of birth and death. Because the darkness is inevitable is no reason to surrender the opportunity to kindle the flames as brightly as possible.

Thus Arthur and his companions ride forth again and again, full of hope and promise. Eternally they are destroyed, their achievements cast down. As they ride forth they may discover that nothing has been solved by the centuries of grief and sacrifice, for the old follies still hinder us in our quest for the Grail in Percy's *Lancelot*; and the old mistakes are still repeated in Cherryh's *Port Eternity* and Lewis' *That Hideous Strength*. They may discover that the dark force of fate cannot be resisted, for Tristan and Iseult must love again and suffer again in *Castle Dor* by Quiller-Couch and du Maurier; Mordred and Arthur must meet at Camlann in Stewart's *The Wicked Day*; Morgan le Fay and Arthur must love and hate in Bradley's *The Mists of Avalon*. They may find their hopes shattered by a bleak and anti-romantic world, as ambitious kings contest Arthur's leadership in Gloag's *Artorius Rex*; as violent warriors rage with unrestrained violence in Treece's novels; and as selfish men and women frustrate the noble endeavors of Arthur and Lancelot in Steinbeck's *The Acts of King Arthur*. They may fall to deception and betrayal, as Medraut turns against Arthur in Frankland's *The Bear of Britain*; as evil sets its agents to work against Merlin and the Old Ones in Cooper's series, *The Dark Is Rising*; as cruel tyrants selfishly sacrifice their followers in Drake's *The Dragon Lord*; and as proud knights seek one another's lives in Monaco's Grail trilogy. Despite these defeats, they continue to ride forth, eternally reborn for each generation, and they do so with a defiance that is as heroic as their optimism. If the old struggles must be fought again, the will to do so is still strong. If fate remains inexorable it can still be boldly acted out or bravely resisted. If darkness and deception continue to frustrate hope, they nevertheless warn us that a better way must be found.

That way is compassion and self-sacrifice. This is the answer offered again and again, be it the lesson learned by a child in Stone's *Page Boy for King Arthur*, or that taught us by Arthur's last desperate ride to Camlann at the head of a loyal few in Sutcliff's *Sword at Sunset*. Those who hang back and watch forgo the opportunity to achieve their own Grail, we learn from Mitchison's *To the Chapel Perilous*.

This answer, too, is part of the paradox inherent in the Arthurian legend. Arthur and his companions win undying fame because they sacrifice themselves so entirely: Arthur to his kingdom, Gawain and Bedivere to their king, Lancelot and Tristan to their ladies, Perceval and Galahad to the Grail, Merlin and Morgan le Fay to their magical arts. By giving themselves so fully, they are rewarded most richly. It is the reality of achievement behind the illusion of failure.

The impact of these thematic patterns upon tradition is, as we have seen, varied. Fiction set in the Dark Ages, whether historical or fantasy, is usually heroic in mood. As in the medieval chronicles Arthur and his followers are predominantly warriors, with the virtues and weaknesses of warriors engaged in a grim struggle for survival.[2] Under fierce pressures, qualities such as valor and loyalty are crucial, while treachery poses the most serious threat to success. In most of these works Arthur is a charismatic leader with a dream of order that inspires his followers. Sometimes he is limited by a naivete that leaves him vulnerable to deception and betrayal, as Babcock, Frankland, and Trevor observe. Occasionally his ambition can drive him to needless cruelty, as Vansittart, Treece, and Drake show.[3] When his leadership ability is matched by compassionate insight, however, then he develops into the hero worthy of both love and respect whom we meet in the novels of Sutcliff and Godwin.

Arthur's followers are judged largely in terms of their service to the goals that he pursues, hence the emphasis upon loyalty. This is particularly noticeable in the case of Tristan. He appears in the novels of Canning and Godwin as Arthur's loyal companion, his love for Iseult confined largely to the background. In order to focus upon the love story Taylor removes Arthur early in her novel, *Drustan the Wanderer*. Other figures tend to divide into the devotedly loyal, like Christian's Bedivere and Treece's Cei, or the treacherously ambitious like Turton's Merlin and Marshall's Vivain. Most fascinating, however, are those whose wavering loyalties are the source of genuine struggle: Viney's Cai, Sutcliff's Bedwyr, Stewart's Mordred, Bradshaw's Gwalchmai, Vansittart's Lancelot, and Bradley's Morgaine, to name but some.[4]

In general the figures preserve their familiar roles: Arthur is the great leader, Kay proud and aggressive, Gawain courteous and likeable, Bedivere loyal, Mordred treacherous. However unlike the medieval chronicles and heroic tales, modern fiction explores the psychological motivation of its characters. This deepens our understanding of them and explains apparent inconsistencies in their behavior. Thus Bradley does a masterly job of accounting for the love-hate relationship between Arthur and Morgaine, while Sutcliff, Bradshaw, and Godwin offer convincing reasons for Guenevere's betrayal of Arthur.

Just as fiction set in the Dark Ages recalls medieval chronicle, so that set in the High Middle Ages recalls medieval romance. Arthur is usually a noble monarch, though not immune from criticism, as Housman, Borowsky, and Nye demonstrate. He is often the target of irony, but it is almost always tempered with the affection found in White's *The Once and Future King* and in Berger's *Arthur Rex*. In many of the stories, he recedes into the background, becoming little more than a vague presence, as in Newman's *Merlin's Mistake*, Priestley's *The Thirty-First of June*, and French's *Sir Marrok*.[5] Instead the focus falls upon the knights who venture forth from his court to achieve their quest, like

Karr's Kay, Roberts' Dinadan, and Steinbeck's Lancelot; or, less frequently, upon those who seek it, like Hunter's Percival.

The characters have more time for self-discovery and growth than they do in the Dark Age setting. This may be achieved through love, as in Erskine's *Tristan and Isolde,* Closs' *Tristan,* and Chapman's trilogy of The Three Damosels; or on the Grail quest, as in Hunter's *Percival,* Mitchison's *To the Chapel Perilous,* and Monaco's Grail trilogy. As the authors explore character psychology they reveal new possibilities inherent in traditional roles. Thus Percival discovers the existential dilemma of the Grail quest in the novels of Hunter and Monaco, just as does Gawin in Roberts' *Kinsmen of the Grail;* the family tensions of Gawain and his brothers are traced to their childhood roots in White's *The Witch in the Wood;*[6] and we are invited to ponder the paradoxes of illusion and reality in figures like Housman's Aglovale, Cabell's Guenevere, and Karr's Morgan le Fay. Rather than rationalize the contradictions found in tradition, many novels discover in them profound lessons about the contradictions of human nature.

Fiction in a modern setting shows least connection with the literary forms of the Middle Ages. In the fantasies we encounter figures with supernatural abilities, notably Merlin and Morgan le Fay, though Arthur too is invested with awesome, and at times threatening, powers as in Mayne's *Earthfasts* and Cooper's series, The Dark Is Rising. The response of the modern protagonists to these Arthurian figures is crucial to their development. However, the Arthurian figures themselves remain static and largely symbolic presences, despite the occasional interesting explanation offered for traditional conduct, such as occurs in Laubenthal's *Excalibur.* By introducing them into a later setting, fantasy, realistic, and science fiction all pay tribute to the continuing power and fascination, not only of Arthurian figures, but also of traditional patterns like the Grail quest and the love triangles formed by Lancelot-Guenevere-Arthur and Tristan-Iseult-Mark.

Modern treatments of Arthurian legend not only deepen our understanding of existing tradition, but also spawn new features that may become traditional in their turn. Sutcliff was the first to give Lancelot's role to Bedwyr, the companion who with Kay is most closely linked to Arthur in earliest tradition, but her lead has been followed by both Bradshaw and Stewart. Lancelot is usually a rather sombre and intense figure, but both Berger and Godwin stress his lack of humor, while Monaco makes him stupid. Arthur's naivete is regularly acknowledged, but White, Nye, and Borowsky make him rather simple-minded. Laubenthal borrows the concept of the pendragonship from Lewis, but she herself anticipates Bradshaw with the idea that Morgause is consumed by the evil power she worships, and anticipates Marion Zimmer Bradley when she makes Morgan le Fay a priestess of the Mother Goddess. Christian and Bradley both use the names Merlin and Lady of the Lake as titles: the former combines the functions of bard and druid, the latter is held by a priestess of the Mother Goddess. Elaine of Corbenik and Elaine of Astolat are fused by authors like Christian and Godwin. Mordred's mother is Morgan le Fay, rather than Morgause, in the novels of Lindsay, Godwin and Bradley, though Sutcliff and Christian name her as Arthur's half-sister Ygern. Arthur is not always the father, however, for many authors omit the incest motif entirely, including Godwin, Canning, Christian and Treece.

The extent to which these are conscious borrowings is uncertain and indeed unimportant, except insofar as they provide evidence that modern authors are now influenced by each other as well as their medieval predecessors. It is further proof of the vitality of Arthurian legend, and the respect that these later versions command.

As well as these specific developments in tradition, some broad trends in the modern treatment of Arthurian legend can also be observed. Because the novel form is well suited to the complex analysis of character and motivation, modern fiction tends to humanize traditional figures. One result of this is that characters are less often completely good or bad than in romance. Faults are more noticeable in the good, redeeming features in the bad. Thus Galahad may be a misguided religious fanatic or a complacent and self-righteous prude; Lancelot may be proud and self-centered; Tristan may be irresponsible and unscrupulous; conversely, Mordred and Morgan le Fay may be well-intentioned but ill-fated. The rehabilitation of traditional villains does shift more blame on others. Morgause, Agravain, Gaheris, and Guenevere are frequently at fault, although their motives are usually made clear. Another result of humanizing traditional characters is the greater attention paid to women. Their lack of power in a male-oriented warrior society and their heroic attempts to break with convention by taking an active role in events win our sympathy and admiration, thanks largely to the important contributions of the many fine women writers in the field. Bradshaw's Gwynhwyfar and Bradley's Morgaine are two of the best examples.

The considerable number of novels set in the Dark Ages has given prominence to those warriors whose links with Arthur are of longest standing. Thus we see more of Bedivere, Kay, and Mordred in modern fiction than in medieval romance. The shift is most noticeable in the case of Bedivere who played a very minor role in medieval versions. This allows greater freedom to authors who wish to develop his character. We also see more of Arthur's Saxon enemies, notably Cerdic, who is usually a bold British renegade.[7]

A third major trend is caused by the fact that many Arthurian novels were written for younger readers. To help their readers identify with events in the story, they often introduce young characters, something very rare in medieval romance.[8] These characters are usually invented, but the early years of traditional figures like Arthur, Kay, Bedivere, Gawain, and Gareth are also given greater attention.

A fourth trend is caused by the popularity of the fantasy form. Since the element of the supernatural is central to fantasy, magic workers like Merlin and Morgan le Fay play a crucial role in a wider range of situations than was customary in medieval romance.

Finally, we come to the question of the quality of modern Arthurian fiction. Some writings are indisputably poor: the short stories by Smith, Cox, and Holland are typical of the hastily written adventures used to fill the pages of popular magazines; the novels of Shorthouse and Church are turgidly pretentious; far too many works strike the reader as little more than unambitious attempts to entertain an undemanding audience. The most persistent faults are annoying sentimentality, episodic plot structure, and a failure to integrate the various elements of the stories—in a word, control over the material.

Yet these are common literary problems and no more than we should expect from a tradition with such a broad appeal. Certainly similar charges can be laid against many Arthurian romances of the Middle Ages.[9] They are evidence of the enthusiastic response of writers and readers alike to the Arthurian legend. What gives that legend its appeal, however, is the ability of writers to give powerful expression to its basic patterns. The compositions of Chrétien de Troyes, Wolfram von Eschenbach, the Gawain-Poet, Malory, and Tennyson fill the imagination with the Arthurian vision. No modern novelist has yet achieved their success, but many have explored serious issues with considerable thoughtfulness and skill, while some have written novels of impressive literary merit. Percy, Powys, and Hunter have helped us rediscover the frustrations of the Grail quest, Closs the dizzying passion of Tristan and Iseult; and Sutcliff and Godwin have revealed the warmth and compassion of the Arthurian dream, Cooper and Cherryh its timeless challenge, Twain and Berger its glorious folly, White and Bradley the ache as it slips from our grasp.

They and others have taught us to look for the reality behind the illusion. Arthur is no minor warlord of doubtful authenticity, consigned to irrelevance by the tides of history. He and his companions live in the imagination of all who dream of a better world. Amidst the desolation and despair that darken about us as the twentieth century draws to its close, he is the dream of peace and justice, of love and laughter. He is the unquenchable spark of hope in the human spirit. It may be defeated but can never be completely extinguished. For Arthur has returned from Avalon to ride with us. Whether it be to Badon or to Camlann matters little—just so it pushes back the Darkness for a while.

NOTES

1. As seen above, the Arthurian element in some of these is very minor. Exclusion of novels where the Arthurian borrowings are vague or unimportant could reduce their total by as many as thirty, depending

upon how rigorously the criteria are applied. Conversely, some novels will inevitably have been missed.

2. For the code of the warrior in medieval Arthurian romance, see Sidney Painter, *French Chivalry* (1940; reprint, Ithaca: Cornell University Press, 1964), pp. 28–64.

3. This is a criticism also voiced in some medieval works, e.g., *The Awntyrs off Arthure* and the alliterative *Morte Arthure*.

4. Among untraditional characters torn by conflicting loyalties, the most memorable are found in Powys' *Porius*.

5. Similar tendencies occur in thirteenth-century French romance: for example Arthur is criticized in the Vulgate Cycle (see also note 2 above), he is the object of irony in Raoul de Houdenc's *La Vengeance Raguidel*, and he fades into the background in Froissart's *Méliador*.

6. Cf. Bradshaw's *Hawk of May* and Stewart's *The Wicked Day*.

7. Scholars have noted that the name of Cerdic, King of the West Saxons and thus ancestor of King Alfred and the present British royal family, is British: see, for example, Morris, *The Age of Arthur*, pp. 103–4.

8. The *enfances* of heroes such as Perceval, Gawain, and Lancelot are usually passed over rapidly in order to dwell upon their experiences as knights.

9. See, for example, Dorothy Everett, "A Characterization of the English Medieval Romances," in *Essays on Middle English Literature* (Oxford: Oxford University Press, 1955), pp. 1–22, especially p. 22.

APPENDIX: VARIANT SPELLINGS OF CHARACTERS' NAMES

Arthur, Artorius, Artos, Arturo, Artyr. King of Britain, son of Uther Pendragon and Ygraine

Bedivere, Bedwyr. Arthur's close companion; occasionally the lover of Guenevere

Cai, Cei. See Kay

Drustan. See Tristan

Elaine, Eleyne. (1) Of Astolat, who dies for love of Lancelot; (2) Of Corbenik, mother of Lancelot's son Galahad

Essylt. See Iseult

Ewen. See Ywaine

Gawain(e), Gawin, Gwalchmai. Oldest son of King Lot(h) of Orkney and Morgause; Arthur's favorite nephew

Guenever(e), Guenevera, Gueneva, Gueneviere, Guenhumara, Guenivere, Guinevere, Gwenhywfar, Gwenhwyvar, Gwenyfer, Gwinfreda, Gwynhwyfar, Winifrith. Arthur's wife; loved by Lancelot

Igraine. See Ygraine

Iseult, Essylt, Isolde, Isolt, Isoud, Yseult, Ysolt. (1) Of Ireland and Cornwall, wife of King Mark; loved by Tristan; (2) Of Brittany, of the White Hands, wife of Tristan

Kay, Kei, Cai, Cei. Arthur's foster-brother and seneschal

Lancelot, Lancelet, Launcelot, Olans, Wlenca. Son of Ban, a king in France; Arthur's close friend and foremost knight; lover of Guenevere

Mark, Marc. King of Cornwall, uncle of Tristan; husband of Iseult of Ireland

Margawse. See Morgause

Medraut, Medrawt. See Mordred

Merlin, Merd(d)in, Merdyn, Myrdhin(n). Prophet and magician; tutor and counsellor of the young Arthur, to whom he is occasionally represented as being related

Mordred, Modred, Medraut, Medrawt. Son of Morgause or, occasionally, Morgan or Ygraine, and nephew of Arthur; usually the illegitimate issue of his mother's incestuous union with her half-brother Arthur, whom he eventually kills

Morgan le Fay, Morgana, Morgaine. Younger daughter of the Duke of Cornwall and Ygraine; mother of Ywain by her husband King Uriens; in some versions the only true love of her half-brother Arthur, to whom she incestuously bears a son Mordred; wields magic powers, sometimes benevolent but usually evil

Morgause, Margawse, Morgawse. Older daughter of the Duke of Cornwall and Ygraine; mother of Gawain, Agravain, Gaheris, and Gareth, by her husband King Lot(h) of Orkney; usually mother of Mordred by incest with her half-brother Arthur; sometimes wields evil magical powers

Nimiane, Nimue. See Vivien

Olans. See Lancelot

Perceval, Percival(e), Parzival, Peredur, Parsival. Of Wales or York, usually the son of Pellinore; Grail quester

Tristan, Tristram, Trystan, Drustan. Nephew of Mark of Cornwall and lover of his wife Iseult of Ireland; later marries Iseult of Brittany

Uwaine. See Ywain

Vivien, Vivain, Vivayn, Viviane, Nimiane, Nimue. Lady of the Lake, usually a benevolent worker of magic, in which role she succeeds Merlin as counsellor to Arthur; occasionally evil, seducing and imprisoning Merlin; marries Pelleas, one of Arthur's knights

Winifrith. See Guenevere

Wlenca. See Lancelot

Ygraine, Igraine, Ygern, Igrayne. Wife of the Duke of Cornwall, by whom she is mother of Morgause and Morgan; mother of Arthur by King Uther Pendragon whom she later marries; occasionally the half-sister of Arthur and mother of Mordred

Yseult, Ysolt. See Iseult

Ywain, Ewen, Owain, Uwaine. Son of Morgan le Fay and King Uriens; nephew of Arthur

SELECTED PRIMARY BIBLIOGRAPHY

This bibliography is based primarily upon the work done by Northup, Parry, Brown, and Reimer (see note 3 to Chapter 1), supplemented by my own researches. Unfortunately, the forthcoming Arthurian bibliography being prepared by Edmund Reiss and Beverly Taylor for Garland Press was not available when this study was completed. I have examined copies of Arthurian books in my own collection, those borrowed through the services of Inter-Library Loan, and those in the collections at the Newberry Library, Chicago (for whom I compiled an Index of their holdings in Arthurian Literature from the Nineteenth and Twentieth Centuries); at the Clwyd Library in Mold, Wales; at the Science Fiction Foundation Library of the North East London Polytechnic in Dagenham, England; at the British Library, London; and (for T. G. Roberts) at the Harriet Irving Library of the University of New Brunswick in Fredericton, New Brunswick. I would like to repeat here my gratitude to the many librarians whose courtesy made my task easier.

Items that I was unable to locate are marked with an asterisk. Because they are cited in this study, a few items are included which are retellings of traditional versions or else contain no more than passing references to Arthurian legend.

Anderson, Poul. *Three Hearts and Three Lions.* Garden City, N.Y.: Doubleday, 1953.
Babcock, William H. *Cian of the Chariots: A Romance of the Days of Arthur Emperor of Britain and his Knights of the Round Table, How They*

Delivered London and Overthrew the Saxons after the Downfall of Roman Britain. Boston: Lothrop Publishing, 1898.

Baring, Maurice. "The Camelot Jousts." In *Dead Letters*. London: Constable; Boston: Houghton Mifflin, 1910. (Note: First published in the *Morning Post*.)

Berger, Thomas. *Arthur Rex: A Legendary Novel*. New York: Delacorte Press/Seymour Lawrence, 1978; London: Magnum, 1979.

Bishop, Farnham, and Arthur Gilchrist Brodeur. *The Altar of the Legion*. Boston: Little, Brown, 1926.

Bond, Nancy. *A String in the Harp*. New York: Atheneum, 1976.

Borowsky, Marvin. *The Queen's Knight*. New York: Random House, 1955; London: Chatto and Windus, 1956.

Braddon, Mary Elizabeth [Mary Elizabeth Braddon Maxwell]. *Mount Royal*. London: John and Robert Maxwell, 1882.

Bradley, Marion Zimmer. *The Mists of Avalon*. New York: Alfred A. Knopf, 1982.

Bradley, Will. *Launcelot and the Ladies*. New York and London: Harper, 1927.

Bradshaw, Gillian. *Hawk of May*. New York: Simon and Schuster, 1980.

———. *In Winter's Shadow*. New York: Simon and Schuster, 1982.

———. *Kingdom of Summer*. New York: Simon and Schuster, 1981.

Brooke, Maxey. "Morte D'Alain: An Unrecorded Idyll of the King." In *Rogues' Gallery: A Variety of Mystery Stories*, ed. Walter B. Gibson. Garden City, N.Y.: Doubleday, 1969, pp. 264–74.

Broun, Heywood. "The Fifty-First Dragon." *The Golden Book*, 13 (May 1931), 60–63.

Brunner, John. *Father of Lies*. New York: Belmont Books, 1968. (Note: Bound with Bruce Duncan, *Mirror Image*, as a Belmont Double.)

Bulla, Clyde R. *The Sword in the Tree*. New York: Thomas Y. Crowell, 1956.

Burnham, Jeremy, and Trevor Ray. *Raven*. London: Corgi Books/Carousel, 1977.

Cabell, James Branch. *Jurgen, a Comedy of Justice*. New York: McBride, 1919; London: John Lane, The Bodley Head, 1921.

Campbell, Alice Ormond. *The Murder of Caroline Bundy*. New York: Farrar and Rinehart, 1932.

Canning, Victor. *The Circle of the Gods*. London: William Heinemann, 1977.

———. *The Crimson Chalice*. London: William Heinemann, 1976.

———. *The Crimson Chalice*. New York: William Morrow, 1978. (Note: Includes *The Crimson Chalice*, *The Circle of the Gods*, and *The Immortal Wound*.)

———. *The Immortal Wound*. London: William Heinemann, 1978.

Carlsen, Chris. *Berserker: The Bull Chief*. London: Sphere Books, 1977.

Carmichael, Douglas. *Pendragon: An Historical Novel*. Hicksville, N.Y.: Blackwater Press, 1977.

Chant, Joy. *The High Kings*. Toronto, New York, London, Sydney: Bantam Books, 1983.

Chapman, Vera. *The Green Knight*. London: Rex Collings, 1975; New York: Avon Books, 1978.

————. *King Arthur's Daughter*. London: Rex Collings, 1976; New York: Avon Books, 1978.

————. *The King's Damosel*. London: Rex Collings, 1976; New York: Avon Books, 1978.

————. *The Three Damosels: A Trilogy*. London: Magnum Books/Methuen, 1978. (Note: Contains *The Green Knight, The King's Damosel*, and *King Arthur's Daughter*.)

Chase, Mary Ellen. *Dawn in Lyonesse*. New York: Macmillan, 1938.

Cherryh, C. J. *Port Eternity*. New York: DAW Books, 1982.

Christian, Catherine. *The Sword and the Flame: Variations on a Theme of Sir Thomas Malory*. London: Macmillan London, 1978. Published in the United States as *The Pendragon*. New York: Alfred A. Knopf, 1979.

Church, Alfred J. *The Count of the Saxon Shore or the Villa in Vectis: A Tale of the Departure of the Romans from Britain*. London: Seeley; New York: Putnam's, 1887.

Clare, Helen [Pauline Hunter Blair]. *Merlin's Magic*. London: John Lane, The Bodley Head, 1953.

Closs, Hannah. *Tristan*. London: Andrew Dakers, 1940.

Cohen, Matt. *Too Bad Galahad*. Toronto: Coach House Press, 1972.

Colum, Padraic. *The Boy Apprenticed to an Enchanter*. New York: Macmillan, 1920; reprinted 1966.

Cooper, Susan. *The Dark Is Rising*. New York: Atheneum, 1973.

————. *Greenwitch*. New York: Atheneum, 1974.

————. *The Grey King*. New York: Atheneum, 1975.

————. *Over Sea, Under Stone*. New York: Harcourt, Brace and World; London: Jonathan Cape, 1965.

————. *Silver on the Tree*. New York: Atheneum, 1977.

Cox, Irving E. "Lancelot Returned." In *Fantastic Universe Science Fiction*, 8, no. 4 (October 1957), 58–68.

Curry, Jane. *The Sleepers*. New York: Harcourt, Brace and World, 1968.

Davies, Andrew. *The Legend of King Arthur*. London: Fontana/Armada, 1979.

*Dawson, Coningsby. *The Road to Avalon*. London: Hodder and Stoughton; New York: Doran, 1911.

Deal, Babs H. *The Grail: A Novel*. New York: David McKay, 1963.

Deeping, Warwick. *The Man on the White Horse.* London, Toronto, Melbourne, and Sydney: Cassell; New York: Alfred A. Knopf, 1934.

————. *Uther and Igraine.* New York: Outlook, 1903; London, Toronto, Melbourne, and Sydney: Cassell, 1927; New York: Alfred A. Knopf, 1928.

Dickinson, Peter. *The Weathermonger.* London: Victor Gollancz, 1968.

Dickson, Gordon R. *Secret under the Caribbean.* New York, Chicago, and San Francisco: Holt, Rinehart and Winston, 1964.

Ditmas, E.M.R. *Gareth of Orkney.* London: Faber and Faber, 1956.

Doyle, Arthur Conan. "The Last of the Legions." In *The Last Galley: Impression and Tales.* London: Smith and Elder; Garden City, N.Y.: Doubleday, Page; Leipzig: Tauchnitz, 1911, pp. 91–101.

Drake, David. *The Dragon Lord.* New York: Thomas Doherty Associates, 1982. (Note: Copyright listed as 1979.)

Duggan, Alfred. *Conscience of the King.* London: Faber and Faber, 1951.

Eager, Edward. *Half Magic.* New York: Harcourt, Brace, Jovanovich, 1954.

Endersby, Clive. *Read All About It!* Toronto, New York, London, Sydney, Auckland: Methuen, 1981.

Erskine, John. *Galahad: Enough of His Life to Explain His Reputation.* Indianapolis: Bobbs-Merrill; London: Nash and Grayson, 1926.

*————. "The Tale of How Sir Lancelot Slew Sir Agravaine." In *American Weekly* (March 17, 1940).

*————. "The Tale of King Arthur's Sword 'Excalibur.' " In *American Weekly* (February 4, 1940).

*————. "The Tale of Merlin and One of the Ladies of the Lake." In *American Weekly* (March 10, 1940).

*————. "The Tale of Sir Galahad and the Quest of the Sangreal." In *American Weekly* (February 25, 1940).

*————. "The Tale of Sir Launcelot and the Four Queens." In *American Weekly* (March 3, 1940).

*————. "The Tale of Sir Tristram and the Love Potion." In *American Weekly* (February 11, 1940).

*————. "The Tale of the Enchantress and the Magic Scabbard." In *American Weekly* (February 18, 1940).

————. *Tristan and Isolde: Restoring Palamede.* Indianapolis: Bobbs-Merrill, 1932.

Faraday, W. Barnard. *Pendragon.* London: Methuen, 1930.

Fergusson, Adam. *Roman Go Home.* London: Collins, 1969.

Finkel, George. *Twilight Province.* Sydney: Angus and Robertson, 1967. Published in the United States as *Watch Fires to the North.* New York: Viking Press, 1968.

*Francis, Gerard. *The Secret Sceptre.* London: Rich and Cowan, 1937.

Frankland, Edward. *The Bear of Britain*. London: MacDonald, 1944.
———. "Medraut and Gwenhwyvar." In *England Growing*. London: MacDonald, 1944, pp. 15–21.
French, Allen. "Sir Marrok: A Tale of the Days of King Arthur." In *St. Nicholas Magazine*, 29 (May 1902) 592–620. (Note: Republished as a book, New York: Century Co., 1902.)
Garner, Alan. *The Moon of Gomrath*. London: William Collins, 1963.
———. *The Wierdstone of Brisingamen: A Tale of Alderley*. London: William Collins, 1960; rev. ed. Harmondsworth, Middlesex: Penguin Books, 1963.
Gash, Jonathan [John Grant]. *The Grail Tree*. London: William Collins, 1979.
Geoffrey Junior [William John Courthope]. *The Marvellous History of King Arthur in Avalon and of the Lifting of Lyonnesse: A Chronicle of the Round Table Communicated by Geoffrey of Monmouth*. London: John Murray, 1904.
Gloag, John. *Artorius Rex*. London: Cassell; New York: St. Martin's Press, 1977.
Godwin, Parke. *Firelord*. Garden City, N.Y.: Doubleday, 1980.
Greeley, Andrew M. *The Magic Cup: An Irish Legend*. New York: McGraw-Hill, 1979.
*Groom, Arthur. *The Adventures of Sir Lancelot, Book 2*. London: Adprint, 1958. (Note: The first book was written by John Paton.)
Haldeman, Linda. *The Lastborn of Elvinwood*. Garden City, N.Y.: Doubleday, 1978.
Hamilton, Ernest. *Launcelot: A Romance of the Court of King Arthur*. London: Methuen, 1926.
Holland, Rupert Sargent. "The Knights of the Golden Spur." In *St. Nicholas Magazine*, 39, no. 1 (November 1911), 43–47; no. 2 (December 1911), 127–32.
Housman, Clemence. *The Life of Sir Aglovale de Galis*. London: Methuen, 1905; rev. ed., London: Jonathan Cape, 1954.
Hunter, Jim. *Percival and the Presence of God*. London and Boston: Faber and Faber, 1978.
Jewett, Eleanore. *The Hidden Treasure of Glaston*. New York: Viking Press, 1946.
Jones, Gwyn. "Gwydion Mathrafal." In *Penguin Parade II*, ed. Denys Kilham Roberts. Harmondsworth, Middlesex: Penguin Books, 1945, pp. 7–17.
Kane, Gil, and John Jakes. *Excalibur!* New York: Dell, 1980.
Karr, Phyllis Ann. *The Idylls of the Queen*. New York: Ace Books, 1982.
*Keith, Chester. *Queen's Knight*. London: Allen and Unwin, 1920.
Kuncewicz, Maria. *Tristan: A Novel*. New York: George Braziller, 1974.

Landis, Arthur H. *Camelot in Orbit*. New York: DAW Books, 1978.
———. *Home—To Avalon*. New York: DAW Books, 1982.
———. *The Majick of Camelot*. New York: DAW Books, 1981.
———. *A World Called Camelot*. New York: DAW Books, 1976.
Laubenthal, Anne Saunders. *Excalibur*. New York: Ballantine Books, 1978.
Le Cain, Errol. *King Arthur's Sword*. London: Faber and Faber, 1968.
Lewis, C. S. *That Hideous Strength. A Modern Fairy-tale for Grown-ups.* London: John Lane, The Bodley Head, 1945; New York: Macmillan, 1946.
Lindsay, Philip. *The Little Wench*. London: Ivor Nicholson and Watson, 1935.
Lively, Penelope. *The Whispering Knights*. London: William Heinemann, 1971.
McGowen, Tom. *Sir MacHinery*. Chicago: Follett Publishing, 1971.
Machen, Arthur. *The Great Return*. London: Faith Press, 1915.
———. "Guinevere and Lancelot." In *Notes and Queries*. London: Spurr and Swift, 1926, pp. 1–18. (Note: First published as "Many-Tower'd Camelot." In *T.P.'s Weekly*, 13, April 2, 1909, 431–33.)
———. *The Secret Glory*. London: Secker; New York: Alfred A. Knopf, 1922.
McIntosh, J. F. "Merlin." In *Fantastic*, 9, no. 3 (March 1960), 6–49.
MacLeod, Mary. *King Arthur and his Knights*. New York: Parents' Magazine Press, 1964. (Note: Reprint of edition first published in 1900. This is a retelling, not a work of modern fiction.)
Manning, Rosemary. *The Dragon's Quest*. London: Constable, 1961.
———. *Green Smoke*. London: Constable, 1957.
Marquis, Don [Robert Perry]. "King O'Meara and Queen Guinevere." In *Saturday Evening Post*, 202, no. 37 (March 15, 1930), 6–7, 146, 149, 152, 154, 156; no. 38 (March 22, 1930), 22–23, 110, 114, 119, 121.
Marshall, Edison. *The Pagan King*. Garden City, N.Y.: Doubleday, 1959.
Masefield, John. *Badon Parchments*. London and Toronto: William Heinemann, 1947.
———. *The Box of Delights*. London: William Heinemann, 1935.
Mason, Charles Welsh. *Merlin: A Piratical Love Study*. London: Neville Beeman, 1896.
Mayne, William. *Earthfasts*. London: Hamish Hamilton, 1966.
Mitchell, Mary. *Birth of a Legend*. London: Methuen, 1956.
Mitchison, Naomi. *To the Chapel Perilous*. London: George Allen and Unwin, 1955.
Monaco, Richard. *The Final Quest*. New York: Putnam's, 1980; London: Sphere Books, 1982.

———. *The Grail War*. New York: Pocket Books, 1979; London: Sphere Books, 1981.

———. *Parsival or a Knight's Tale*. New York: Macmillan; London: MacDonald and James, 1977.

Moorcock, Michael. *Gloriana, or the Unfulfill'd Queen: being a Romance*. London: Allison and Busby, 1978; New York: Avon Books, 1979.

Moore, George. *Perronik the Fool*. Mount Vernon, N.Y.: Rudge, 1926; rev. ed. Chapelle-Réanville, Eure, France: The Hours Press, 1928.

Morgan, Charles. *Sparkenbroke*. London: Macmillan, 1936.

Munn, H. Walter. "King of the World's Edge." In *Weird Tales*, 34, nos. 3–6 (September–December 1939). (Note: Republished as a book. New York: Ace Books, 1966.)

———. *Merlin's Godson*. New York: Ballantine Books, 1976. (Note: Includes *King of the World's Edge* and *The Ship from Atlantis*.)

———. *Merlin's Ring*. New York: Ballantine Books, 1974.

———. *The Ship from Atlantis*. New York: Ace Books, 1967. (Note: Bound together with Emil Petaja, *The Stolen Sun*, as an Ace Double.)

Myers, John Myers. *Silverlock*. New York: Dutton, 1949.

Nabokov, Vladimir. "Lance." In *The New Yorker*, 27 (February 2, 1952), 21–25.

Newman, Robert. *Merlin's Mistake*. New York: Atheneum, 1970; London: Hutchinson, 1971.

———. *The Testing of Tertius*. New York: Atheneum, 1973.

Newman, Sharan. *Guinevere*. New York: St. Martin's Press, 1981.

Nichols, Ruth. *The Marrow of the World*. New York: Atheneum, 1972.

Norton, Andre [Alice Mary Norton]. *Here Abide Monsters*. New York: Atheneum, 1973.

———. *Merlin's Mirror*. New York: DAW Books, 1975.

———. *Steel Magic*. Cleveland: Collins-World, 1965; New York: Archway, 1978.

———. *Witch World*. New York: Ace Books, 1963.

Nye, Robert. *Merlin*. London: Hamish Hamilton, 1978; New York: Putnam's, 1979.

O'Meara, Walter. *The Duke of War*. New York: Harcourt, Brace and World, 1966.

Owen, Francis. *Tristan and Isolde: A Romance*. Ilfracombe, Devon: Arthur H. Stockwell, 1964.

Paton, John. *The Adventures of Sir Lancelot*. London: Adprint, 1957. (Note: A second book in this series was written by Arthur Groom.)

Peare, Catherine Owens. *Melor, King Arthur's Page*. New York: Putnam's, 1963.

Percy, Walker. *Lancelot*. New York: Farrar, Straus and Giroux, 1978.

Peters, Elizabeth [Barbara Gross Mertz]. *The Camelot Caper*. New York: Meredith Press, 1969.

Phillifent, John T. *Life with Lancelot*. New York: Ace Books, 1973. (Note: Bound with William Barton, *Hunting on Kunderer*, as an Ace Double.)

Powers, Tim. *The Drawing of the Dark*. New York: Ballantine Books, 1979.

Powys, John Cowper. *A Glastonbury Romance*. New York: Simon and Schuster, 1932; London: John Lane, The Bodley Head, 1933.

———. *Morwyn or the Vengeance of God*. London: Cassell, 1937; reprinted by Arno Press, 1976.

———. *Porius: A Romance of the Dark Ages*. London: MacDonald, 1951.

Price, Anthony. *Our Man in Camelot*. London: Victor Gollancz, 1975.

Priestley, J. B. *The Thirty-first of June: A Tale of True Love, Enterprise, and Progress, in the Arthurian and Ad-Atomic Ages*. London: William Heinemann, 1961; Garden City, N.Y.: Doubleday, 1962.

Quiller-Couch, Arthur, and Daphne du Maurier. *Castle Dor*. Garden City, N.Y.: Doubleday, 1961.

Robbins, Ruth. *Taliesin and King Arthur*. Berkeley: Parnassus Press, 1970.

Roberts, Dorothy James. *The Enchanted Cup*. New York: Appleton-Century-Crofts, 1953.

———. *Kinsmen of the Grail*. Boston and Toronto: Little, Brown, 1963.

———. *Launcelot, My Brother*. New York: Appleton-Century-Crofts, 1954.

Roberts, Theodore Goodrich. "By My Halidom." In *Blue Book Magazine* (December 1947). (Note: Data supplied from author's records.)

———. "Daggers in Her Garters." In *Blue Book Magazine* (1952?).

———. "The Disputed Princess." In *Blue Book Magazine* (1948?) (Note: Author's records indicate that his novelette was accepted for publication, April 1948, and was subsequently published.)

———. "For to Achieve Your Adventure." In *Blue Book Magazine*, 93, no. 6 (October 1951), 2–11.

———. "The Goose Girl," In *Blue Book Magazine*, 93, no. 4 (August 1951), 32–40.

———. "The Madness of Sir Tristram." In *Blue Book Magazine* (Canadian Edition) 92, no. 2 (December 1950), 2–12.

———. "The Merlin Touch." In *Blue Book Magazine* (1948?). (Note: Author's records indicate that this novelette was accepted for publication, November 17, 1947, and was subsequently published.)

———. "A Mountain Miracle." In *Blue Book Magazine*, 94, no. 2 (December 1951), 42–51.

———. "A Purfle for a King." In *Blue Book Magazine* (Canadian Edition), 91, no. 3 (July 1950), 2–9.

———. "A Quarrel for a Lady." In *Blue Book Magazine* (Canadian Edition), 90, no. 4 (February 1950), 14–21.

———. "A Quest of the Saracen Beast." In *Blue Book Magazine* (Canadian Edition), 92, no. 1 (November 1950), 42–50.

———. "Sir Dinadan and the Giant Taulurd." In *Blue Book Magazine*, 92, no. 6 (April 1951), 94–104.

St. John, Nicole [Norma Johnston]. *Guinever's Gift*. New York: Random House, 1977.

*Senior, Dorothy. *The Clutch of Circumstance: or the Gates of Dawn*. London: Black; New York: Macmillan, 1908.

Seton, Anya. *Avalon*. Boston: Houghton Mifflin, 1965.

Sharpe, Ruth Collier. *Tristram of Lyonesse: The Story of an Immortal Love*. New York: Greenberg, 1949.

Shorthouse, J. H. *Sir Percival: A Story of the Past and of the Present*. London and New York: Macmillan, 1886.

Smith, Arthur D. Howden. "The Last Legion and Gray Maiden, the Sword." In *Adventure*, 61 (December 31, 1926), 170–90.

Sobol, Donald J. *Greta the Strong*. Chicago: Follett Publishing, 1970.

Steinbeck, John. *The Acts of King Arthur and his Noble Knights, from the Winchester MSS. of Thomas Malory and Other Sources*. Ed. Chase Horton. New York: Farrar, Straus and Giroux; London: William Heinemann, 1976.

———. *Tortilla Flat*. New York: Grosset and Dunlap, 1935.

Sterling, Sara Hawks. *A Lady of King Arthur's Court: Being a Romance of the Holy Grail*. Philadelphia: George W. Jacobs, 1907; London: Chatto and Windus, 1909.

Stewart, Mary. *The Crystal Cave*. London: Hodder and Stoughton; New York: William Morrow, 1970.

———. *The Hollow Hills*. London: Hodder and Stoughton; New York: William Morrow, 1973.

———. *The Last Enchantment*. London: Hodder and Stoughton; New York: William Morrow, 1979.

———. *The Wicked Day*. London: Hodder and Stoughton; New York: William Morrow, 1983.

Stone, Eugenia. *Page Boy for King Arthur*. Chicago: Follett Publishing, 1949. (Reprinted as *Page Boy of Camelot*. New York, London, Richmond Hill, Ontario: Scholastic Book Services, 1967.)

———. *Squire for King Arthur*. Chicago: Follett Publishing, 1955.

Sturgeon, Theodore. "Excalibur and the Atom." In *Fantastic Adventures*, 13, no. 8 (August 1951), 8–51.

Sutcliff, Rosemary. *The Lantern Bearers*. Oxford: Oxford University Press; New York: Henry Z. Walck, 1959.

———. *The Light Beyond the Forest: The Quest for the Holy Grail*. London, Sydney, Toronto: The Bodley Head, 1979. (Note: This is a retelling, not a work of modern fiction.)

———. *The Road to Camlann*. London, Sydney, Toronto: The Bodley Head, 1981. (Note: This is a retelling, not a work of modern fiction.)

———. *The Sword and the Circle*. London, Sydney, Toronto: The Bodley Head, 1981. (Note: This is a retelling, not a work of modern fiction.)

———. *Sword at Sunset*. London: Hodder and Stoughton, 1963.

———. *Tristan and Iseult*. London, Sydney, Toronto: The Bodley Head, 1971. (Note: This is a retelling, not a work of modern fiction.)

*Tatum, Edith. "The Awakening of Iseult." In *Neale's Monthly*, 2 (August 1913), 177–85.

Taylor, Anna. *Drustan the Wanderer: A Novel Based on the Legend of Tristan and Isolde*. Harlow, England: Longman, 1971; New York: Saturday Review Press, 1972.

Taylor, Keith. *Bard*. New York: Ace Books, 1981. (Note: Portions of this novel first appeared in *Fantastic Stories*, 1975, published under the pseudonym Dennis More.)

Treece, Henry. *The Eagles Have Flown*. London: John Lane, The Bodley Head, 1954.

———. *The Great Captains*. London: John Lane, The Bodley Head; New York: Random House, 1956.

———. *The Green Man*. London: John Lane, The Bodley Head; New York: Putnam's, 1966.

Trevor, [Lucy] Meriol. *Merlin's Ring*. London: Collins, 1957.

Turner, Roy. *King of the Lordless Country*. London: Dennis Dobson, 1971.

Turton, Godfrey. *The Emperor Arthur*. Garden City, N.Y.: Doubleday, 1967.

Twain, Mark [Samuel L. Clemens]. *A Connecticut Yankee in King Arthur's Court*. New York and London: Harper, 1889; New York: Webster, 1889. (Note: Parts of the story were printed in *The Century*, 39 [N. S. 17; November 1889], 74–83; they include the destruction of Merlin's tower and Hank's participation in the tournament.)

Vance, Jack. *Lyonesse*. New York: Berkley Books, 1983.

Vansittart, Peter. *Lancelot: A Novel*. London: Peter Owen, 1978.

Viney, Jayne. *The Bright-Helmed One*. London: Robert Hale, 1975.

White, T. H. *The Book of Merlyn*. Austin: University of Texas Press; London: Collins, 1977.

———. *The Ill-Made Knight*. New York: Putnam's, 1940.

———. *The Once and Future King*. London: Collins; New York: Putnam's, 1958. (Note: Includes *The Sword in the Stone*, *The Witch in the Wood*, both in revised form, and *The Ill-Made Knight*, with the addition of a conclusion.)

———. *The Sword in the Stone*. London: Collins, 1938; New York: Putnam's, 1939.

———. *The Witch in the Wood*. London: Collins; New York: Putnam's, 1939.

Wibberley, Leonard. *The Quest of Excalibur*. New York: Putnam's, 1959; reprinted San Bernardino, Calif.: Reginald, The Borgo Press, 1979.

Williams, Charles. *War in Heaven*. London: Victor Gollancz, 1930.

*Wodehouse, P. G. "Sir Agravaine. A Blithesome and Knightly Tale, Throwing New Light upon the Mystery of Affinities." In *Chicago American* (July 8, 1923).

Yunge-Bateman, Elizabeth. *The Flowering Thorn*. Published by the author, 1961.

Zelazny, Roger. *The Courts of Chaos*. Garden City, N.Y.: Doubleday, 1978.

———. *The Guns of Avalon*. Garden City, N.Y.: Doubleday, 1972.

———. "The Last Defender of Camelot." In *The Last Defender of Camelot*. New York: Pocket Books, 1980, pp. 271–94.

INDEX

About the Author
RAYMOND H. THOMPSON is Professor of English at Acadia University, Nova Scotia. He is the author of *Gordon R. Dickson: A Primary and Secondary Bibliography* and of numerous articles appearing in *Studia Neophilologica, Extrapolation, Folklore, Atlantis,* and *Forum for Modern Language Studies.*